# ALTHUSSER'S LESSON

**Also available from Continuum:**

# ALTHUSSER'S LESSON

*Jacques Rancière*

---

*Translated by* Emiliano Battista

continuum

**Continuum International Publishing Group**

| | |
|---|---|
| The Tower Building | 80 Maiden Lane |
| 11 York Road | Suite 704 |
| London SE1 7NX | New York NY 10038 |

www.continuumbooks.com

Originally published in French as *La Leçon d'Althusser* © Jacques Rancière, 1974
This English translation © The Continuum International Publishing
Group Ltd., 2011

**British Library Cataloguing-in-Publication Data**
A catalogue record for this book is available from the British Library.

ISBN: 978-1-4411-0805-0

**Library of Congress Cataloging-in-Publication Data**
A catalog record of this book is available from the Library of Congress.

Typeset by Newgen Imaging Systems Pvt Ltd, Chennai, India
Printed and bound in Great Britain

# Contents

# Acknowledgements

Writing a Translator's Preface has seemed superfluous to me, as I discuss problems of terminology and justify my choices – where they need justification – in the endnotes. Nevertheless, I welcome the opportunity to acknowledge my gratitude to the 'travelling-companions' who have seen me through this intellectual adventure into the heart of the May 68 storm and of what Kristin Ross calls its 'after-lives': in the fields of theory, politics and—considering a trajectory that begins with this book—in the politics of theory.

Jacques Rancière read and annotated the translation as it was in progress, and was always willing to indulge my overly zealous desire to annotate the text, supplying a number of notes which, I hope, will help open up the text and its contexts to the reader. I would like to thank Stathis Kouvelakis and Alberto Toscano for so generously guiding me through many conceptual and terminological issues; the notes on the differences between 'the left', 'communists' and 'leftists' and on the difference between 'workerism' and *'ouvrièrisme'* are really their work. Katja Diefenbach's inexhaustible knowledge of Marx and the Marxist tradition led me to passages in Marx and others Rancière alludes to that I would never have found on my own; more often than not, when I refer the reader to Marx, it is with Katja's help. M. G. Goshgarian and Warren Montag, experienced Althusser translators, were kind enough to look over my translations of passages Rancière cites from texts by Althusser not available in English (unless otherwise indicated, all translations in the book are my own). Fabien Gerard's nose for subtle differences in the French language saved me from many blunders, and Peggy Donnelly's for English from many transliterations.

## ACKNOWLEDGEMENTS

While I was in constant contact with all the people just mentioned, there were many others who lent a helping hand. I am grateful to Gregory Elliott for referring me to Michael J. Gane, who had been involved with the journal *Sublation* and who was kind enough to search for, and find, a copy of the partial translation of Althusser's 'Student Problems', a text Rancière returns to time and again in the course of the book. It seems I am one of the few people ever to have seen this translation! I am also indebted to Joseph Tanke, Tzuchien Tho, Peter Thomas, John Hymers, Jacques Marx, and Pedro Leal, in ways that I need not bother the reader by enumerating. And to Molly Morrison and Heather Hambleton for their meticulous copy-editing.

Finally, I am grateful to Sarah Campbell, Tom Crick, David Avital and Nicholas Church at Continuum; their patience with me and with the delays this project was heir to was almost holy.

# List of Abbreviations

## WORKS BY LOUIS ALTHUSSER

DMAa = 'Dear M. A.' (letter of 2 April 1968) in: Maria Antonietta Macciocchi, *Letters from inside the Italian Communist Party to Louis Althusser*, trans. Stephen M. Hellman, London, 1973.

DMAb = 'Dear M. A.' (letter of 15 March 1969) in: *Letters from inside the Italian Communist Party to Louis Althusser.*

ESC = *Essays in Self-Criticism*, trans. Grahame Lock, London, 1976.

EYM = 'On the Evolution of the Young Marx', in ESC, 151–63.

FM = *For Marx*, trans. Ben Brewster, London, 1996.

ISA = 'Ideology and Ideological State Apparatuses', in LPOE, 127–87.

IT = 'Introduction: Today', in FM, 21–41.

LP = 'Lenin and Philosophy', in LPOE, 27–68.

LPOE = *Lenin and Philosophy and Other Essays*, trans. Ben Brewster, London, 1971.

MD = 'On the Materialist Dialectic', in FM, 161–218.

MH = 'Marxism and Humanism', in FM, 219–47.

MVME = 'A propos de l'article de Michel Verret sur "mai étudiante"', in *La Pensée*, no. 145, June 1969, 3–14.

OYM = 'On the Young Marx', in FM, 49–86.

PE = 'Problèmes étudiants', in *La Nouvelle Critique*, no. 152, January 1964, 80–111.

PRW = 'Philosophy as a Revolutionary Weapon', in LPOE, 13–25.

## LIST OF ABBREVIATIONS

PSP = 'Philosophy and the Spontaneous Philosophy of Scientists', in PSPS, 69–165.

PSPS = *Philosophy and the Spontaneous Philosophy of Scientists and Other Essays*, ed. Gregory Elliot, trans. Warren Montag et al., London, 1990.

RC = *Reading Capital*, trans. Ben Brewster, London, 1970.

RJL = *Reply to John Lewis*, in ESC, 35–99.

SC = 'Elements of Self-Criticism', in ESC, 101–61.

SP = 'Student Problems' (partial translation of PE), trans. Dick Bateman, *Sublation* (Leicester: University of Leicester, 1967) 14–22.

TPF = 'Theory, Theoretical Practice, and Theoretical Formation: Ideology and Ideological Struggle', trans. James Kavanagh, in PSPS, 1–42.

## WORKS BY OTHERS

C1 = Karl Marx, *Capital*, vol. 1, trans. Ben Fowkes (London, 1976).

LCW = V. I. Lenin, *Collected Works* (Moscow and London, 1960–).

MECW = Karl Marx and Friedrich Engels, *Collected Works* (Moscow and London, 1970–).

PO = Alain Faure and Jacques Rancière (eds), *La Parole ouvrière* (Paris, 2007 [1976]).

SWM = Mao Tse-tung, *Selected Works* (Peking [Beijing], 1967–).

## POLITICAL ORGANIZATIONS OR MOVEMENTS

CGT = Confédération générale du travail; General Workers' Confederation, a large trade union

CMLF = Centre marxiste-léniniste de France; Marxist-Leninist Centre of France

FCML = Féderation des cercles marxistes-leninistes; Federation of Marxist-Leninist Circles

FGEL = Fédération des groupes d'études de lettres; UNEF student group which represented the Sorbonne

GTU = Groupes de travail universitaire; collaborative research groups

JC = Jeunes communistes; Young Communists

JCR = Jeunesse communiste révolutionnaire; Revolutionary Communist Youth

MCF = Mouvement communiste français; French Communist Movement

MRG = Mouvement des radicaux de gauche; Movement of Left-Wing Radicals

NRP = Nouvelle résistance populaire; New Popular Resistance

PCF = Parti communiste français; French Communist Party

PCI = Partito communista italiano; Italian Communist Party

PS = Parti socialiste; Socialist Party

UEC = Union des étudiants communists; Union of Communist Students

UJC (ML) = Union des jeunesses communistes (marxiste-leniniste); Union of Communist Youth (Marxist-Leninist); this was the first Maoist student organization in France (often just UJC)

UNEF = l'Union nationale des étudiants français; National Union of French Students

# Foreword to the English Edition

This book appeared in France in 1974. The English-speaking reader discovering it today will find an explanation of the circumstances that led me to write it in the original Preface. He or she, however, will need some additional indications to be able to resituate the circumstances themselves. Althusser is now counted as one of the representatives of a French theory generally said to be endowed with a twofold power of subversion: theoretical and political. The problem with this view of it is that it all too easily blurs the disparities in the theories joined under that rubric, while also forgetting the intellectual and political contexts within which those theories were developed and wherein they produced effects. Thus, the reader who associates Althusser's name with the theory of ideological state apparatuses may be surprised to read here a critique of his theory of ideology in which that notion plays no role. Similarly, the reader should not expect to find anything about the 'aleatory materialism' of Althusser's late texts in a book written in 1974. In recalling this date, I am not trying to excuse the absence of references now commonly attached to Althusser's name. It had not been my intention to write a monograph explaining a thinker's ideas. What I wanted, instead, was to study the politics of a system of thought and the way in which this system seized upon the signifiers and the political stakes of a moment, and in so doing defined the specific scene and time for thought to be politically effective.

In Althusser's case, we can pinpoint quite precisely the moment of this effectivity: it spans the decade between the publication of the texts collected in *For Marx* and the seminar on *Capital* at the beginning of the 1960s, and the *Reply to John Lewis* in 1973. Althusser continued to publish all manner of texts in the years that followed, texts that have been carefully read and studied and that have stimulated a variety of positions and ideas. But Althusserianism, as a form of theoretico-political intervention, as the creator of a specific scene for the effectivity of thought, unfolded in the decade just indicated. It was in that order that Althusserianism became the dominant figure among the renewed Marxisms that were then trying to keep pace with the dynamics being exhibited by new forms of the workers' struggle, by anti-colonial liberation conflicts, by anti-imperialist movements and by the uprising of the student youth. Althusserianism distinguished itself within that ambit in two ways: theoretically, by calling for a return to Marx's thought against those who wanted to modernize Marxism, and politically, by displaying, in the face of the various rebellions that were then rattling communist apparatuses, a faithfulness to the Party that was not without ulterior motives. Althusser wanted, in effect, to guarantee an autonomy for theory that would make it capable of investing Marxism with the theoretical edge to generate political renewal. The idea of a Marxism in lockstep with the structuralist revolution of thought and thus able to overcome such old aporias as the individual and the collective, or determinism and freedom, was defined from inside this project, as was the development of new militant energies which assimilated this rediscovered Marxist rigour to the force of anti-imperialist struggles and the Cultural Revolution. This project exploded in the storm of May 68 in France. It is true that the Althusserian definition of ideology as a system of representations that automatically subjects individuals to the dominant order suggested, to some, the idea of a radical cultural revolution. But its more widespread effect was different: in the intellectual class, it underwrote the condemnation of the student uprisings as a petit-bourgeois movement, one whose actors were in fact the victims of the bourgeois ideology they imbibed without knowing. They had to be re-educated by the authority of Science and the Party.

*Althusser's Lesson* tries to trace the genealogy and offer an assessment of this effective Althusserianism. The book's undertaking coincided, as it happens, with Althusser's own attempts to glue the pieces of Althusserianism back together, and thus to seal up the breach that had been opened up by the event. The timing here is by no means accidental. I wrote the book as the efforts to give long-term life to the rupture of 1968 were succumbing to exhaustion and as the resulting disenchantment was taking the form of a radical critique of militantism, its male and patriarchal

forms of power, and its ascetic rigour. This same period saw the flourish-
ing of calls to party and to liberate desire, for which some, too hastily,
thought they found the formula in Deleuze and Guattari's 'desiring
machines'. Not much later, we saw the 'new philosophy', which read all
of revolutionary history as the appetite for the power of master thinkers,
unleash its offensive.[1] Marxist organizations, not surprisingly, were
encouraged by this exhaustion to come up with ways to give shelter and
direction to all these newly orphaned energies. The patching up of
Althusserianism, after it had been blown up during the storm, took place
in this context of a return to order. The critique I develop in the pages
that follow, consequently, should by no means be treated as a personal
settling of scores. What the book, it seems to me, succeeds in identifying
more or less accurately is the beginning of an intellectual counter-
revolution that has continued to radicalize its principles and effects by
working on two different fronts: one denounces the entire revolutionary
tradition in the name of Marxist crimes; the other recycles all the principles of the Marxist critical tradition into weapons for the dominant
order.[2] This explains why the book does not turn the critique of Althusser
into the opportunity to validate a rectified Marxism, or any other good
theory of emancipation. The point is not to condemn a discourse, as I say
in concluding the book, but to reinscribe its argumentation, to bring it
back 'into the concatenation of words used, now as in the past, to articulate both the inevitability of oppression and the hopes for liberation'.[3]
The book, in sum, attests to a double objection: a political objection to
following the theories and strategies of the 'reflux' – whether in their
Marxist or anti-Marxist variety – which went hand in hand with the
desire to keep open, in its very indecision, the space for the subversion of
thought, institutions and practices opened up by the event of 1968; and
a theoretical objection, expressed in the decision to abandon the field of
'theory' – and with it the rhetoric of the 'critique of the subject' and the
empty discussion of the relationship between theory and practice – and
to study, instead, the multiple ways thought assumes form and produces
effects on the social body. This includes studying the set of material forms
of dominant thought – decisions, regulations, buildings, techniques and
exercises – that Foucault's archaeology of knowledge was then bringing
to light, as well as the materiality of the discourses and practices of those
who were then engaged in opposing dominant thought, those who were
commenting on the letter of discourses of domination, turning its regula-

tions on their heads, unhinging its machines and subverting its space. The book confronts the shadow fights between 'materialist' and 'idealist' philosophies with the rationality of thought at work, as it is embodied in *dispositifs*, institutions and – not least – in the words (stolen from the enemy, interpreted, transformed, inverted) constantly exchanged in the struggle. I wanted to pit this topography of possible discourses and positions against the teleological discourses about historical evolution that sustained revolutionary hopes for so long, and whose transformation into the doleful discourse of the end of utopias, politics or history we have all seen first hand.

From the very beginning, my concern has been with the study of thought and speech there where they produce effects, that is, in a social battle that is also a conflict, renewed with each passing instant, over what we perceive and how we can name it. From the beginning, I have confronted the philosophies of the end of history with the topography of the possible; indeed, we can see the contours of this project appearing in the framework, and the limits, of the book's polemic. Above and beyond the theses specific to Althusser, the book has its sights trained on the much broader logic by which subversive thoughts are recuperated for the service of order. The principle of this process of recuperation is the idea of domination propagated (*véhiculer*) by the very discourses that pretend to critique it. These critiques in fact all share the same presupposition: domination functions thanks to a mechanism of dissimulation which hides its laws from its subjects by presenting them with an inverted reality. The sociology of 'misrecognition', the theory of the 'spectacle' and the different forms assumed by the critique of consumer and communication societies all share with Althusserianism the idea that the dominated are dominated because they are ignorant of the laws of domination. This simplistic view at first assigns to those who adopt it the exalted task of bringing their science to the blind masses. Eventually, though, this exalted task dissolves into a pure thought of resentment which declares the inability of the ignorant to be cured of their illusions, and hence the inability of the masses to take charge of their own destiny.

My book declared war on the theory of the inequality of intelligences at the heart of supposed critiques of domination. It held that all revolutionary thought must be founded on the inverse presupposition, that of the capacity of the dominated. It did so at the price of identifying this capacity with the slogans of China's Cultural Revolution. The prevailing view of the Cultural Revolution at the time, and it is a view the book shares, was that of an anti-authoritarian movement which confronted the power of the state and of the Party with the capacity of the masses. This view, in its turn, was encompassed by the notion that Maoism was a radical critique both of state domination and of the model of development instituted by Russian communism. There can be no doubt that we were bending the manifestations of the Maoist revolution a bit too quickly to our own desires for a communism radically different from the Stalinist one. We cannot be satisfied, today anymore than yesterday, with the inverse thesis, which essentially reduces the mass movements of the Cultural Revolution to a simple manipulation carried out by Mao Tse-tung to recover a power he had lost in the apparatus of the Party. But it is also equally impossible to justify the zeal with which we tried to validate the official image and discourse of the Cultural Revolution. In the intervening years, history has taught us not only the limits of the autonomous capacity for initiative attributable to the actors of the Cultural Revolution, it has also revealed the penitentiary realities that accompanied the theses about the re-education of intellectuals through manual labour which, at that time, seemed so consonant with some Western critiques of the division of labour. On this point, the book bears out, at its own expense, the thesis that there is no theory of subversion that cannot also serve the cause of oppression.

More generally, the book bears witness to a palpable tension between the conviction of some of its objections and the uncertainty about the arguments used to found them. It is clear that I would not subscribe to some of its claims and analyses today. Still, I have not changed when it comes to the principle which guided them, namely, that only the presupposition of a capacity common to all can found both the power of thought and the dynamics of emancipation. For these two reasons, I have made no changes to the original text. The only difference between this edition and the original concerns 'On the Theory of Ideology', which is presented here as an appendix. I had thought it useful to include this text, an analysis of the politics of Althusserianism written in the heat of the moment five years earlier, as an appendix in the French edition. But the editor, who did not like books composed from assembled parts, asked me to turn it into an actual chapter. To mitigate the disparity between it and the rest of the volume, I added a number of footnotes, in which I formulated my reservations about many of the propositions elaborated in the body of the text. As these circumstantial reservations were themselves of the sort to prompt new reservations, I have thought it best to omit the footnotes and to present the text as it was written in 1969, and as it was published, a year later, in a Spanish translation.[4]

Paris
June 2010

# Preface

This book is intended to be a commentary on the lesson in Marxism that Louis Althusser gives to John Lewis.[1] It is a reflection on what this lesson wants to teach us, and on what it actually teaches us, not about Marxist theory itself, but about the present reality of Marxism, that is to say, about what constitutes the discourse of an acknowledged Marxist in 1973. It is a reflection on the conditions of possibility of Althusser's lesson, and of its resonance with intellectuals, politicians, 'communists' and 'leftists'.[2]

My commentary on this lesson does not claim to be objective, at least not if we understand by 'objective' the process of weighing good and bad sides, favourable and unfavourable opinions, and so forth. The starting point of my commentary is, rather, an experience that a great many intellectuals of my generation lived through in 1968: the Marxism we had learned at Althusser's school was a philosophy of order whose every principle served to distance us from the uprisings which were then shaking the bourgeois order to its core.

Most of us did not want to turn this experience into the principle for an open critique of Althusser, and there were good reasons for that. A sense of decency, for one. Althusser had misled us, yes, but he had also opened up paths that we might never have known without him. Was it not Althusser, after all, who freed us in the 1960s from the phenomenological fog that dominated philosophy? And was it not also Althusser who cleared the way for a Marx who was neither the guarantor of Soviet state power nor the partner of theologians and armchair philosophers? As for the equivocal Marxist rigour that we came to regard, in 1968, as consonant with the more blatant rigours of bourgeois order, had not it too led more than one person to the toils of combat? What good could there be in submitting to a theoretical trashing a philosophy that practice had already condemned? Althusserianism had died on the barricades of May 68, along with many other ideas from the past, and we had more important things to do than stir up old ashes.

The rare texts Althusser published during this time only served to confirm this. In them, we could see Althusser struggling, somewhat pitifully, to reconcile his old ideas with the lessons offered up by the events themselves, and to whisper a subversive idea or two into the ears of a hopeless Party.

A surprise awaited us in 1973, however. With the publication in France of the *Reply to John Lewis*, Althusser resumed the thread of an interrupted discourse. What was even stranger was the fact that Althusser only broke his silence to dress up in 'popular' garb an idea that he had defended eight years earlier – that Marxism is a theoretical anti-humanism – and to accommodate, as best he could, some of the considerations on Stalinism that were making the rounds in the streets. In June 1973, the very month Lip workers took over the management of the Lip factory, such a wet fuse was not likely to make much noise.[3]

But there was another surprise in store for us. We could hear the very same rumour being spread by philosophical circles and the mainstream media, by 'leftist' circles and those of their opponents. The *Reply to John Lewis* was the book of the year: 'a political event of the very first order', said one; 'the best Marxist treatise in years', said another. At the precise moment when we were singing in Besançon that nothing would ever again be the same, we found ourselves being forced to face our illusions. Apparently, when it came to Marxist discourse, everything was exactly the same as before. We had declared Althusserianism dead and buried in May 1968. And what but Althusserianism should come along now to tell us that the rupture of that May had actually changed nothing? In an era marked by the Union de la Gauche,[4] by the decline of leftist organizations and by the return en masse of the old parties, what but Althusserianism should reappear to sign the theoretical death certificate of leftism?

These are the questions at the origin of this book. It should be clear, then, that it aims for something a bit different than a straightforward refutation. It is not my intention to suggest which concept best replaces the 'process without a subject' or to spell out what Althusser's political position should be. Experience has taught us the futility of such appeals to the norm. Instead of refuting – whether in the name of the Front Uni or of the dictatorship of the proletariat – the theses of the PCF, it may prove more useful to examine how the Party works, concretely and in fact. Instead of showing that Althusser 'is not' a Marxist, it may be better to try to analyse *what* Althusser's Marxism is. In this commentary, when I juxtapose what Althusser says with what Marx says, the aim is never to denounce an act of treason, but to examine the function or role of the gap between their statements. This procedure, I hope, will allow us to raise the following, more general question: what use of words, what modes of reasoning and what forms of knowledge characterize a recognized Marxist discourse today? In other words, what does it mean to speak *as a Marxist* today?

Such an inquiry may perhaps contribute something to the examination of a number of questions that have become urgent as a result of our present theoretical and political conjuncture. This conjuncture is marked by a decline of classical leftism accompanied by a rise in favour of major left-wing parties and of a certain 'theoretical' Marxist discourse; by the steady proliferation of forms of revolt; by the increasingly evident inadequacy, on the part of leftists and of left-wing parties, to translate them; and by the development of forms of combat and of unionizing that are as remote from Marxist theory as from classical leftism in practice (the Lip strike, the Larzac gathering).[5] Some of the questions this particular conjuncture raises are: Does *our* Marxism allow us to understand and translate the uprisings going on today? What weapons does it give us to unify these revolts or prepare future ones? These questions open up the space for a reflection, not about the foundations of Marxism, or about its forms of rationality and the conditions for their application, but about the *practice* of Marxism. What does it mean, exactly, to be a Marxist? To read and teach Marx? To apply Marx and create 'Marxist', 'Marxist-Leninist' or 'Maoist' organizations? What can we do with a theory? What purpose does it serve? For whom? What is really at stake, politically, in the defence of theory or its application? What are the actual power relations at work in 'Marxist' organizations? Over the past ten years, Althusserianism, the crisis of the UEC, May 68 (especially) and the history of leftism have supplied Marxist intellectuals with plenty of material with which to reflect upon the questions raised above.

What happens, though, when the actors of this story want to spell out its lesson? Instead of analysing objective conditions, they theorize their state of mind, giving us a discourse of *justification*. Whether it is through Marx, Lenin and Mao, or through Nietzsche, Freud and Deleuze, what they do is explain, for example, why they believe, why they have stopped believing, why they were right or wrong, or why this or that did not work. This theorization produces a strange displacement of the scene. Instead of militants – new or old – trying to think their histories, what we find are students reciting the old lessons they learned in their philosophy classes. They want to make us believe that they are talking about May 68, or about leftism, when in fact all they are doing is resuming the thread of an interrupted academic discourse, dressing up as 'facts' the phantoms of their speculations. Consider, for example, those tired leftists who avail themselves of the Deleuzean machinery and operate it after their own fashion. Abandon Marx, the old illusions and the old books, they tell us. And what does such daring get them? Essentially, it clears the way for them to go on and on about *The Genealogy of Morals*: the revolution, the proletariat – it's all reactive libido, debt, resentment.[6] Ossified Leninists had thought it possible to understand our problems by reducing them to a single concept, the oscillation of the petite bourgeoisie; tired leftists, for their part, think that all will be clear if only we can bring everything back to the category of resentment. What they suggest, in short, is that we change authors. If Marx doesn't work, try Nietzsche; not happy with Althusser, read Deleuze. It is no surprise that these discourses of impotence echo one another: 'Everything is class struggle,' says Althusser; 'Everything is libido,' replies Lyotard and the thinkers of the CERFI. In the end, both sides say the same exact thing: 'It's all in vain. We've tried in various way to change the world; the point now is to interpret it.'

It is as if the education we received in university classrooms or in the ranks of political organizations has rendered us incapable of speaking about our history without recourse to the phantoms of speculation. The lessons given by 'practice' do not, it seems, transform consciousness quite as easily as we were told.[7] We may have to revisit our education, however briefly, to see if our pretensions to having left it behind are really justified.

These questions and these problems define the three aims of this book: to analyse what the recognized discourse of Marxist philosophy tells us in 1973, to re-examine the history of a certain contemporary adventure of Marxism and to reflect upon the effects of this school where a generation of intellectuals learned to frame the relationship between Marxist theory and class struggle.

The starting point of my discussion is the lesson in orthodoxy Althusser inflicts on John Lewis. It seemed to me that this orthodoxy, praised by some and decried by others, bore a strange figure, and that, in its paradoxes, it allowed us to make out the real political stakes of Althusser's lesson: the relationship between theory and politics that is at the heart of Althusser's whole project. With this as my starting point, I try to give a genealogy of Althusser's present discourse, to seize at its origin the relationship between politics and theory that his thought puts into play. The goal is not to give an exhaustive overview of Althusser's writings, but to pinpoint the displacements in the political position of his discourse that resulted from the effects of class struggle in the two places from which he speaks: the university and the PCF.[8] If we follow the thread of this story closely, it brings us back to the present, that is, to the *Reply to John Lewis*.

A note about the order of the argument. To bring out the full political significance of Althusser's 'orthodoxy', I thought it best to begin with a systematic deconstruction of its problematic by attending to the roles it ascribes to a handful of characters: the bourgeoisie, the petite bourgeoisie, Feuerbach and M-L. I do not deny that the 'pedagogy' of this deconstruction is slow going, and I suspect that a good many readers of the *Reply to John Lewis* may have no interest in retracing, once more, the adventures of 'man' and the 'masses'. I advise these readers to begin with Chapter 2 and eventually to return – or not – to Chapter 1.

At the end of this book, I have included an older text, 'On the Theory of Ideology', which I wrote in 1969 for a collection of essays published in Argentina. The text appeared for the first time in France in 1973, in the journal *L'Homme et la societé*.[9] Although I have changed my mind considerably since writing 'On the Theory of Ideology', I have decided to include it here, as readers may perhaps be intrigued by this first attempt at formulating a critique of Althusserianism on the morning of the events of May 68.

Lastly, I would like to thank everyone whose documentation, reflections and criticisms have helped me write this book.

# CHAPTER ONE
## A Lesson in Orthodoxy: M-L Teaches John Lewis That It Is the Masses Which Make History

> *It is just as absurd to think that workers can do without a foreman as it is to think that kids can do without teachers and the sick without doctors.*

*Georges Séguy*[1]

There was once a puzzled journalist, who could not understand why his desperate search for a photo of John Lewis for an article about the *Reply to John Lewis* had turned up nothing. This journalist, it seems safe to say, had not studied much philosophy. Otherwise he would easily have recognized in John Lewis that character – essential to every handbook in the field – who says what must not be said and, in so doing, lays the ground for philosophy to put down roots and flourish by problematizing his naïveté. In philosophy handbooks, John Lewis is generally known, quite simply, as 'common sense'.

His interlocutor, who calls himself 'M-L', is more mysterious. This curious character relentlessly tracks down everything that, from near or far, might resemble a 'subject'. And yet, he never addresses or questions his own identity; these thin initials evidently suffice on their own to preserve it. If Althusser's method in the *Reply to John Lewis* is fairly simplistic, it is because he works by ranging good and bad points side by side – all the while reproaching John Lewis for doing the same. But it is also, more importantly, because these imperious initials foreclose at the outset most of the questions that could be asked of Althusser concerning the coherence of the theses he presents in the text as Marxist-Leninist 'orthodoxy'.

1

What do the detractors of the 'orthodoxy' Althusser claims to be defending usually argue? Very briefly put, they pit Marx's historicism against Engel's naturalism, Lenin's democratic centralism against Stalinist terrorism, Mao's revolution of production relations against Lenin's insistence on the primacy of productive forces, Lenin's libertarian reveries in *The State and Revolution* against the realities of Leninist power. Althusser can of course challenge the coherence of all these oppositions, but he cannot simply make them disappear by virtue of the hyphen that joins M to L. This is especially so given that Althusser is speaking from *within philosophy*, so that what he holds up for scrutiny are not conflicting analyses of concrete situations, but 'orthodox' and heterodox theses.

But let us hear the speakers themselves. What does John Lewis say? 'It is man who makes history.' What does 'M-L' say? 'It is the masses which make history.' As Althusser likes to say: everyone can see the difference. On one side, we have the thesis that the bourgeoisie tirelessly inculcates upon the incurable minds of the petite bourgeoisie; on the other, we have the scientific, proletarian thesis. But there is something amiss here. The two theses are different, certainly, but are they speaking about the same thing? Does 'make history' have the same meaning in both instances? This question takes us back to the question raised earlier concerning the subject of these statements, and the fact is that John Lewis is nothing more than a straw man, while 'M-L' needs a more precisely defined identity. The question we must ask, then, is: behind this dialogue between an unknown philosopher and an undefined character, who is actually speaking and what is really at stake?

Who first suggested to John Lewis that it is man who makes history? Althusser tells us: it was the growing bourgeoisie of the eighteenth century, represented by the 'great bourgeois Humanists', and the declining petite bourgeoisie of the nineteenth century and beyond, represented by Feuerbach or Sartre. In this passage, Althusser explains what the thesis meant to the bourgeoisie:

> To proclaim *at that time*, as the great bourgeois Humanists did, that it is *man* who makes history, was to struggle, *from the bourgeois point of view* (which was then revolutionary), against the religious thesis of feudal ideology: it is *God* who makes history.[2]

Things are clear: the bourgeoisie proclaims that it is man who makes history as a reaction against feudalism and its providential ideology. The problem, though, is that the bourgeoisie proclaims nothing of the sort. It is one thing to show the progress of the human mind *in history*; it is quite another, however, to say that man *makes history*. Kant demonstrates that it is possible to describe 'the progress of the human mind' while working within a providential economy. As for the feudal lords attacked by the Revolution, they are very careful not to say that it is God who makes history, since that would only legitimize the revolution. What they do say, with their prophet Burke, is that society is a purely human creation, that tradition alone can give a society its justification and that natural rights and laws are a metaphysical dream. Neither Kant nor Burke, nor the 'bourgeois Humanists' more generally, raise the question of the *subject* of history, for the simple reason that this question only makes sense in light of a concept of history which they did not have. *Man* is not the answer to the question, Who makes history? Rather, he is himself the object of the question, *What is man*? Kant, whom Althusser regards as the mirror that reflects the bourgeoisie's ideological revolution, added this fourth question to his three well-known ones: What can I know? What should I do? What may I hope? The question, *What is man*? became the foundation for the development of philosophical anthropology. The most radical bourgeois answer to the question is that of materialists like Claude-Adrien Helvétius, and it goes as follows: man is a material being prompted to think and act by the impressions materially produced upon his sensory apparatus. This answer not only splits man in half at the outset, it also joins, at the root, the twin problem of private interest and of how to produce the power effects necessary to its exercise. It brings to the fore the link between the satisfaction of the interests of the minority and the effects to be produced on the sensory apparatus of the majority. Man is a material being. Here we have, spelled out, the principle of domination – private interest – and the means of its exercise. The proper means for subjecting the sensory apparatus can be known, and so too can the distribution of times, places, objects and words that secures, for the minority, a maximum of knowledge and power over the majority. This principle can be perfectly deduced from Jeremy Bentham's *Panopticon*:

> If it were possible to find out a method of making ourselves masters of all that can happen to a certain number of men, to dispose of all that surrounds them, so as to produce on them the very impressions

we wish to produce, and to determine their actions, their connexions, all the circumstances of their lives, according to a certain pre-conceived plan, there can be no doubt that such a power would be a most effectual and useful instrument in the hands of governments, and which they might apply to various objects of the highest importance.[3]

The *man* of bourgeois thought is not the grand, unified being whose figure masks exploitation. He is split in principle. Similarly, the practical ideology of the bourgeoisie, formed through the reproduction of bourgeois power relations, is not the ideology of the free person and of man as the maker of history. It is an ideology of surveillance and assistance. At its core, bourgeois *man* is far from being the conquering subject of *humanism*. He is, instead, the man of *philanthropy*, of the *humanities*, of *anthropometry* – he is formed, assisted, kept under surveillance and measured.[4]

The true heart of bourgeois ideology is not man as the maker of history, but sensible nature. And this implies a much more complex relationship between 'feudalism' and bourgeois ideology than Althusser imagines, one that is not entirely determined by the opposition between man and God. Hence Bentham's astonishment – or that of his translator – when he hits upon what he believes to be the most adequate institutional model for the young French Republic to emulate: the Inquisition.

> It is very singular that the most horrible of all institutions is in this respect an excellent model. The Inquisition in its solemn procession, its emblematic dresses, its frightful ornaments, discovered the true secret of overpowering the imagination, and speaking to the soul.[5]

Here we have a more precise idea of what we are to understand by 'Freedom, Equality, Property, and Bentham',[6] and it is something quite different from the complicity between humanism and economism. What is reflected here, on the side of the bourgeoisie, is something that workers would repeatedly denounce in the century that followed, namely, the tendentious identification of bourgeois domination and feudalism, of wage labour and serfdom. We shall have to return to this point. For now, it is enough to note, with Marx, that the central problem of the bourgeoisie is not the subject of history, but human nature. Against this background, it is important to bring into sharp relief Marx's real rupture with bourgeois ideology in the 'Theses on Feuerbach', where he pits a new materialism against the old.

> The materialist doctrine that men are products of circumstances and upbringing, and that, therefore, changed men are products of other circumstances and changed upbringing, forgets that it is men who change circumstances and that the educator must himself be educated. Hence this doctrine is bound to divide society into two parts, of which one is superior to society (in Robert Owen, for example).[7]

The point of view of the old materialism was that of 'education' and 'circumstances'; it was the point of view of a superior class that takes in charge the surveillance and the education of individuals by reserving for itself the ability to dictate every determining circumstance: the use of time, the distribution of space, the educational planning. Bentham's *Panopticon*, Owenite colonies and Fourierist phalansteries, for example, all find their models in the reformist practices of the bourgeoisie and their principles in bourgeois philosophy.[8]

This is where the decisive rupture between revolutionary thought and the hierarchical thought of the bourgeoisie is played out. Let's compare the third of Marx's theses on Feuerbach with the pages he devotes to eighteenth-century materialists in *The Holy Family*. There, Helvétius's materialism appears as the very foundation of communism: if man depends upon circumstances and education, all that is needed to change man is to change society, 'to arrange the empirical world in such a way that man experiences and becomes accustomed to what is truly human in it'.[9] In the 'Theses on Feuerbach', however, Marx raises the singularly decisive question: Who will 'arrange' this world, who will educate the educators? The 'Theses' confront the hierarchical point of view of the educators with the revolutionary transformation of the world.

But can we at the very least attribute the thesis that 'It is man who makes history' to the petite bourgeoisie – exemplarily represented by Feuerbach – that Marx had to break with in order to found historical materialism?

'The matter is also clear when we are confronted with the *philosophical* petty-bourgeois communitarian *anthropology* of Feuerbach (still respected by Marx in the *Manuscripts* of 1844), in which the Essence of Man is the Origin, Cause and Goal of history.'[10] Clear indeed. Everybody 'knows' that. In fact, everybody knows it so well that no one bothers to check its accuracy. As it happens, this well-known 'truth' is absolutely false.

Feuerbach does not say that the essence of man is the origin of history. What he says is that an alienated human essence is the origin of Hegel's speculative history. This essence, however, is not historical. Rather, it is defined in a relationship to *nature* which Feuerbach conceives either in terms of a spatial coexistence designed to be the very opposite of temporal exclusivity, or in terms of a communication between self and other that is, likewise, at the opposite pole of the temporal dialectic of negation. (If there is a philosopher opposed to the 'negation of the negation', it is Feuerbach.) History reaches this essence through an *accident* of representation, but it does not constitute or shape its development. This is so clearly the case that Marx, in the *Manuscripts* of 1844, finds himself obliged to double the man he finds in Feuerbach's thought. He writes, 'Man is not merely a natural being: he is a *human* natural being.'[11] By himself, Feuerbach's man is neither the cause nor the goal (*fin*) of any history. Marx's critique turns essentially on the fact that Feuerbach defines the essence of man by means of an atemporal relation – whether man/object, self/other, man/woman – and on the fact that, for Feuerbach, sensible experience is not historical. Marx doesn't object to the fact that Feuerbach's history has a subject; he objects to the fact that his subject has no history. If history reaches this subject, closed in as he is in the *contemplation* and *interpretation* of the world, it is purely by accident. History in Feuerbach, and in the young Hegelians in general, is the history of *representations*.

Feuerbach's philosophy is indeed humanistic, but his humanism does not go hand and in hand with any historicism. Marx's method here is quite remarkable: he does not refer Feuerbach's man to the category of the *subject*, even though such a move, coupled with the mediation of bourgeois rights, would have sealed the relationship between this man and bourgeois economism. Instead, Marx points out that Feuerbach's man is German. This is far from being the 'simplistic' observation it is sometimes taken to be. Indeed, it tells us a few things about this humanism, notably that it is not the philosophy of the bourgeois actors of class struggle, but the philosophy of a people *on the sidelines* of the major developments of class struggle. In the 'overdeveloped' philosophy of a politically 'underdeveloped' country, the inegalitarian ideology of bourgeois philanthropy can be resolved in the idyll of 'communication'. Here is a question that might reward further investigation: in general, isn't humanism – as a theory of the realization of the human essence – a marginal ideology, the result of certain discrepancies produced by the class struggle?

That is how Marx understands it. In his critique of Feuerbach, Marx does not pit the good subject of history against the bad; rather, he pits history – with its real, active subjects – against the contemplative and interpretative subjects of German ideology. He does not defend the 'good' thesis that 'It is the masses which make history' against the 'bad' thesis that 'It is man who makes history'. He is satisfied to pit against Man 'empirical' individuals, that is, the men who are brought into specific social relations as a result of their need to reproduce their existence. In other words, it is not Man who makes history, but *men* – concrete individuals, those who produce the means of their existence, the ones who fight in the class struggle. That is as far as Marx goes in his critique of Feuerbach. It is enough for him to show that the *man* Feuerbach saw as the key to the critique of speculative history is in fact another abstraction, produced by the division between manual and intellectual labour, from the historical existence of individuals.

But why should it be necessary to recall this whole story to the very person who had taught us not so long ago to distinguish between what Marx, Feuerbach and some others really say, and what we make them say as a result of our impatience or our reliance on hearsay? John Lewis is naive, certainly, and the goal here isn't to show that Althusser does not know Marx's thought and its history. Althusser, like Kautsky, certainly *knows* Marx's texts. If Althusser needs to displace the terms of the opposition between Feuerbach and Marx by attributing to Feuerbach the theses of the *Manuscripts* of 1844, and if this displacement obliges him to act as if he had forgotten all he knows about Feuerbach, it is because there is something in all of this that he does not want to know, something that cuts much deeper than the opposition between knowledge and ignorance. He is like the frustrated sleeper in Gramsci, who imagines that, by slaying a few fireflies, he can put out the moonlight keeping him awake.[12]

Let's look at what is at work in this displacement. The fundamental opposition in Marx, which he adheres to all the way to *Capital*, is between the historical and the atemporal: the bourgeoisie transforms the categories expressive of historical forms of life into the atemporal features of nature. Althusser suspects this opposition of 'historicism', hence his efforts to send the ball back to the bourgeois side of the court: the ideology of man as maker of history is the ideology of the bourgeoisie. And

Althusser does not beat around the bush to get it done: if Marx cannot come to the aid of 'orthodoxy', then 'M-L' will. This substitution occurs at a decisive moment in Althusser's argument, when the question of the 'subject' of history becomes intertwined with the question of the object of knowledge.

At this point in the text, we find Althusser dealing with the problem of how to defend the good thesis, 'One can only know what exists', against the bad thesis, 'Man only knows what he makes'. To do so, and to guarantee the primacy of the 'materialist' over the 'dialectical' theses,[13] Althusser rejects the notion that history has a privileged status, that history 'is more easily known' than nature because it is man who makes it. He writes:

> 'One can only know what exists.' As far as nature is concerned, there ought not to be much problem: who could claim that 'man' had 'made' the natural world which he knows? Only idealists, or rather only that crazy species of idealists who attribute God's omnipotence to man. Even idealists are not normally so stupid.[14]

Indeed, they are not so stupid, these idealists who – we might add – would have had no trouble showing in Althusser's argument the crudest paralogism: the idea that nature is by definition that which is not man-made. Those who insist on the artificiality of knowledge do not argue that man 'makes' the nature he knows. What they argue, instead, is that *scientists* find in the effects elicited by their experiments that which they had put into their hypotheses, or that the results they get are relative to the instruments they use for measuring, and so on. With such arguments, they suggest either that 'nature' is a rational construct or that it cannot be known in itself. Be that as it may, this whole discussion in Althusser serves only one purpose: by introducing a false symmetry, it clears the way for the idea that, when it comes to history, there are enough illusions to require the *intervention* of philosophy.

> But what about history? We know that the Thesis: 'it is man who makes history' has, literally, no sense. Yet a trace of the illusion still remains in the idea that history is *easier* to understand than nature because it is completely 'human'. That is Giambattista Vico's idea. Well, Marxism-Leninism is categorical on this point: history is as difficult to understand as nature. Or, rather, it is even more difficult to understand.

Why? Because 'the masses' do not have the same *direct practical* relation with history as they have with nature (in productive work), because they are always *separated* from history by *the illusion that they understand it*. Each ruling exploiting class offers them 'its own' explanation of history, in the form of its ideology, which is dominant, which serves its class interests, cements its unity, and maintains the masses under its exploitation.[15]

It is a good thing, surely, that 'M-L' is 'categorical' about this, since, when it comes to this question, and to Vico in particular, Marx is equally categorical. Except, he says the exact opposite:

Darwin has directed attention to the history of natural technology, i.e., the formation of the organs of plants and animals, which serve as instruments of production for sustaining life. Does not the history of the productive organs of man in society, of organs that are the material basis of every particular organisation of society, deserve equal attention? *And would not such a history be easier to compile, since, as Vico says, human history differs from natural history in that we have made the former, but not the latter?* Technology reveals the active relation of man to nature, the direct process of the production of his life, and thereby it also lays bare the process of the production the social relations of his life, and of the mental conceptions that flow from them.[16]

Citing a passage proves nothing, and we would be wasting our time if our purpose was to remind Althusser that he should respect the texts. No one is obliged to stick to what Marx says, and Althusser has every right to show us what concepts have to be criticized, abandoned or improved in the interests of revolutionary theory and practice. But that is just what he is not doing. Althusser is an implacable champion – a martyr even, he would have us think – of orthodoxy, ready to defend all its riches tooth and nail. What is, then, this Marxist-Leninist orthodoxy that supports Marx as the noose suspends a hanged man?[17]

The next phase of the argument gives a clear answer. The masses, Althusser explains, know nature better because they have a direct relationship to it in 'productive work', whereas they are separated from history by the ideology imposed upon them by the ruling classes.

It is not clear what keeps the ruling classes from offering the exploited an explanation of 'nature' that blurs the evidence of this direct relationship. Indeed, we thought we knew that the ruling classes have, from the dawn of time, offered just such a thing to the masses: religions, Feuerbach reminds us, were not made for elephants. Moreover, is it not the case that the masses do have something of a 'direct relationship' to 'history', for example, in their dealings with the lord, the tax collector, the foreman or the police officer? Or in the practical experience of corvées and discrimination, of exploitation and oppression? Is it not the essence of Marxist 'orthodoxy' that all production is simultaneously the reproduction of social relations? Is this not the touchstone that separates Marxism from bourgeois or petit-bourgeois 'philistinism'?

> Mr Proudhon understands perfectly well that men manufacture worsted, linens and silks; and whatever credit is due for understanding such a trifle! What Mr Proudhon does not understand is that, according to their faculties, men also produce the *social relations* in which they produce worsted and linens.[18]

'Men' again … Marx is decidedly hopeless. But he had an excuse: he believed in the revolution. It is thanks to that belief that we can hear in Marx the song Althusser sings here with his 'direct relationship to nature…', and which is nothing other than the old bourgeois song which ascribes 'nature' to the masses: theirs is the nobility of artisanal production, the concrete experience of matter and the charms of the rustic life; ours is the hard labour of organizing and thinking.[19] Althusser's masses remind us less of Mao's combatants than of the workers with dirty but honest faces that Lords Fleurville and Rosbourg loved to meet during their country walks.[20]

We now have a better sketch of this unfaithful orthodoxy. Althusser needs the opposition between the 'simplicity' of nature and the 'complexity' of history: production is the business of workers, whereas history is too complex an affair for them, one they must entrust to the care of specialists from the Party and from Theory. The masses produce – and so they must, otherwise we scholars would have to do it. In that predicament, how could we defend 'our right and duty to know'?[21] But when it is a matter of organizing to make history, the masses must rely on the wisdom of the Party. As for knowing history, the masses should wait for the 'theses' that specialists in Marxism work out for their benefit. Roll up your sleeves and transform nature; for history, though, you must call on us.

The 'order of reasons'[22] here is clear: if this 'orthodoxy' is 'unfaithful' to Marx, it is because it restores the *old materialism*. In so doing, it restores the bourgeois view that splits the world in two, putting producers in charge of 'nature' at the bottom and the 'men of leisure' in charge of dissipating the producers' illusions about history on top. Politics, under Louis-Philippe, was said to be the business of 'men of leisure'. History, Althusser teaches, can only be known or 'made' through the mediation of intellectuals. The 'masses' make history, certainly, but not the masses in general, only the ones *we* instruct and organize.[23] They only make history on the condition that they understand, at the outset, that they are separated from it by the thickness of the 'dominant ideology', by the stories the bourgeoisie is constantly feeding them and that they, stupid as they are, would forever be eating up, were it not for the fact that we are there to teach them how to tell the good theses from the bad. Out of the Party, no salvation for the masses; out of philosophy, no salvation for the Party.

In 1964, in order to justify the hierarchical order of the university structure, Althusser found the 'Marxist' concept of the 'technical division of labour' (proof that if one is willing to look, there is no concept that 'cannot be found' in Marxist theory).[24] This concept provided 'theoretical' backing to hierarchies in factories, to the separation between manual and intellectual labour, and to the authority of professors.[25] After the Cultural Revolution and May 68, Althusser became more prudent: he no longer told students that they must respectfully listen to their professors, or that there will always be engineers and unskilled workers. But he did not say the opposite either. His 'rectification' amounted to reproducing the very same thesis, only now cast under the modest guise of a proposition for 'scientific understanding':[26] it is more difficult to know history than nature. But this thesis can only hold if it is formulated in its true terms: politics is 'more difficult' than production. A thesis for scientific understanding. A thesis for 'scientists'.

The stakes are clear: preserve philosophy – 'Marxist philosophy' in particular – as the exclusive business of academically trained specialists by upholding a division of labour that safeguards its place. This goal, diametrically opposed to Marx's, finds its way into theory through the restoration of the 'old materialism', the materialism of educators, of those who think for the masses and who develop theses for 'scientific understanding'. The hunt for humanist fireflies is the smokescreen that gives

Althusser cover to restore the philosophical form of bourgeois philanthropy: *workers need our science*. The moonlight that keeps Althusser awake is that of the warm nights at Tsinghua University or the Sorbonne; of the thought that workers *don't need our science, but our revolt*; of the threat of a serious job crisis on the philosophical market.

This crisis had already received its theoretical formulation 130 years ago in the 'Theses on Feuerbach'. In these theses, which Althusser always found so enigmatic, Marx proclaims the end of the era of philosophers and philanthropists, of the world's well-intentioned reformers and interpreters. He announces that the time had come for the study of the real world and for its transformation, that the time was ripe for a new intelligence, one different from that of professors. Althusser, however, knows how to get around this: what Marx announces, he explains, is a 'new philosophical practice'. And this new practice, as we can see in the *Reply to John Lewis*, is thoroughly committed to the general policing of theoretical statements. But that is not what Marx has in mind. In the 'Theses on Feuerbach', he proposes a departure from philosophy, one that establishes a *politics* of theoretical statements that is essentially at odds with Althusser's. It is true that Marx is uncompromising when he wants to defend statements that belong to the academic sphere but are implicated in political practices. Thus the defence of surplus value against the 'iron law of wages', thus his claim – against Wagner – that his starting point is not 'man' but an era of social production (that is the starting point of *Capital*, not the origin of history). Still, he can affirm, with Vico, that man knows his history better than he knows natural history because he makes it, or that the origin of social relations is to be found in the 'active relation of man to nature'.[27] Marx, in other words, pits a new materialism, founded on the human history of production, against the old materialism, the 'abstract materialism of natural science'.[28] That is why Marx can say that 'man' – or 'men' – make(s) history, without first getting clearance from the control bureau for proletarian statements, and without incurring any of the catastrophic scientific and political consequences Althusser predicts will befall anyone who dares utter such horrors. Marx is no longer speaking from within philosophy, and this allows him to say that man makes history without being obliged, in the same breath, to offer a thesis about the 'subject' of history. Marx is arguing against 'abstract materialism', and so he places himself there where Althusser's problem – the primacy of 'materialist' over 'dialectical' theses – makes no sense. 'One can only know what exists,' Althusser declares. Marx's point is entirely different: he argues that the consciousness of men is determined by their 'social being',[29] and that the point of view of the relationship of 'knowledge' to 'being' characterizes the non-dialectical thought of the old materialism, the materialism expressive of the bourgeois world view. There is no possible hierarchy between two indissociable terms, according to Marx. What this means, among other things, is that there is not, opposed to the idealist tradition, a materialist tradition which has dialectical materialism as one of its forms. Both the old materialism and idealism belong to the same theoretical configuration. The new materialism sets itself over and against this configuration just as the transformation of the world sets itself over and against its interpretation. This renders useless the derisory philosophical court where Althusser separates the good theses from the bad, and where he pursues a philosophy that seems less entitled to its independence the more zealously it seeks to stake it. What, after all, does philosophy have to tell us? That 'It is the masses which make history'? Do we really need philosophy to tell us this? 'The fact that scientific propositions may *also*, in the context of a philosophical debate, "function philosophically" is worthy of thought,' says Althusser.[30] But wouldn't it be more accurate to inverse the problem? Is it not rather this philosophy, whose jurisdiction is said to be so indispensable to historical materialism even though it appears to have nothing better to do than rehearse its talking points, that is 'worthy of thought'? The question could easily be related to a number of other questions. How is it that the people who pocket the surplus-value of wage workers can at the same time 'function' like wage workers? The answer to this question lies in the fact that factory labour functions, simultaneously, as labour that produces surplus value. Could the 'labour' of philosophy be something of the same order? Does it produce a certain 'surplus' through the appropriation of the concepts of historical materialism and of the slogans of class struggle? Can we not recognize, in the zealous agent of this appropriation, the anonymous and omnipresent M-L, the silhouette of a character – half-worker, half-bourgeois – indispensable to any extortion of surplus: the foreman?

Let us take a closer look at this. What does 'M-L' say here? 'It is the masses which make history.' That is the reply Althusser has M-L give to the idealist proposition that 'It is man who makes history.' If this reply is not to be found in Marx, as we have seen, it is because the fundamental opposition for him is between the approach from 'nature' and the approach from history.[31] In other words, it is enough for Marx to pit concrete men – or man – against the man of the old materialism. Additionally, 'the masses' was not a concept with a defined theoretical status in Marx's work; indeed, it did not acquire that status in the Marxist tradition until much later. Lenin exalts the creative initiative of the masses in 1905 and 1917, but the Menchevist and Luxembourgian opposition between 'masses' and 'leaders' also made him suspicious of the notion. The reply only gained its credentials with Maoism: 'It is the masses which make history' is not a 'philosophical thesis of Marxism-Leninism'; it is, essentially, a political thesis of Maoism, even if it was not Mao who coined the phrase. What does Mao say, exactly? 'The people, and the people alone, are the motive force of world history.'[32] It is understandable that, here too, Althusser prefers to have 'M-L' speak: this 'world history' is a bit too Hegelian, this 'creativity' a bit too humanistic.[33] But that is what is being talked about, and we cannot simply try to put all the blame for such language on translators, who also give us, incidentally, this emblematic sentence from the Cultural Revolution: 'It is the masses of people who push history forward.'[34] The whole problem really turns on the *competence of the masses*, not on the *subject of history*. To say, in 1945, that the people alone are the creators of history is to affirm the imminent and immediate defeat of fascism; it is to announce to future generations that the means of struggle forged by the intelligence of the oppressed will triumph over the death machine Chiang Kai-shek and his powerful army put in place with the support of the world's imperialist powers. Mao's thesis is this: it is the oppressed who are intelligent, and the weapons of their liberation will emerge from their intelligence (as an illustration, consider the admirable narratives gathered by Snow or Myrdal).[35] The thesis spells out a double superiority: that of the people's fighters over imperialist and feudal armies and that of the peasants of Tathai, the workers of Shanghai and the students at Tsinghua University over the specialists who want to teach them the art of leading the class struggle, of producing, of cultivating the land and of studying Marxism. 'The masses are the real heroes': that is not at all a self-evident 'Marxist-Leninist thesis'. It is, for the most part, a *new* thesis, one quite clearly opposed to the Kautskyist tradition founded on the conviction that the masses are unable to elevate their intelligence beyond what it takes to get a pay raise. It is a political thesis that goes hand in hand with a new conception of the development of productive forces and the methods of communist leadership: the intelligence of the class struggle, much like the intelligence of production, does not belong to specialists. Workers who invent a new machine, peasants who devise an economic irrigation system, unarmed villagers who frighten powerful enemy armies with their snares: all of them create history. The 'duty' of workers is no longer to exceed productivity norms; it is, instead, to invent a new world through their barely perceptible gestures. This is a new thesis, and it calls into question two conceptions of Marxism: the mechanistic conception tied to the 'development of productive forces' and the authoritarian conception tied to 'democratic centralism' and the 'dictatorship of the proletariat'.[36]

All of this is at play in the claim that the masses, and the masses only, are the creators of history, and it cannot but raise some questions about the 'Marxist philosophy' of 'communist intellectuals'. For what is stated here quite clearly is that the masses have as 'direct' a 'relationship' to history as to nature and that, conversely, a 'direct relationship to nature' could perhaps disabuse the educators of the masses of a good many of their own illusions. This is not a philosophical thesis in which a 'simple' subject – man – is confronted with a more complex subject that essentially explodes the concept of 'subject'. The thesis does, indeed, reject bourgeois ideology, but in a completely different way: it rejects the idea that the oppressed must be *assisted*, either by the charity of philanthropists who relieve them of their misery, or by the science of philosophers who dispel their illusions. This new thesis actually inhabits the space designated by the 'Theses on Feuerbach', that is, the space of a new intelligence – the intelligence formed in the struggle, the knowledge reclaimed from the hands of the exploiters.[37] This new intelligence, forged over there, obliges every 'Marxist philosopher' over here to rethink the question of his practice and his knowledge; it obliges him to reconsider his place in the distribution of the spaces of power and knowledge that reproduce bourgeois domination. An uncomfortable question. Behind the mediocre jokes about John Lewis's 'man', his 'little human god' who is 'up to his neck' in reality, but who manages now and then to step out of that reality and 'change its character', are phenomena quite contrary to 'science': mountains to be moved, workers who storm the heavens[38] ... when will we be done with this sort of nonsense?

Althusser's manoeuvre here is as classical as can be. He transforms the expression of a practice of the masses into a philosophical thesis that he defends with the 'heroes' of theory. We thought we were talking about the Cultural Revolution when, in fact, the whole thing turns out to be about the 'process without a subject'. Philosophy makes this new thesis, born from a practice which calls philosophy itself into question, a part of its machinery, and it makes its enunciation of this thesis a confirmation of its own power. The challenge Mao Tse-tung's army of beggars represented to the overwhelming forces of the Kuomintang, or the challenge represented by the Chinese peasants and workers who were abandoned to their 'incompetence' by Soviet experts, becomes in Althusser's hands another piece of evidence in the philosophical trial convened to settle an old family feud: the undoing of the 'Kantian heritage'. Althusser wants to make us believe that the 'Marxist theoretical revolution' is ultimately a critique of the subject, as if philosophy had not made the undoing of the subject its bread and butter for two centuries already. What begins with the purification of the subject through the all-out war against the substantiality of the cogito and the finitude of the mental powers, leads – somewhat later – to an attack on the subject itself. Nietzsche detects in the subject a grammatical illusion, and Heidegger later accuses him of being the last representative of the dissimulation operated by the old 'subject' of Western metaphysics. From Schelling to Feuerbach, from Feuerbach to Nietzsche, from Nietzsche to Heidegger, from Heidegger to structuralism ... it's a while now that philosophers have been entertaining us with the subject's descent into hell. But what purpose does this process without a subject serve, exactly? It is, in truth, hard to say anything else about this absence of the subject, other than that it presents philosophers with a new recipe for their old problem: how to be done with the subject? If the philosophical community accepted Althusserianism so readily, it is because that community could easily see its own concerns reflected in it. These concerns, for reasons indicated below, had at that very moment acquired a certain urgency.

This family feud is not played out independently of the class struggle; it has political implications. If we are to grasp them, however, we have to reject the speculative practice that operates by divorcing statements from their political and theoretical context so as to be able to pit them, in an imaginary class struggle, against statements that they would never have confronted in practice. In order to analyse the political effects of a particular thesis, we must oppose what practice itself opposes. Let's examine, for example, the 'political effects' of the claim, 'It is the masses which make history':

> You do not have to be a great thinker to see that, when one tells workers that 'it is men who make history', one sooner or later contributes to disorienting or disarming them. One tends to make them think that they are all-powerful as men, whereas in fact they are disarmed as workers in the face of the power which is really in command: that of the bourgeoisie, which controls the material conditions (the means of production) and the political conditions (the state) determining history. By feeding them this humanist line, one turns workers away from the class struggle, one prevents them from making use of the only power they possess: that of their *organization as a class* and their *class organizations* (the trade unions, the party), by which they wage *their* class struggle.[39]

The method never changes. For the theoretical debunking of 'humanism', Althusser brings 'M-L' into action. But when it is a matter of refuting it in practice, he relies on the 'one' of the passage above.[40] When 'one' tells workers that it is men who make history, 'one' disarms and disorients them. (To what extent one arms and orients workers by telling them that the bourgeoisie is all powerful is a question we shall return to.) Althusser 'talks about politics' and reproaches John Lewis for not doing so.[41] However, the political discussion of Lewis's theses resolves to nothing more than a description of their probable effects. Apparently, the organization John Lewis belongs to, Great Britain's Communist Party, cannot lay claim to a practice that is sufficiently spectacular as to invite debate on the effects of this or that thesis discussed in its theoretical journal. Consequently, Althusser can give his forecasts without risking much. But there are other communists who have developed theses of this sort and who have made sure that they produced verifiable political effects (Gramsci, for example). As it happens, though, it is precisely when Althusser has communist leaders in his sights that he is satisfied with offering a strictly philosophical critique of their positions; political practice, if it intervenes at all, serves only as an *excuse* for their theoretical errors. Hence, in *Reading Capital*, Gramsci and Lukács see their leftism excused by the failure of the Second International.[42] Gramsci's theses, however, do not rely – on the theoretical side – solely on Croce, nor – on the practical side – solely on the fall of Kautskyism. They also rely on a quite specific proletarian practice (the factory councils), and they have produced visible political effects. If the 'theoreticism' of *Reading Capital* had foreclosed the discussion of those political effects, is this not one opportunity to put 'rectification' into practice?

But there is no need to go back so far. After all, doesn't Althusser suspect John Lewis of being nothing more than Sartre's British double? This gives Althusser the occasion to wax ironic, in the 'witty' tone that has endeared him to his more refined readers, about the philosopher 'of man-projecting-himself-into-the-future' and of an ethics that is always still to come.[43] But shouldn't this be the place to discuss the political effects of Sartre's theses? In Sartre, the whole problematic of 'men' making history is bound up with a perfectly clear set of political problems, all of which are ultimately related to the political role of intellectuals. What part can intellectuals without a party take in revolutionary political combat? What relation can they have to the working class, when they are neither the 'importers' of theory, nor Party functionaries? How can they reconcile the demands of their own practice (the 'objectivity' of research, the 'universality' of truth, etc.) with the demands of organized political combat? Is it right not to say what one thinks or knows to be true because the party line says that such 'petit-bourgeois' scruples or malaises are to be subjected to the discipline of the class struggle? And what status should one give to a discipline whose effects are not intended to restore the old constraints of *raison d'état*? If the 'communist' intellectuals of our generation can only laugh at the naïveté of all these questions, it is because they think they have succeeded in settling all of these problems by introducing the following arrangement: we leave the Party alone in questions of politics, and it leaves us alone when it comes to epistemology and other issues of theoretical practice.

But all of these questions were integral to the existentialist problematic of man as maker of history. They were, moreover, on the horizon of the major overarching question about the history of the Soviet Revolution, that of its trajectory from October to concentration camps. It also worth mentioning that there have been real confrontations between existentialism and Marxism over the years: the polemics of 1946–1947, when the PCF accused existentialism of being anti-humanistic, thus obliging Sartre to respond by proving his humanism;[44] the articles Merleau-Ponty and Sartre published in *Les Temps modernes*; the debate in 1961 about dialectics in history and in nature. Wouldn't the analyses of these debates be full of interesting lessons?[45] Sartre's theses have also had quite precise political effects. During the Algerian War, for example, they were behind the propaganda in favour of insubordination and behind the establishment of a network of direct support to the FLN.[46] In May 68, they legitimized support for the student uprisings. After May 68, they were implicated in the alliance Sartre forged with Maoist militants, in the editorship of *La Cause du peuple*,[47] in the Lens tribunal, in the establishment of new forms of interaction between intellectuals and the popular masses and in the creation of a new daily paper (*Libération*).[48] Are not all of these political practices right under our noses? And do they not attest to some sort of convergence between Sartre's theoretical questions and the questions the Cultural Revolution raised? This is what has to be discussed if we want to have a conversation about the political effects of Sartre's thought. But it is impossible to discuss any of this without making a *political choice*. If we were to examine the policy of providing direct aid to the Algerian struggle, we would have to speak about the politics of the Communist Party and about the vote to give full powers to Guy Mollet – a vote justified, as it were, on a certain interpretation of the thesis that it is the masses which make history.[49] But are these masses and Althusser's the same? Similarly, if we were to speak about May 68 or later, we would have make a choice: we would have to say who we thought was right at the beginning of May 68, Marchais or the students; we would have to discuss the role the Communist Party played in restoring order to the university; we would have to say whether we thought Sartre associated with a gang of provocateurs and whether we thought the project of a free press was a dream. To speak about all this is inevitably to take a political position; it is, ultimately, to take a position for or against the politics of the apparatus of the Communist Party. Althusser is evidently not too keen on doing this. For he cannot very well allow himself to be against the Party, nor can he, given the consideration he owes to his 'leftist' public, allow himself to justify the Party's political positions. If the Party tolerates Althusser's pranks, it is not just because they are harmless; it is, more importantly, because they act as a magnet that attracts the leftist fringe to the Party. This only works, though, if Althusser's 'leftist' public has some reason to believe, or pretend to believe, that Althusser agrees with it politically and that it is the Party that is being played. This fringe accepts Althusser's PCF membership, provided he never justifies its political positions.[50] This double game is not only necessary for

Althusserianism to be able to bring leftists back into the Party fold, it is also essential to its theoretical status. Indeed, the latter is entirely dependent upon Althusserianism's double role: part militant–communist and part Maoist, anti-revisionist theoretician. Had they been written by an unknown intellectual or by the theoretician of some groupuscule or other, would anyone pay any attention to the theses of the *Reply to John Lewis*? The only way to preserve the balance of this double role is to go on at length about the political effects of imaginary statements devoid of context, while saying nothing at all about the real political practices immanent to these 'philosophical' theses.

This non-political stance is a political choice. But if Althusser deliberately sidesteps any discussion of the political effects of the theses he attacks, he unwillingly tells us quite a lot about the political foundations of his own theses. When 'one' tells workers that 'it is men who make history', 'one' makes 'them think that they are all-powerful as men, whereas in fact they are disarmed as workers in the face of the power which is really in command: that of the bourgeoisie, which controls the material conditions (the means of production) and the political conditions (the state) determining history'.[51] Is that really what the Maoist claim that the masses make history means? Does it not mean, rather, that in the last instance the 'determination' of history belongs to the revolt and intelligence of the oppressed, and not to the paper tigers who control the means of production and the bourgeois state?[52] 'By feeding them this humanist line, one turns workers away from class struggle, one prevents them from making use of the only power they possess: that of their *organization as a class* and their *class organizations* (the trade unions, the party), by which they wage *their* class struggle.'[53] Here we have it: the *only* power of workers is their organization, which is to say – lest there be any doubt – the trade unions and '*the*' Party.[54] This silly multitude has nothing going for it; nothing, that is, other than its numbers and the organization it acquires – as we all know – in the schools of the factory.[55] Let us not, then, join hands in criticizing this, their only power. These reservations aside, Althusser is ardent about the Cultural Revolution.[56] 'What is this "man" who "makes" history?' he asks, and answers: 'A Mystery.'[57] But the well-organized and – according to the *Reply* – history-making 'masses' hold no mystery at all: they are the 'non-monopolized strata', united – thanks to the good graces of the Champigny program[58] – around the 'Party of the working class'.

It is to get to this point that Althusser undertakes all of these manoeuvres, imputes to the bourgeoisie a problem it does not have (Who makes history?), attributes to Feuerbach a thesis that actually belongs to the young Marx, transforms a Marxist thesis into the core of bourgeois ideology, debunks this 'bourgeois ideology' by way of an M-L that effectively restores a most banal materialism through its commendation of old principles and of the old wisdom of the rich ('One can only know what exists'; 'You can't step out of reality to change its character'; 'It is difficult to know history') and transforms the fighters of Mao's army into the voters of the Union de la gauche.[59]

This is where the twists and turns of this paradoxical orthodoxy lead us: the mediation of philosophy was necessary to bring Mao to Marchais. But, at the same time, the philosopher needed Marchais's mediation in order to bring the slogans of the Chinese people into the folds of philosophy books and to implicate the Cultural Revolution in an academic debate in which the proponents of a new trend (which stresses epistemology, rupture, the process without a subject, or writing) are locked in battle with the proponents of the old trend (which insists on intentionality, critique, praxis and hermeneutics). Is this a debate with nothing at stake? No, certainly not. But what is at stake – the relationship of the producers of university ideology to their consumers – is *extrinsic* to the debate itself. If there is so little rigour in Althusser's definition of the 'humanism' he is critiquing, if this critique forces him to deal more harshly with Marx than with John Lewis, it is because his fight against a 'revisionist' humanism is to only a screen. (All we have to do to convince ourselves of this is to look at how Régis Debray today puts Althusserian rhetoric at the service of Mitterand's humanist outbursts.) From the beginning, though, something more important has been at work behind the fight Althusser the philosopher wages against a declining existentialism and the one Althusser the 'communist' wages against those of his 'comrades' who have been corrupted by bourgeois humanism. All along, this has been the fight of a 'communist philosopher' against that which threatens both the authority of his Party and of his philosophy: Cultural Revolution on a global scale, and students who contest the authority of knowledge on a local scale.

# CHAPTER TWO

## A Lesson in Politics: Philosophers Did Not Become Kings

*I was forced to admit that humanity's ills would only end when the class of true and authentic philosophers came to power, or when rulers were moved by some divine inspiration to philosophize in earnest.*

*Plato*[1]

*Youth counts enthusiasm, dedication, the taste for action, the thirst for the new and generosity among its natural qualities. But, rich as youth is made by these qualities, they do not give the young the power [faculté] to master all their problems spontaneously .... If these natural qualities are to work towards their happiness, the young have to be guided with a sure hand.*

*Roland Leroy*[2]

In February 1968, Althusser addressed the members of the Société française de philosophie, and through his voice Lenin entered the lecture halls of the Sorbonne.[3] On 13 May of that same year, thousands of students made a less solemn entry into those same halls and pitched there the flags of their revolt. The proximity of these two infringements of 'class struggle' upon the university can perhaps help us define the space wherein the *political* history of Althusserianism was played out.

It is strange to note that this political history is entirely *forgotten* in the 'self-critique' that leads Althusser to proclaim the need for 'partisanship' in philosophy.[4] The history of Althusserianism, as told in his self-critical essays, goes as follows: Althusserianism arose from the desire to combat the revisionist tendencies that had seeped into philosophy following the Twentieth Congress, but was eventually led into a 'theoreticist' deviation by the need to restore Marxism to its status as a science and by the period's predominantly 'structuralist' environment.[5] This deviation, which defines Marxism as a theory of the production of scientific knowledges,[6] succeeds in claiming for Marxism the status of a science with its own norms of verification, but also cuts Marxism off from political practice. Althusser rectifies this 'theoreticist' deviation with the notion, introduced in *Lenin and Philosophy*, of 'partisanship' in philosophy. From that moment on, philosophy ceases to be the science of science and becomes political intervention. Philosophy will be class struggle's representative in the sciences, and the sciences's representative in class struggle. As such, philosophy traces a political line of demarcation in its relationship to the sciences that effectively separates the *idealist* from the *materialist* exploitation of scientific practices. Everything suddenly becomes clear: 'theoreticism' had forgotten politics, and 'partisanship in philosophy' restores politics to its governing role.

This apologetic history, however, forgets an important fact: it is *precisely* the 'theoreticist' discourse of *For Marx* and of *Reading Capital* that produced political effects, both on the practices of communist organizations and on the student uprisings. And its effects were quite contradictory. The Marxist science and 'rigour' of Althusser's 'theoreticism' strengthened the PCF apparatus by recruiting communist students to the Party. But it also created a fissure, as this very science and rigour provided support to the Maoist students who founded the first Maoist *student* organization in France, the UJC (ML).[7] 'Theoreticism' not only produced a broad range of political effects, it also contributed to specific political operations within the UEC: reversals of power, returns to power, the formation of factions, secessions. Moreover, after May 68, as the critique of theoreticism drew Althusser into what he describes as a fierce class struggle over the question of the reality of matter, those university students who were card-carrying members of the PCF were brandishing 'theoreticist' texts as they called for the re-establishment of order at the university.

These political effects were not produced in spite of theoreticism, or *alongside* it. Certainly, we must distinguish between Althusser's politics and the politics of Althusserianism; Althusser may very well always have kept his distance from the latter, but that very distance was a political position. The supposed 'theoreticism', in other words, didn't forget politics for a minute; quite the contrary: it was an actual partisanship, and not only 'in philosophy'. Differently put, theoreticism was the meeting point for a number of political contradictions, all of which harboured the possibility for contradictory political effects. The important point, in any case, is that all these contradictions were woven together by, and all these effects produced through, the interpretation of one concept: the *autonomy of theoretical practice*. The politics of Althusserianism was played out in the assertion of this autonomy, in the implications and political effects of that assertion.

Althusser's theoretical and political project, the one that began with the publication of 'On the Young Marx' in 1961, is staked on the bet that it is possible to effect a *political* transformation inside the Communist Party through a theoretical investigation aimed at restoring Marx's thought. There was no political solution outside the Party (because it was *the* party *of* the working class), but there was no political solution within the Party either, as it was at the time undergoing a liberal *aggiornamento*[8] inspired by the PCI and representative of the hopes of intellectuals opposed to the Party line. This liberalism was essentially the other side of Zhdanovian terrorism, a different expression of the very same principle, the very same subjectivist repression of Marxist *dialectic*. The only way to keep the liquidation of Stalinism from resulting in eclecticism in theory and revisionism in practice was restore Marx's theory, that is to say, restore the scientific ground upon which new political problems could be discussed. The key to the success of this project, according to Althusser, was 'the *investigation* of Marx's *philosophical* thought'.[9] If there was anything good to have come out of the Twentieth Congress, it was the space of *relative* freedom for the study of Marxism opened up by the end of Stalinism, and it was important to make the most of that opening. It would now be possible to speak about Marx again, to dust off the major texts, to read everything around the passages we had only seen cited, to situate these cited passages in their theoretical and political context, to look with fresh eyes at the major lines of philosophical filiation (Hegel, Feuerbach, Marx), to return the texts to their nudity and the interpretations to their history. To see this as nothing more than a palaeographic exercise that turned its back on politics would be a mistake, for the whole project was in fact directed at rediscovering, whether in the scientific practice of *Capital* or in Lenin's political practice, the *bases* upon which political problems could be raised, at unearthing the site wherein those problems could each be defined and the instruments suited to resolving them found. Simply returning to the texts that held the key to the correct political positions was never the point. The goal, rather, was to find anew the *dialectical* practice at work in Marx's text and Lenin's actions. The polemic with Mury is revealing in this respect.[10] There, Althusser confronts the retrospective knowledge of historians with the dialectic at work in the political determination of the combination of contradictions that define 'the current situation'.[11] In one or another note or allusion in the texts from this period, we catch a glimpse of the political aspirations that inform Althusser's project: to confront the 'debate of ideas' that had taken root in France as a result of its theoretical and political misery (its 'provincialism', as Althusser is fond of saying)[12] with the political rationality of the revolutions then underway, in China and in Cuba.

Theoreticism didn't forget politics at all. What happened, rather, is that it took a *detour* in order to recover what is specific to Marxist politics. Everything was played out in this detour, and not in the simple opposition of theory to practice or dream to reality. The key was the double relationship this detour established between philosophy and politics – local politics (French misery in need of a solution), and distant politics (the revolutions of long ago or of distant places, whose specific dialectic had to be thought through). Everything was played out in this double relationship. If we were to find a way out of the opposition of dogmatism to opportunism that characterized the political situation at the time, then we had to look for the solution *elsewhere*: in the updated rationality of revolutionary politics in action that we find in Lenin in 1917 and Mao in 1937. The operation split politics into two camps, one blind and empirical, the other rational. This rational politics, however, had not revealed the principle of its rationality: Marx never wrote the 'Logic' of *Capital*, and Lenin and Mao only give us sporadic hints of the logic of their politics. It was up to philosophy, then, to release the dialectic at work in their practice. It was here that philosophy justified its necessity: in the relationship between blindness and silence – between an irrational politics and a rational politics that does not speak the principle of its rationality–and on the radical silence looming on the horizon – the silence of the masses.

Philosophy's new status becomes fully visible in the introduction to *For Marx*, written in 1965. Also clearly sketched out in this text is the historical figure of political irrationality which haunts Althusser's reflections – as it haunts those of every communist intellectual of his generation: Zhdanovism, the time when philosophers could only choose between silence or the deliriums of 'proletarian science'. The importance Althusser attaches to Marx's philosophy is a response to the experience of that time. We should, of course, distinguish what the introduction to *For Marx* owes to the philosopher's self-defence and what it owes to political intuition. Under the first heading, we might underline Althusser's recollections of the humiliation suffered by philosophers 'without writings of [their] own' and without an audience among their 'peers'; the resentment at the insults from enemies who, he writes, 'flung in our faces the charge that we were merely politicians'; the regret for not having defended 'our right and duty to know'.[13] All these formulations make Althusser's defence of the integrity of the university sound a little forced. It is true, though, that one of the noteworthy effects of Althusserianism is that it secured a royal place for communist intellectuals in that cohort, the university elite. Thanks to Althusser, Party intellectuals have enjoyed the undivided attention and consideration of their peers. But we should not focus solely on this aspect of the issue and ignore the deep-seated political meaning of this historical recollection. Althusser's thesis is this: to reduce Marx's *philosophy* to historical materialism would be to subordinate theory to the whims of politics all over again. When confronted with the whims of subjectivism, it is not enough to carve out a safe haven for theory; one must also fortify this haven with the difference between science and philosophy. (To have historical materialism without dialectical materialism would be to run the risk of reducing theory to a form of ideology; it would be to 'treat science, a status Marx claims [for his work] on every page, as merely the first-comer among ideologies'.[14])

This analysis gives the following name to the perversion of Marxism it denounces: *leftism*. 'To defend Marxism, imperilled as it was by Lysenko's "biology", from the fury of bourgeois spite, some leaders had relaunched this old Left-wing [Leftist] formula, once the slogan of Bogdanov and the Proletkult.'[15] The crux of the matter is here, in the view of 'leftism' that

Althusser imports wholesale from the official self-critique of 'proletarian science' offered by the Soviet Communist Party: it had all been a leftist error. Behind Lysenko and Zhdanov is Bogdanov; behind the cold rigours of Soviet *raison d'état* and of the Soviet Communist Party is the old leftist folly of wanting to subject all truth to historical and political criteria. Faced with such circumstances, the only alternative was to assert the autonomy of Marxist *philosophy*. The first order of business, after asserting this autonomy, was to give it a foundation, and that is what Althusser does with his elaboration of a new concept of politics and history – the concept of overdetermination, of the heterogeneity of historical time. The introduction of this concept clears the way for Althusser to advance the thesis that the concept of leftism, in its general form, is the concept of a bad totality, one that denies the autonomy of philosophy, the heterogeneity of times and the distinctions among instances of the social whole.

It is easy to follow the development of this concept of leftism from 'On the Young Marx' to the introduction to *For Marx*. At first, Althusser is still thinking within the categories of *The German Ideology*: the suppression of philosophy, the primacy of historical materialism and the opposition of historical reality to the illusions of ideologues. 'Contradiction and Overdetermination', however, opens a new period in which Althusser questions the appeal to 'history' in the name of what is specific to politics (overdetermination). Althusser's first political target had been economism, but in the texts from 1965 the political target became leftism, understood as the general form of a bad totality. These texts describe the historical experience of Zhdanovism as a particular form of the leftist deviation, one whose defining trait is philosophy's loss of theoretical and political *identity*: theoretical – philosophy is an ideology that stems from historical materialism; political – politics is realized philosophy. Althusser chases this deviation across a number of its avatars: Bogdanov – truth is a form of ideology; Gramsci – all men are philosophers; Lukács – Marxism is the self-consciousness of the proletariat; Zhdanov – class struggle permeates everything. And he detects its effects in the budding student movement of 1963: students are productive labourers and should be able to control the knowledge of their professors.

It is essential for Althusser to be able to group all these political positions under the single model of subjectivism (voluntarism, historicism, leftism). It is likewise essential for leftism to appear as nothing other than the flip side of rightist economism, fruit of the same tree of history, as continuous and homogeneous. Revisionism and leftism are the same thing for Althusser. If he treats leftism as public enemy number one, it is because leftism is the *philosophical* form – reduction of the theoretical to the political, affirmation of time as homogeneous and continuous – assumed by this deviation. This explains why the main theoretical targets of *Reading Capital* are 'leftists' such as Gramsci and Lukács. The political struggle against revisionism must pass through the philosophical struggle against leftism. This principle will of course have some political consequences when leftism, initially only a philosophical tendency, becomes a *political* force.

There is little doubt that this evocation of the terrible times of Zhdanovism reveals Althusser's core intuition. If theory has to be fashioned out of the unpredictable meanderings of daily politics and if history is a homogeneous field, so that everything that is said or written in it draws its authority from historical materialism, then there can be no rationality to Marxist politics. From Bogdanov to Kautsky, from Kautsky to Lukács, from Lukács to Stalin, from Stalin to Garaudy, there is only a movement from right to left, from Charybdis to Scylla, from the similar to the same. If theory is to escape this, its time of elaboration cannot be the same as the time of political campaigns or Cold War manoeuvres. Nor can the norms of theoretical truth be the norms of Party discipline. Here we come upon the roots of Althusser's entire theoretical apparatus, of the whole system of differences he sets in motion: the distinction among instances, the construction of the time specific to each instance, the severing of science from ideology, the epistemological break that allows him to discard all the themes of leftist subjectivism as part of Marx's personal prehistory. This system of heterogeneities, with which Althusser eludes the simple liberalism that many an intellectual survivor of difficult times regarded as the only solution, is in some ways a guarantee against the return of the old nightmares. But it is also a substitute, one that conflates a particular politics, time and history with another, and one that produces a double exclusion in its search for the actualization of Marxist philosophy in political practice. Althusser's recourse to Lenin is marked by the double denial of politics as a systematization of the ideas of the masses and as the set of operations of one *power*. The analysis of the Zhdanovian period illustrates this double denial perfectly, for it is entirely pitched around the relationship between the madness of particular leaders (thus effectively reducing the mechanisms of power to Bogdanovian subjectivism) and the lack of theory: our leaders were so crazy because they didn't have a 'theoretical tradition'.

Absence, the void, is the only explanation Althusser gives for the 'madness' of a 'period summed up in caricature by a single phrase, a banner flapping in the void: "bourgeois science, proletarian science".'[16] 'A banner flapping in the void' – the expression is not random. It is, on the contrary, strangely reminiscent of Althusser's mockery of the slogan, 'Sorbonne to the students', on the banners and signs that student strikers in 1963 brandished, as he says, 'in the sky, that is to say, in a utopian void'.[17] The place of ideology is the void, the absence of science. Everything that flaps in the sky of political storms is necessarily flapping in the void filled by ideology.

'Proletarian science' might have been hopeless in biology, but it was not so bad when it came to physics, nor did its banners flap in the void. Indeed, if they flapped so loudly, it is because they were filled with the same wind that held aloft the banners of the conquerors of Stalingrad and of Mao's army as it marched towards Nanjing. It is, above all, because they flapped in the same sky against which rang out the slogans of striking miners and the bullets of Jules Moch's fusillades.[18] It would be good to reread the texts from this period, particularly those in the first issue of *La Nouvelle Critique*,[19] for they show clearly enough that the issue was not the void, but the positivity borne by the manifest sense of a struggle. The large miner strike of 1948 and the furious way in which it was repressed had an impact on the consciousness of Party intellectuals, not simply because it showed an enthusiasm that justified delirium, but because it produced a double evidence:

1. It is impossible that there should be anything in common – not even the science and culture we once claimed as a common heritage – between the world of the miners and the world of Jules Moch.

2. The very dialectic of class struggle refuted the existence of needs that stand above classes: the same miners who had accepted the 'Coal Battle'[20] in 1945 refused in 1948 to put the need to provide the French population with heating and to protect the basis for an economic activity above their class struggle. Their practice affirmed that there is no need to produce that stands above the class struggle. Why didn't intellectuals put their 'productions' to the same

test? Why didn't they ask themselves about the absolute need of their modes of verification? The miners's practice brought forth the ideological matrix that made the idea of a 'proletarian science' *acceptable* to intellectuals: no production that stands above classes for workers, and no science that stands above classes for intellectuals. It rendered the idea acceptable because, at the end of the day, intellectuals had no choice but to accept it. 'Petit bourgeois' that they are, they can only challenge the authority of the Party by insisting on intellectual 'scruples' that betray their resistance, as a class, to 'go over to working class positions'.[21] All of this has little to do with a 'lack' of science or of a 'theoretical culture'.[22] It is important to analyse all the pieces of the puzzle: the systematization of the ideas and practices of the masses, the rechanneling of these ideas and practices by an organizational power, the mechanism of subordinating intellectuals by preying on their guilt at being petit bourgeois and the political function of philosophy (it befell to philosophers to take up the task, rejected by biologists, of defending Michurian biology).[23] All these pieces disappear in the simple opposition of the lack of science and the delirium attributed to ignorance – if only our leaders had known ... The slumber of reason is responsible for engendering these monsters, and empirical history is nothing other than this slumber: it is the home of subjectivity, of the delirium of leaders and of banners flapping in the void – in sum, it is a history of sound and fury that is the very opposite of the enlightened politics based on the distinction of levels. What this means is that we must *rediscover* Marxist dialectic. There is no hope of articulating a just politics by systematizing the ideas and practices of mass revolt which constituted the reality of life in France in the 1960s. The solution has to be sought elsewhere. People will no doubt say that 'the masses' are not a magic cure effective upon mere invocation, or that the reality in France during this period did not provide examples of mass practices that could have suggested to Althusser the solution he felt he had to cast out so far in order to find. The problem, though, is that this objective situation led the Althusserian project down a particular path, obliging it to find the rationality of political practice outside that practice and *to invent* theoretical solutions to problems that political practice could not solve. The return to Marx, the autonomy of theoretical practice, the theory of the autonomy of instances: all of these are attempts to find a solution, *from above*, to the revisionist crisis. The autonomy of instances, a substitute for the autonomy of the masses, was, in essence, a new figure of utopia. True, it was not a utopia populated by phalansteries or Icarians ready to welcome workers, but it still gave the thinker's solution there where the real movement seemed to come up short. If Marx describes utopian socialism as the *infancy of the proletarian movement*,[24] a thought or idea from a moment when workers themselves had not yet developed solutions to their exploitation as workers, Althusser's theory of history can perhaps be described as a modern form of utopia, as the substitute for the self-emancipation we no longer believe in. This may perhaps explain why a research project as ambitious as this has by and large only inspired academic discussion. The problem, surely, is that its essential effect resides in its own enunciation: it is not a tool to change the world, but one more tool to interpret it with.

There is nothing surprising, then, about the fact that the reflections where Althusser tries to constitute the categories of a history without a subject should be accompanied by a constant valuing of *singularity*. This permeates even the understanding of Leninist politics. Leninism shows Marxist dialectic in action, but it does so only at the price of being seen as a singular science of contradiction in which the relationship to the masses entirely disappears behind the work of a solitary hero. From the 'one man standing there in the plain of History' to the 'petty' and 'dogmatic' intellectual of *What is to be Done?*, this strange figure of Lenin keeps coming back, a specular image in which theory is reflected as political action.[25] Even the definition of practice is caught up in this specular relationship: for philosophy to be able to express the theoretical and political rationality of practice, the latter has to be defined in relation to an *object* that is thinkable within the researcher's model of discovery. Hence the insistence on the *discovery* of Marx, the explorer of a new territory, as well as on the colossal individual effort Karl Marx, the person, undertook to free himself from bourgeois ideology, to evade the contingency that obliged him to be 'born somewhere'.[26] Hence the rather stunning depiction of Leninist solitude, as well as the steadfast defence of an individualistic approach to research against the criticisms of the students themselves.[27] This omnipresent valuing of singularity, rupture and discovery will find its most caricatured expression in the texts that followed May 68, texts in which Althusser pretends to discover in the course of his research something that the action of the masses had already amply demonstrated, but which he advances as a very daring hypothesis: the function of the school as an ideological state apparatus. What is outlined in these texts, parallel to the repression of every creative action of the masses, is a certain image of theoretical heroism: the masses can make history because the heroes make its theory.

The line that separates the politics of delirium from its enlightened counterpart thus gives to political *practice* – where the elements that had been split asunder are supposed to be brought back together – and to the political intervention of Althusserianism a very specific status: that of ruse. The logic of Althusserianism implied a certain suspension of political judgement. In order to resolve political problems, one had to learn to raise them by giving oneself the autonomous time of theory. But, as Descartes had already taught long ago, it was also important not to remain indecisive in our actions while we pondered our judgements. In other words, we needed a provisional moral code [*une morale par provision*].[28] We didn't know if the decisions of the Party were just; indeed, we had some doubts about that, but we didn't *know* yet. Hence the solution prescribed by Althusser and adopted by those among us who saw it only through the lens of political struggle: to defend the positions of the Party, not because they were just but simply because they were the Party's positions. To defend them, that is, without justifying them or trying to give them a theoretical foundation. This attitude represented in some ways an inversion of the attitude that had once upon a time been assumed by communist intellectuals who treated politics as the realm of the certain and theory as the realm of the uncertain and secondary. The Party had then been obliged to insist that these intellectuals commit themselves on the theoretical level, on the level of an aleatory theoretical activity which they saw as distinct from the certainties of politics. The high priests of proletarian science had thus thrown themselves into what they regarded as a risky theoretical task, only to serve a politics whose justness was already evident to them. Althusser turned this on its head: there was no longer evidence of the justness of the political struggle. With the Algerian War over – it was the Algerian War that had led us to the UEC – all the Party had to offer us, in the calm of Gaullist France, were periodic elections and the fight for the Langevin-Wallon Plan.[29] Certainty was now entirely on the side of theory, and our relationship to the Party, rather than being sustained by the justness of one or another struggle, was instead of the order of a provisional morality.[30]

If this theoretical project was to produce political effects in the long term, the Party had to approve and accept its credentials. But there was the problem: deep down, the PCF had no reason in the world to look favourably upon Althusser's project. The notion that it was necessary to 'go back to Marx' outlined a highly suspect approach, one that could not be defended simply by pleading that it was high time somebody showed Marx's bourgeois exegetes the error of their ways. The Party line on Marx was that Marx's thought had been incorporated into the political and cultural experience of the worker's movement and that the theoretical authority of Marxism ultimately depended upon the political authority of the 'Party of the working class'. There was no room to grant autonomous status to Marx's texts. Those who had tried to give a certain autonomy to Marxist thought, like Henri Lefebvre, wound up making this very attempt the focus of their self-critique during the heroic period.[31] In the 1960s, the only ones who went back to Marx were those who had left the Party, or those who had never joined it but who wanted anyway to pit the letter of Marx's philosophy against its political avatars. Going back to Marx could only mean the recourse to a political authority other than the Party. And who could possibly need such a thing, except those who were not satisfied with the Party's political authority? Traditionally, the functions assigned to Party intellectuals were threefold: justify the Party's politics to their peers, illustrate the excellence of Marxist methods in their respective fields of expertise and bathe the Party in the aura of their intellectual prestige. Pretending to bring to workers the philosophy necessary to their practice was not part of the picture. Kautsky's theory about 'importing' consciousness to the working classes was accepted, but as something of the past. The critique of spontaneity did indeed outline the need for organization, but not for a science brought by intellectuals. As it happened, UEC leaders were at that very moment returning to Kautsky's thesis and using it to shore up their desire for political autonomy and for the freedom to discuss the Party's political positions. To be accepted by the Party, Althusser's project had to distance itself from this initiative. More than that, even: it had to be seen as a concerted critique of misguided initiatives of that sort.

33

We should revisit here the effects of the Twentieth Congress, as these put into play a more complicated political game than the one we find in Althusser. The Congress's repudiation of Stalinism was not accompanied by an actual critique of it, and that opened the door for calls for liberalization (pluralism, the right to form tendencies, the right to free research) and for modernization (shake up the old dogmas, take new realities – the transformations of the working class, a new ideological style – into account, etc.). The new theses about peaceful coexistence and the peaceful transition to socialism being advanced at the time led those who wanted to ground these theses to come up with fairly risky theories. The PCF, in particular, was all the more susceptible to such erring theoretical and political ways because it accepted the Soviet theses – the critique of the 'cult of personality', peaceful coexistence, peaceful transition to socialism – without attempting to take them further and without being willing to risk a debate about them. By refusing to theorize its political positions, the Party was constantly faced with the risk of a break, whether to the right or the left. More specifically, revisionism carried within it a double seed of dissolution. A dissolution to the right in the case of those who wanted to *theorize* the 'peaceful transition to socialism' and spell out its political consequences. This is exactly what happened with the UEC's 'Italian' leadership. It insisted on the need to give a thoroughgoing analysis of the peaceful transition and spell out all its practical consequences; on the need to avail oneself of the means to convince the majority of the population and win the people over to the communist side by showing them the *alienation* that was everyone's lot; on the need to repudiate 'dogmatism' of every sort and to reach the people where they were; on the need to bring the Marxist themes of humanism and disalienation to the forefront. According to the 'Italians', in sum, it was imperative not only to destroy communism's forbidding face, which frightened away the people to be won over, but also to give greater autonomy to 'mass organizations' and to establish the open discussion of political problems within the Party.

This break 'to the right' (the 'Italianism' of Kahn and Forner,[32] followed later by Garaudy's humanism) was already quite disturbing in itself. But, furthermore, in attempting to spell out the consequences of Khrushchev's theses, it inevitably elicited a counter-effect, or break, to the left. This took the form of a critique of revisionism modelled on China's (by then) quite explicit critique of Soviet revisionism, a critique that, among the students, only intensified the conflict between new, 'qualitative' claims and the PCF's policy on higher education. Revisionism, especially among intellectuals, carried this double effect of dissolution, and the Party found itself with no theoretical weapons to contain it. With the old Zhdanovian orthodoxy expired, the orthodoxy had to be reinvented.

This situation gave Althusserianism the space to introduce a new orthodoxy, one that replaced Zhdanov's machine guns with *warning signs* and met the aspirations of the Italians, not dogmatically, but by laying out a critique of the implicit philosophy of their position. This new orthodoxy was not based on Stalin's words, but on Marx's texts. Althusser's *detour* foreclosed the possibility of providing the politics of the Party with a theoretical foundation. But giving its politics a theoretical foundation was decidedly not the point; others had already tried, much too assiduously, to do so. The real task was to keep its politics from being contested. If Althusserianism could serve the Party, it was because it warned against the dangers of hasty theorizations – insisting instead on the need to learn to raise the problems before arriving at conclusions – and against the risk that by attempting to 'modernize' Marxism, one might actually restore the tendencies of bourgeois humanism.

Still, it took some time for part of the Party apparatus to perceive the political usefulness of Althusserianism. Indeed, Althusser's project was at first the source of some perplexity among the PCF's intellectual authorities. It is easy to detect a certain hesitancy on how to read the whole affair in the critiques originally raised by Besse, Garaudy and Mury. Similarly, it is easy to see, with the benefit of hindsight, that the most spirited reactions came from future detractors of the orthodoxy, from the humanist Garaudy and the Marxist-Leninist Mury, both of whom wanted the Party to have the theory of its practice or the practice of its theory. At the time, though, they were simply underscoring more forcefully what was already the common opinion of their peers. It was only in 1965, when our actions within the UEC started to give some intimation of the effects that were to follow, that a fraction of the Party apparatus came to perceive the appeal of going back to Marx and of the 'autonomy of theory'. This fraction, represented by Guy Besse and the young team of *La Nouvelle Critique*, sensed the danger of Garaudy's humanism and the usefulness of a return to Marxist rigour. To restore the Party's authority with intellectuals, its 'Marxist' facade, threatened as it was by the all-too-visible efforts of Garaudy's revisionism, had to be redone. Equally important, to attract intellectuals and keep them in the Party was to give them a certain autonomy and the space for discussion.[33]

In December 1963 we were still very far from such an alliance. It was in that year, though, that two events, two meetings of theory and politics, pushed Althusserianism in the direction of that alliance by leading it to a choice of theoretical targets which reconciled the general interests of theory with the particular interests of the Party: the attacks against Althusser's essay, 'On the Materialist Dialectic', and the conflict between the PCF and the theses defended by the students of the syndicalist left.[34]

In 'On the Materialist Dialectic', Althusser not only comments at length on Mao at a time when the Chinese–Soviet polemic was at its peak, he also puts great emphasis on the concept of the *displacement of the contradiction* – and he does so at the precise moment when Chinese communists were bringing to the forefront the struggles of oppressed peoples from the 'zone of storms' against imperialism.[35] Lucien Sève raised questions about this particular conjuncture, and Althusser found himself having to justify his words to *La Pensée*'s editorial board. For his defence, Althusser set in motion an inversion mechanism that is a regular feature of his rhetoric: there is no relationship at all between his theoretical position and the political argumentation of the Chinese. If Sève thought there was, it must have been because the Chinese and their tricks duped him. In his essay, Althusser explained, he develops the *Marxist* principles contained in Mao's *On Contradiction*, while the Chinese, for their part, only *pretend* to be applying these principles. They give the illusion of offering *a scientific demonstration* when what they produce is, in fact, only *political reasoning*.[36] Sève had fallen into the trap. He saw theory, when empirical politics is all there really was. (The concept of *oversight* [*bévue*], an essential piece in the Althusserian reading of Marx, finds its pragmatic origins here, in the efforts to deny the political implications of a theoretical discourse.)[37]

Althusser met the accusation of Maoism by divorcing Maoist theory from Maoist practice. The warning he got, however, must have led him to choose his targets with a specific goal in mind: to bring about the coincidence of theory's long-term interests (the interests of rational politics, in other words) with the immediate interests of the Party, that is to say, with the fight against the dissolution sparked by the Party's politics. This is where Althusser's grand strategic design and his tactical calculation converged. His critique of humanism offers a good illustration. Strategically, Althusser treats humanism as one of the figures of political subjectivism against which our only weapon is the restoration of theory. Marxist humanism and the cited passages from the *young* Marx had contributed their fair share to the suppression of theory and the Zhdanovian delirium. Tactically, the critique of humanism could serve to halt the Party's break to right because it assumed the acceptable form of an attack against the 'right-wing' humanism of some communist intellectuals. This game, however, put Althusser's rescue operation in the paradoxical position of a doctor who can only save his patient by saving the illness that afflicts him. Political practice (the Algerian War, the Chinese–Soviet conflict, the student uprisings) was constantly poking holes in whatever authority revisionism had among intellectuals, and the task of theory was to seal up those holes, to thwart the objective effects of dissolution borne by an illness whose name would eventually become quite clear: revisionism. As nothing could be expected from below – the solution, after all, had to pass through the *medicine* of theory – the only way to treat the illness was by thwarting its effects.[38] A paradox that reveals the complicity between the illness and the doctor. In other words: not simply the doctor's interests, but his 'illness'. Or, in Marxist terms: the education of the educator.

This is where the solidarity, or alliance, was eventually sealed: in the *education* Althusserianism advanced as propaedeutic to all transformation, in the link between this education and Althusser's twin education as a scholar and a party militant, in the question that students in their first protests were suddenly raising about their professors. The materialization of the solidarity between theory and the politics of the Party's leadership became manifest in the position Althusser took towards the student problems at the end of 1963, particularly in his offensive against the syndicalist left. 'Student Problems', the text which gives expression to this partisanship, should by no means be seen simply as a political intervention prompted by a current event, the fruit of irritation or opportunism. That it should have remained, to date, Althusser's only *political* intervention, in the strict sense, not only speaks volumes about its decisive character but also reveals the shared sensibility that allowed Althusser's philosophy spontaneously to join hands with the politics of the PCF. This intervention cannot be justified simply by the fact that it was among students that the effects of dissolution mentioned earlier were most clearly visible. What troubled Althusser, rather, is the fact that these effects of dissolution, by their very nature, called his project into question. By questioning the knowledge of *educators* and the ties between that knowledge and the existing order, and by introducing a new dividing line – between the producers and the consumers of knowledge – into the intellectual community, the students attacked Althusserianism from the 'bad' side, the leftist side.

The Algerian War was over. The communist students who had mobilized the student population to take to the streets to protest the war, against the directives of the Party, had gained a certain independence, which the 'Italian' leaders of the UEC wanted to consecrate with the creation of an autonomous political programme. The end of the Algerian War, moreover, put the actions of the students of the syndicalist left on a new path. The student left had been formed at the UNEF and at the UEC through the anti-war efforts, but now it wanted to use whatever power it had acquired to carry out its own struggle. The students were eager to move beyond the opposition between a corporatism limited to economic issues and a politics limited to supporting the struggles of others to be able to focus their attention on the problems of student labour, of the modes for acquiring knowledge and the ends of knowledge. These initiatives, for the most part the work of the UEC's 'syndicalist left', drew attention to the following topics: the ends of academic knowledge, which seemed to be to educate future auxiliaries of the bourgeoisie; the forms for the transmission of knowledge – the 'pedagogic relation' – tied to this objective (lecture courses which inured students to being docile); individualism (which the UNEF had opposed with its proposal for research groups, the GTUs); and the arbitrary nature of exams. Students saw their overall situation within the university through the categories of student alienation and dependence (the financial dependence on the family, compounded by the pedagogical dependence on professors). And it was to offset this situation of assistance that the students demanded *student wages*, a demand that clashed with the PCF's advocacy of scholarships for underprivileged students.

There is no need to re-evaluate these aspirations today, and we would be hasty to see them as the forerunners to May 68. At the time, all of this was more of an inquiry led by specialists in student syndicalism than the beginning of a mass movement. Not only was its language a bit confusing, its systematization was also somewhat reformist in nature (the ideology of the counterplan and of the 'alternative', recently imported from Italy and embraced by the innermost ranks of the PSU, enjoyed a certain prestige at the time). Even so, there was something important in all of this, something that would tilt Althusserianism – and other ideologies – towards what came to be called 'structuralism', namely, the beginning of a certain fissure within the intellectual world. A new element had been introduced to the game, one that could not be absorbed into the opposition between intellectuals (teachers and students) with conflicting political opinions and practices: knowledge itself, the forms of its transmission, the power relations it implies, the links between these power relations and the power relations which ensure the reproduction of class exploitation and oppression. The time when students identified their struggle with the well-intentioned fight of left-wing intellectuals for justice and freedom for the people was over. The question of the relationship to power was pushed back into the heart of the university itself, and the opposition between the producers and the consumers of knowledge drove a wedge through the front line of progressive intellectuals. There can be little doubt that 'structuralist' ideology played a larger part in precipitating this fissure than the Gaullist 'technocratism' that its adversaries associated it with. If we were to study how the rules of the academic trade bundled into one and the same ideology the problematics of thinkers who have little to do with one another (Foucault, Lacan, Althusser) but also, each in their way, have little to do with 'structures', what we would see – *among other determinations* – is the reaction to this 'fissure' on the part of a certain academic 'elite'. The themes that flourished then – the death of man, the subordination of the subject to the law of the signifier, the staging of the subject through production relations, the opposition of science to ideology – reflected, in their way, not only the end of the war (in Algeria), and with it the end of the old problems of the intellectual coping with politics (responsibility, engagement, bearing witnessing), but also the appearance of politics in a new form – in the question of knowledge, its power and its relationship to political power. This would become the ground for a 'civil war' among intellectuals in which the question of whether one *should* be committed could no longer be posed.

This theoretico-political conjuncture crystallized in Althusser's intervention against the syndicalist left. Two events provoked his reaction: the student strike led by the FGEL[39] in November 1963, whose main – and notable – slogan was, 'Sorbonne to the students', and the intervention by FGEL's secretary, Bruno Queysanne, during the inaugural lecture of Bourdieu and Passeron's seminar at the École Normale Supérieure.[40] In Queysanne's intervention, in his questioning Bourdieu and Passeron about the political status of a sociological research project about academic learning that protracted the authoritarian division of academic labour, Althusser recognized his enemy: here was leftism, the subordination of science to politics, the aggression of illiterate politicians against researchers. In the students's questioning of the privileges of knowledge, Althusser saw the resurgence of the obscurantism of proletarian science, and against this threat there was nothing to do but state in no uncertain terms that the scientific knowledge of an object has nothing to do with its political transformation.[41] The strategic, long-term defence *against the authority of the Party* demanded, in the short term, a tactical intervention *in support of its authority*. In 'Student Problems', published in *La Nouvelle Critique*, Althusser combats the rallying cries of the syndicalist left essentially by rehearsing the Party line: scholarships, improved material conditions, critique of 'student wages'. The article displaces the line of class division from the forms of knowledge to its contents – science or ideology – in a move that allows Althusser to reserve the critique of content to experts. As the fundamental pedagogical relation was that between knowledge and ignorance, there was only one way for the students to be able to criticize their professors from the point of view of class, and that was to become their peers.

My analysis of 'Student Problems', written on the morning after May 68, is reprinted at the end of this book,[42] so I shall not rehearse it now. What matters to me here is to stress the decisive character of this one instance of political intervention on Althusser's part. The intervention was neither tangential to theoretical activity, nor a simple application of theory to politics. As Althusser himself stressed in his reply to Queysanne, what was at stake, a problem 'of the highest importance', was nothing less than the very foundation of theoretical practice. In practice, this intervention was responsible for making Althusserianism a politically active ideology, both in the field of theory and in practice. It made Althusser's efforts, which had till then been enigmatic and marginal, political. The politics of this intervention gave Althusserianism its systematic face, it tilted the open and undecided research of his texts for *La Pensée* towards the orthodoxy eventually cemented in the texts from

1964 and 1965: 'Marxism and Humanism', 'Theory, Theoretical Practice and Theoretical Formation', *Reading Capital*, the introduction to *For Marx* and 'Historical and Dialectical Materialism'. This political intervention created a major terrorist figure, a sort of terrorizing ghost: the battle of science (revolutionary) against ideology (bourgeois). The historical weight of this figure will reach well beyond the alliance sealed then between the decrees of theory and the interests of the Party apparatus and bear heavily upon the future of what might be called *authoritarian leftism*. The most decisive effects of this intervention, in the long term, are probably not the immediate assistance it brought to the leadership of the Party, but the lasting divisions it produced within the anti-revisionist left. For it bore the principle of a split, one that would be played out many times over, between the slogans of the students' 'petit-bourgeois' uprising, and the *enlightened politics* of Marxist scholars and the builders of 'proletarian' parties. Later on, once the policing of 'Science' had been unmasked, things would come to be called by another name: ideology then became petit-bourgeois ideology and 'Science' became Marxism-Leninism or proletarian ideology. The mechanism, however, remained the same, viz.: the indefinite censuring of the slogans of revolt in the name of an authority represented by a group of intellectuals. A new mechanism for accepting any authority whatsoever had been produced.

This mechanism, which transformed Althusserian prudence into theory's police force, was established through our political actions within the Cercle d'Ulm.[43] Althusser's article is in fact what convinced some of us to join the political battle inside the UEC to restore Marxist rigour as the way to chase out the prevailing eclecticism. The Cercle d'Ulm, like many others, had been in something of a vegetative state since the end of the Algerian War. Here, though, was a political cause that could reanimate it: the defence of Science against Ideology.

It would be easy to give a reductive reading of this battle (and of Althusser's project, for that matter), to see in it nothing more than the simple ideology of a student aristocracy. Treated like heirs to the throne by our professors, we had no objections to the 'pedagogic relation'; the winners of a fiercely selective competition, trained to compete from very early on, we could not but look upon the critique of individualism and the calls for collective work groups as the reveries of illiterate minds. We were not short on arguments to show the absurdity of the notion of student wages, but, then again, our salary was not a theoretical problem for us. Undoubtedly, we shared the established view that the fees for the reproduction rights of our labour force were particularly high. Comfortably settled at the ENS, relieved of every worry, we had a pretty good time making fun of the descriptions in *Clarté* of the miseries of the students' 'daily life'. Our privileged situation allowed us to make science the only important thing and to push everything else – the petty academic, financial or sexual grievances of students – into that realm of illusion known in our discourse by the term *lived experience* (*le vécu*).

The problem with this analysis is that it overlooks the exact distribution of the pieces on the game board and the contradiction specific to our ideology. We were not confronted with a mass movement but with theoreticians like ourselves, and the psychosociology that underwrote the demands for GTUs gave us some grounds to suspect them of being avatars for the way capitalist companies managed human relations. We thought we had reasons for seeing, in the ideology of 'daily life', not so much the aspirations of thousands and thousands of students, but the romanticism of great bourgeois aesthetes. The large political debates that the 'Italian' leadership prided itself on excluded the mass of militant students. Consequently, calls for theoretical formation served as a democratic demand, one capable of reducing the power of the big shots by arming all militants with the weapons of discussion. As for our anger at *Clarté*'s agenda ('to reflect student romanticism in all its aspects'), it was informed by the conviction that the discourse of communist intellectuals had to be not a tool for reflecting or mirroring reality, but a weapon for its transformation.

Our hostility towards 'lived experience' (*le vécu*) also meant waging a battle against the ideologies of impotence that assigned to intellectuals no other role than that of being the conscience or 'reflect' of their world. What we saw in the philosophies of existence was nothing more than the ideologies of fellow-travellers or of the witnesses to the world's ambiguities.[44] In Althusser, however, we found the principle for a different role for intellectuals, one that resolved neither into the role of cultural consumer nor to that of ideological 'reflect'. This different role entailed a real participation, *as intellectuals*, in the transformation of the world. This may perhaps explain why some Althusserians were swimming against the current when the protests of May flared up, and why others were swimming in the opposite direction as the trumpets of 'reflux' started to ring out everywhere. 'Structuralism', in which some people saw only a philosophy of immutable order, represented rather the search for a new power for intellectuals over reality. But this search remained closed up in the professorial ideology borne by our practice. We found this power in 'science', and it was from within science that we tried to undercut every attempt to contest the authority of knowledge (*savoir*). Contrary to what the critiques – superficial or interested – of 'theoreticism' might suggest, it was the desire to act that spurred us on to the defence of the hierarchies of knowledge (*savoir*).

As partisans of science, we campaigned against the theses that ruled the UEC at the time: 'productive' student work, alienation, the notion of the 'reflect' or 'mirror'. And we were all surprised to find that this turned out to be the grounds for agreement with Party authorities. We read the polemical texts Party theoreticians wrote against the leaders of the UEC, and we concluded that, in the end, *they were right*. Where our younger selves had been prone to see the old forces of Stalinism being unleashed to stifle the wind borne by a new generation, we now saw instead an honest defence of Marxist principles against revisionist mistakes. These people demanding that students be paid wages must certainly have been unfamiliar with Marxist wage theory; the students certainly were petit bourgeois and so thoroughly besieged by bourgeois ideology that they lacked the autonomous power to carry out the onslaught of this ideology; they must certainly have been crazy to think that they had any lessons they could teach to the Party of the working class. On these bases, we sided – a bit surprised but without second thoughts – with the Party.

On other fronts, however, the situation was a little more complicated. Things were starting to happen in the East, and the first news of the Chinese–Soviet conflict began to circulate in France. As far as theory was concerned, we knew where we stood: we didn't have to stay awake nights pondering where to locate a real faithfulness to Marx, in Khrushchev's whining sophisms or in Mao's beautiful rigour. We were not Maoists, though. There were no Maoists in France then, only *pro-Chinese* sympathizers. And that was not the same: being pro-Chinese did not entail a *practical* difference – vis-à-vis the PCF – but a difference of opinion concerning problems that exceeded our practice. To make up our minds, we had to wait until we had been sufficiently instructed by science. It was not enough that Mao's texts were more faithful to Marxist principles than Khrushchev's: we also needed to elaborate, and not simply understand, the science of modes of production and of the forms for transitioning between two modes of production.[45] Without that, we could only have opinions, and we didn't want to have opinions. To us, pro-Chinese sympathizers were essentially a sect, one among many, living in the realm of opinion, whereas we, for our part, were fighting against the political dispersion of opinions in the name of unity through science.

We mounted our offensive along three lines: an attack against every concession to the spontaneous ideology of students, support for the Party – on the condition of not discussing its politics – and the primacy of theoretical formation. In his speech to the Seventh Congress of the UEC, held in March 1964 and marked by the entrance of Althusserians into the arena of political struggle, the delegate from the Cercle d'Ulm put the matter in carefully weighed terms: the UEC has a specific practice in the student environment. It is not up to the UEC to discuss the atomic bomb or the Chinese–Soviet conflict; its task, instead, is to secure the bases that allow for the discussion of these problems. We must *support* the positions of the Party, but there is no need for us to ground this support with hasty analyses. Our priority should be to apply ourselves to mastering our theoretical formation, 'The UEC's goal is to guarantee the theoretical formation that allows its members to engage in these discussions and to put an end to the "battle of ideas."'[46] The important stuff, then, was *our* stuff – theoretical formation. Hence the effort the Cercle had us put into the journal *Clarté*. The motion introduced by the Cercle and voted on by the Congress stipulated that *Clarté* would regularly run columns devoted to the commentary of major texts and current theoretical problems. To do that, *Clarté* would have to 'call upon comrades who are experts in their specific fields'. We were these comrades, of course.

It must be said, though, that this speech addressed a real need: a majority of communist students were wary of engaging in long discussions about the atomic bomb or the socialist alternative and instead wanted the UEC to focus primarily on student problems and the study of Marxism. But the Party had other worries. The 'Italians' had managed to persuade the Party that the 'Chinese' threat was the urgent business of the UEC and that they – the 'Italians' – were the only rampart against that threat. The Party temporarily gave them the reins, and they were careful not to call upon our 'expertise'.

The following year we resumed the battle, now on a larger scale. The publication, in December 1964, of the *Cahiers Marxistes-Léninistes* reaffirmed that our vocation was to oversee the theoretical formation of UEC militants. The first issue enjoyed considerable success among militants and was also looked upon favourably by the Party's regulatory authority. Indeed, it was even cited in *France Nouvelle* as evidence of the vitality of the new forces that seemed poised to show the UEC's true colours. For, while we struggled within theory against the spontaneous ideology of students and against the revisionism of the UEC's National Bureau, the Party carried on a parallel struggle with more classical (financial, administrative and political) tools to ensure the triumph of science over ideology. The provinces were treated to an intense 'political effort' to guarantee for the faithful a majority in the Congress of the UEC. This fact changed the rules of the game for us. Up to that point, our politics had worked within the political *dispositif* prescribed by Althusser's project: suspension of judgement concerning the Party's political foundations, support – with no questions asked – for its political positions, insistence upon theoretical work and fight to prevent any breaks to the right. This position was tenable only as long as the Cercle d'Ulm was in the opposition. If Althusserianism had entered politics, it was due to this very particular situation, due, that is, to the existence of a communist organization that was outwardly revisionist and outwardly opposed to the politics of the Party. This situation allowed our Marxist orthodoxy to be anti-establishment and our fight against revisionism to be waged side by side with the Party apparatus. We were fighting against the rightward deviation of *our* organization. We shared common enemies with the Party, but we were not its intellectual functionaries. We would now find ourselves in the majority, and not just any old majority either. The Seventh Congress had left us with the hope of a majority composed of members committed to real research, research that would move beyond the battle of ideas and the need for unconditional loyalty. The Eighth Congress cooled our hopes. The dominant note struck was not that of free research but of cold orthodoxy. All our illusions were gone even before Roland Leroy brought the party to a close with his police discourse. Our 'science' had invested the summary procedures of the apparatus with the theoretical soul they lacked. The great purge had eliminated from the UEC's leadership not only the 'Italians', but the entire old left. The new leaders (Hermier and Cathala[47]) were as far from being the representatives of a more left-wing politics as the 'right-wing' leaders we had waged war on. What they represented, quite simply, was order in all its pettiness. The options open to 'science' were clear: either invest this normalization with its spiritual point of honour or set out on an autonomous path. Both options meant stepping out of the Althusserian game: one meant abdicating autonomy and reverting back to a discourse of justification, while the other was tantamount to abdicating prudence and, in a way, 'actualizing' philosophy.[48]

The Althusserian machine would be unsettled in either case. This machine, though, was itself producing unsettling effects. The very same weapon that had been put at the service of revisionism could be turned against it. In other words, 'theoretical formation' could be a weapon of regeneration. Althusser, in his prudence, may have treated it as a long-term weapon, but there was no reason why it could not be a weapon of the moment, the principle for a different power. 'Theoretical formation', instead of being the acquisition of knowledges with an eye to future transformation, could be the transformation of power relations in the present. Hence the importance assumed, at the time, by the project of creating a Centre de formation théorique. To gather forces around an instance of power specifically devoted to theoretical formation was essentially to transform *the instrument of knowledge* into the *power of truth*. 'Marx's theory is all powerful because it is true': the slogan of the *Cahiers Marxistes-Léninistes* invested theory with a different efficiency than that of a knowledge to be applied.[49] Organizing the theoretical formation of militants meant much more than giving them some useful bit of knowledge: it meant creating Marx's – or his readers's – party within Roland Leroy's UEC.

It was around this time that we were *reading Capital*. As the Eighth Congress was taking place, Althusser was leading the seminar on the rue d'Ulm whose proceedings would be collected and published in *Reading Capital*. His theses provided the quite paradoxical foundations for the possibility of breaking with revisionism. On the one hand, *Reading Capital* presented theses that amounted to a *political* critique of the Party. The break with an evolutionist conception of history, the affirmation of the discontinuity of modes of production, the assertion that the laws of dissolution of a particular structure are not the same as its laws of operation, the radical originality of the problem of transition – all of these theses tended, *logically*, towards a denunciation of the PCF's economism, as well as of the notion of the peaceful transition to socialism and of a 'true democracy'. The clear-cut break established between modes of production attested to the need for violent revolution. What happened, though, is that all of these subversive claims resulted only in the creation of a new field of academic inquiry. Seven years later, we could find Balibar arguing quite calmly in the pages of *La Pensée* for the necessity of revolutionary violence and the destruction of the bourgeois state apparatus.[50]

Subversion had to find another path and, strangely, this path turned out to be the autonomy of theory. *Reading Capital* grounds this autonomy on the thesis that agents of production are necessarily deluded. By agents of production, we are to understand proletarians and capitalists, since both are simply the agents of capitalist relations of production and both are mystified by the illusions produced by their practices. Put bluntly, the thesis that grounds the autonomy of theory is this: *false ideas originate in social practices*. Science, conversely, must be founded on a point extrinsic to the illusions of practice.

This reading of Marx via Althusser and Lacan does little more than give a new sheen to a thesis Kautsky had already defended: science belongs to intellectuals, and it is up to them to bring it to producers necessarily cut off from knowledge. It did not, however, establish a relationship between our science and workers, for the simple reason that there was no practical relation between us. We had no idea what happened 'there'. Nor did we have any pretensions of bringing them our science, which depended for its functioning on a twofold relationship, to the 'petit-bourgeois' student on the one hand and to the Party apparatus on the other. The authority of theory denounced the 'spontaneous' ideology of students, but it also discredited, in the same stroke, the Party's authority. That all 'practitioners' were deluded did not keep us from being militant, but it did mean that Marx's theory was not incorporated into the knowledge, the experience and the general line of the PCF. There is no 'collective intellectual', in other words. And yet, the Party embraced Gramsci's theorization of the collective intellectual and relied on it to seal the identity between the intellectual authority of theory and the political authority of the Party apparatus.

This exacerbation of the Kautskyist thesis freed the relationship to Marx's texts from any and all political subordination. Marx's theory belonged to no one other than its readers, and the only duty these readers had was to the theory itself. Althusser states this point unequivocally in the very text where he resolutely defends the university policies of the Party. The two fundamental duties that together make up the communists' 'morals' are the duty towards Marxist-Leninist science and the duty to know the conditions which govern the application of this science in different domains.[51] There is no discussion of any duty towards 'the masses', 'the people' or any other social instance – and no discussion of a fundamental duty towards the Party. Anybody could read Marx and draw his or her own *conclusions*. The only prerequisite – we shall come back to this – was that these readers had to have passed through the discipline of science. This movement instituted a different authority. For young militant intellectuals, it created another power opposite the power of the apparatus: finally, we would be done with just pitting one line against another, or one interpretation against another; finally, *in this milieu and in this conjuncture*, we would be able to do more than confront our opponents with Trotsky's texts or Chinese theses – now it would be *the thing in itself*, in some ways, that we would be able to pit against its interpretations and political avatars. This is why the effect of this rupture rippled out well beyond the strictly Althusserian circle and affected, in one way or another, an entire generation of militant intellectuals. What really mattered was not the content of the claims, but the opposition of one authority to another.

It may seem amusing today, but the fact is that young communist intellectuals at that time were really looking for an *authority* other than the one represented by the stereotyped discourse of the Party, or by the eclectic blabber that, outside the Party, was regarded as the height of 'Marxist' culture. Eager to have theoretical mastery over the effects of their political and syndicalist fights, these young communist intellectuals needed another authority in order to rethink their relationship to the Party, an authority that would free them from the 'petit-bourgeois' guilt that had always trapped communist intellectuals in the dilemma of submission or betrayal. Althusser played the part of this liberating authority. He was the first to provide an answer to the questions that exercised the most active communist students. He answered the questions with repression, but the important point is that he answered them, that he filled the space left empty by the apparatus of the Communist Party. And this repression didn't have the effect of a call to order. Most of its victims internalized it: Lukácsians and Sartreans became Althusserians, while the theoreticians of student syndicalism carried out their self-critiques and tried to ground syndical action on a critique of the content of the curriculum. The guilt 'petit-bourgeois' militants felt in the face of the 'party of the working class' was internalized in the figure of professorial repression. Here, of course, was the principle of future repressions of the spirit of revolt. But, before being that, it was a principle of rupture. By internalizing the repression, it became possible to take it in a different direction and turn Althusser's double-edged sword against the Party, making Althusserianism a weapon of rupture, not of regeneration. This is how Althusser became a conduit to Mao. For Althusser was speaking at a very specific moment, and the 'double power' he established through the autonomy of theory would have been laughable had it not coincided with the moment when the communist world was being split in half, and when the authority of theory and the return to Marx had, as their counterpart, the charges the Chinese were levelling at the revisionist camp. The defence of theory certainly didn't lead to Moscow.

The apparatchiks of the UEC, for their part, had already made up their minds on the matter, and they were of the opinion that 'the defence of theory' could only benefit the Chinese. The Central Committee at Argenteuil, charged with examining Althusser's and Garaudy's respective cases, did not put things so brutally.[52] It is interesting, however, to see the hierarchy of their concerns. The Committee members were not at all troubled by the conclusions one could draw about the peaceful transition to socialism from *Reading Capital*. The quarrel against theoretical humanism was already more troublesome, because it clashed with the tradition deeply entrenched in the Party of reusing the cultural and scientific heritage of the bourgeoisie. But this problem could be alleviated somewhat through the distinction between two sorts of humanisms, a distinction that had something else in its favour: it served as a counterweight to Garaudy's ecumenical mission, which was starting to become embarrassing. The main problem really was the *autonomy of theory* and the relationship it established between 'scientists' – and, more importantly, their emulators – and the authority of the Party. The same question reappears like a refrain in the intervention of each Committee member: What becomes of practice? What becomes of the Party? It was not a problem that a field of research should find itself entirely cut off from the demands of political practice. The Party, in fact, was at that time working to secure for intellectuals a space where they could play their epistemological or semiological games in peace. But the object of Althusser's thought was nothing less than *the* theory of Marx. Consequently, it unhinged the machine that made each intellectual a specialist in a certain field of knowledge and thereby confined the effects of his or her discourse to the community in that field. Althusser confiscated theory en masse and placed it under the auspices of philosophers, who distributed theory to uninitiated militants in forms that were useful only to the philosophical community. One of the more shrewd people at Argenteuil, Michel Simon, stresses this very point by drawing attention to nothing other than the question of theoretical formation:

> What concerns me about *Reading Capital* is not really what its authors say, provided we read them carefully, that is to say, provided we read them knowing as much as we know. What worries me is the general theory that an uninformed reading of the book might yield. Above all, I worry that such an uninformed interpretation may promote, among our students, a doctrinal view of theoretical formation.[53]

He went on to give a brief illustration of what this 'view' might be, using to that end the syllabus for theoretical formation that had been created in anticipation of the opening of the UEC's Centre de formation théorique. He found the bibliography especially telling:

> To give an example of Marxist methodology in action, the syllabus proposes Lenin's *April Theses*, a very good choice, as well as an essay by comrade Balibar on culture, quite a stunning choice. . . . Surely a more important text could have been found to illustrate dialectics in action. For example: Maurice Thorez's report to the Central Committee from September 1958. Indeed, it is impossible not to note the fact that the syllabus in question includes no documents at all from our Party. It is as if, since Lenin – and putting aside Mao Tse-tung's text from 1937, *On Contradiction* – the international workers's movement had produced nothing at all in the realm of theory and politics.[54]

Balibar's essay contained nothing subversive in itself. The problem lay in the way the syllabus completely overlooked the treasure accumulated by the experience of the Communist Party and its work. This oversight was not just an omission. 'Theoretical formation' created its own memory, its own tradition. And all memory is linked to a power. The omission, in other words, essentially dismissed the Party's entire political tradition:

> The underlying idea, to focus solely on the theoretical level, is not only that Marxism is learned exclusively through books, but also that it is learned only from the classics. It is that every development is a betrayal, that every application of Marxism is a deviation into pragmatism, ideology, and political manipulation.[55]

We can see quite clearly from the phrase, 'to focus solely on the theoretical level', that what was at stake on the practical level was the rejection of the 'developments' that Khrushchev, with his successors and emulators, had introduced to 'classical' Marxism. This was the time, for example, when it was common to teach that peaceful coexistence was the supreme form of class struggle ... The purism of theory could not but have political effects. And that was really all that mattered: we could say everything, provided nothing that we said had practical effects. With this as measure, Althusser and Garaudy each got some high and some low marks, and Aragon[56] concluded by affirming the Party's unshakable commitment to the cultural values and treasures it had inherited from ages past.

While the Party at Argenteuil only spoke about 'theoretical formation' with words covered in danger, the Cercle d'Ulm openly regarded the debates there and the resolution of the Central Committee as blatant manifestations of revisionist degeneracy. The first text of the Cercle d'Ulm's break with the Party – 'Does Marxist-Leninist Theory Have To Be Revised?' – focuses on a single political target: humanism. Its critique of humanism cuts deeper than Althusser's, because it attacks head-on the cultural politics of revisionism, the negation of class struggle among intellectuals and the slavery to the existing values of bourgeois culture. In thus designating and characterizing its targets, the piece breaks away from Althusser's prudence. But as a platform for political opposition (it was defended as such at the Ninth Congress of the UEC), coming as it did after the Cercle d'Ulm decided not to join hands with those who rejected Mitterrand's candidacy,[57] it still functioned within the Althusserian image of politics. Its irony shared with Althusser's prudence the same ground, that of the politics of philosophers, of those who displace the signs of acceptance and rejection.

We can now see how Althusserian politics came to bear on the history of the Maoist student movement, though we should most certainly not treat the latter as the simple continuation of the former. The basis for the rupture that led to the birth of the UJC (ML) in the fall of 1966 was no longer the fight against humanism, but the Cultural Revolution. Indeed, the creation of the UJC, by no means a logical outgrowth of Althusser's project, depended on a split within the core 'politics' of the Cercle d'Ulm, with one faction formed by the group *Cahiers pour l'analyse*, which was first and foremost concerned with working out a theory of the *subject*, and the other by Althusser's faithful followers, who were eager to remain in the Party. This double split was accompanied by a fusion with segments of the student left which had come from other horizons. Conflicts stemming directly from practice, notably the anti-imperialist struggle – the wars in Algeria and Vietnam – were behind this split. But, more importantly, the project of the UJC eluded a strictly Althusserian framework, which could only conceive that project through the category of leftism, of the premature suturing of the time of research and the time of empirical politics. Althusserianism only put so many ruptures in theory to avoid having to put them in political practice. Fundamentally, Althusserianism is a theory of education, and every theory of education is committed to preserving the power it seeks to bring to light. The logical consequence of the Althusserian *dispositif* obliged it always to function within the Party, to play the double game of strategy and tactics by which it supplied revisionism with weapons now, all the while forging the weapons of its future demise. France's peaceful march towards socialism would go hand in hand with the peaceful regeneration of the Party. It was something like an infinite clandestine ideological war, a Kantian *task* that would never be accomplished in this world.

The birth of the UJC was a real rupture, though one still marked by the characteristic traits of the *politics of philosophers*: its condition of possibility was that it not call into question the despotic figure of scientific (*savant*) power. The repression of empirical politics, together with the tactical ruse it implied, had already separated those who wished to openly contest the politics of the Party from those who favoured the prudent position of 'support without justification'. The politics of philosophers held that the science of the conjuncture was the exclusive business of scientists. The absence of an openly political attitude – notably as the Mitterrand affair was ongoing – produced a first break within the student left, one that would later place a part of this left under Trotskyist obedience. Most importantly, though, the unquestioned despotism of 'science' contained the principle of a rupture between the budding Maoist movement and the forms of anti-authoritarian revolt. In the conflict that would explode in May 68, the fight of science (revolutionary) against ideology (petit bourgeois) pushed the Maoists of the UCJ (ML) into the camp of the mandarins.

This is how, at the beginning of the confrontations of May 68, the major thesis of *Reading Capital* – the *manipulation* of the blind subjects of social practice – resurfaced as a political thesis: the students are being manipulated by a social-democratic conspiracy. The very excess of this affirmation denounced the persistent hegemony of Althusserian ideology: the opposition of revolutionary scientists to petit-bourgeois students whose spontaneous ideology delivered them into the trap of bourgeois domination. In sum: we are wrong to revolt. Or, more precisely: we are right, but on certain conditions. In China the students have the right to revolt, but in France the revolt must come from the working class, and the students must put themselves at the service of the workers.

This *ouvriérisme*[58] comes to serve the reaction of the professorial class, a class in love with every revolution except that of its students. Althusser, incidentally, had already forged this solidarity between the professorial repression of the illiterate and the *ouvriériste* repression of the 'petit bourgeois'. Althusserianism's true legacy, the revisionist sign on the forehead of authoritarian leftism, is precisely the kinship between repression-by-science and repression-by-the-proletariat, a kinship that finds expression in the mission, entrusted to a group of intellectuals (representatives of science or of the proletariat), to drag the petite bourgeoisie away from its illusions and into the place of its *theoretical formation*, or its proletarization. The heads of the UJC (ML) reacted like professors being mistreated by *their* students, the petit-bourgeois student body that it was their mission to educate.

This reaction was possible only because of a defining element of the Althusserian problematic: the masking of the question of *power*, the technicist understanding of political organization. In Althusser, the political is seen through a doublet – science/technique – which excludes every consideration of *power effects*. The whole question comes down to whether politics, in different instances, is delirious or rational, whether its line is right or wrong. There are no effects of power, only the effects of the education of the powerful. Organization is a technical instrument. And, as with knowledge, the only problem is figuring out what we put into it. Thus, the political model contained in this problematic is, at the end of the day, nothing more than the very model prescribed by the philosophy of educators: enlightened despotism. This power position allows for two possible relations: either Party leaders became philosophers, which is what Althusser wanted, or philosophers became Party leaders, which is what happened with the UJC (ML). The hierarchy of the UJC's organization mirrored the hierarchy of the university – the Cercle d'Ulm was at the top, and the circle of the Khâgne Louis-le-Grand was the stepping-stone to get there. The Cultural Revolution itself was at first seen as the confirmation of Althusser's theses (specifically of the role of the ideological instance) and as the affirmation of the absolute authority of a system of thought. The nascent French Maoism inherited from Althusserianism the view that political apparatuses are instruments for the application of party lines. The *Reply to John Lewis* was still arguing the same thing in 1973. For Althusserian Maoists, May provided a first lesson by calling into question the power of scientists. But the critique did not go to the heart of the matter. The history of the Gauche prolétarienne is still weighed down by a *neutral* understanding of organization as the instrument for the application of a line founded on the positivity of a class ideology. What this hid from view was the positivity of the organization itself, which in its turn acted on this 'class ideology': the 'proletarian' fight against 'petit-bourgeois' ideology reinstated bourgeois power relations, and with it the bourgeois ideology premised on the repression of revolt.

But here we come upon another history: that of leftism. And Althusser never got there. Nevertheless, his analysis of the Cultural Revolution is identical with that of the founders of the UJC. He sees the Cultural Revolution as the mass ideological revolution that would give socialist China the ideological superstructure necessary to keep political and economic forms of socialism from being stripped of their content and to act as an effective response to the threat of capitalism being restored in every socialist country.[59] But this knowledge (*savoir*) could not be politically effective, since the Cultural Revolution was the one thing it was no longer possible to enlighten the PCF on. The immediate reason for this was that it was a case of excommunication. But the more profound reason, which would become clear later, was that the Cultural Revolution destroyed the very place of the educator. Hence the strange status of Althusser's 'On the Cultural Revolution'. It is conceived as an 'insider' text, written by a militant of the PCF to explain to his comrades the use-fulness of reflecting upon the Cultural Revolution; it is a diplomatic text in which the USSR is left out of the whole problem and the restoration of capitalism is limited to Yugoslavia. And yet, this insider discourse had to be held anonymously and 'outside' the PCF.[60] Althusser's great proj-ect, namely the regeneration of the Party through Theory, through the education of Party leaders, had become impossible in the wake of the Cultural Revolution and the formation of the UJC. The double game of strategy and tactics had reached its limit, and the only options left were subservience or rupture. Althusser agreed with the UJC's analysis of the Cultural Revolution and its implications, but he thought the moment was not yet ripe for them. No doubt, this prudence stemmed from the idea – shared by the UJC – that the creation of the UJC was only the beginning of a long process of secession. At the time, we all thought the Chinese offensive would result in a global redistribution of communist forces that would impact every communist party. But this did not hap-pen. One day we shall have to examine closely why not, but there is little doubt that the ambiguity of the relationship to Stalin is partly responsi-ble for the failure of the Chinese offensive to impact communism glob-ally. Meanwhile, those who were anticipating the success of the Chinese offensive held firm. It was not yet the moment. But, then again, the logic of Althusserian discourse is such that it is never the moment, as the antagonisms of empirical politics never give philosophy the moment to conclude, to bind rational politics to empirical politics. For this to hap-pen, the position of the educator, which sustains this dissociation, would have to be destroyed. But that was not part of the game, hence: *it will never be the moment.*

Althusser kept a benevolent eye on his straying sheep, but he pre-ferred to leave them to their wanderings. What conclusions did the Party draw from the last avatars of 'theoretical practice'? We do not know.[61] All we can see are the effects. For not having gone further, Althusser was obliged to orchestrate his own retreat, what he calls his 'self-criti-cism': he had 'forgotten' politics. That is to say: he had forgotten the Party. He had wanted to place philosophy outside the control of politics, and we could see the results. His only option now was to succumb, to accuse himself of the same wrongs the Central Committee at Argenteuil had accused him of: he had forgotten politics, forgotten practice. *Reading Capital* was reissued with the offending parts – the texts deemed 'too structuralist' – taken out. The announcement was sent out that philosophy would take heed of its modesty and resume its true role: to serve politics. The time had arrived for 'partisanship in philosophy'.

Mockery, surely, or a dark sense of humour. The notion of 'partisanship' was one of the great slogans of the Zhdanovian era, and Althusser's entire project had been formed as a reaction against slogans of that sort. To appropriate it now as his was either an act of courage or a farce. The great project was over. Philosophy had become *partisan* – it had come back to the fold. Althusserianism had played out to exhaustion the double figure of the communist intellectual, and from Kautsky's imperial view (the intellectual as the bearer of science), philosophy was demoted to an auxiliary role (the intellectual at the service of his or her party). Philosophy entered politics as one enters religion – to expiate its faults.

And that is how, on 24 February 1968, Lenin was inducted into the Société française de philosophie, whose 180 members are recruited by cooptation. Non-members are invited to attend the sessions, but not to speak, unless, of course, they have been granted permission by the president.

# CHAPTER THREE
## A Lesson in Self-Criticism: Class Struggle Rages in Theory

---

*All this is supposed to have taken place
in the realm of pure thought.*

*Karl Marx*, The German Ideology

And so, towards the end of 1967 and the beginning of 1968, Althusserian philosophy began its rectification. Philosophy had to be partisan, it declared. The times were uncertain, though, and it opted for the surest side, that of matter. Philosophy announced its entrance into the storms of politics through the battle to defend the spontaneous belief scientists have in the reality of their object.

We could pause to stress how sardonic this 'partisanship' really was. For, clearly, it masks something quite different, namely, the denegation of the political effects of Althusserianism,[1] and the wish to confine philosophical activity to a place where it would be sheltered from such accidents as those that had compromised it during the creation of the UJC (ML). We might also highlight the rather extraordinary view of the political urgencies which seem to motivate this need for partisanship. Althusser's advice to those engaged in political combat – to Régis Debray in South America and to Maria Antonietta Macciocchi in Naples – is the same he had given to the militants of the Cercle d'Ulm, and which they had ignored: learn to wait, to step back, learn to take the time of theory.[2] But when it comes to the exploitation of the sciences, then philosophy simply cannot wait. The urgency of the situation demands that it take risks. The 'theory of the process of production of scientific knowledges', the 'theory of the history of the sciences', the 'theory of the philosophical', the 'theory of the history of philosophies' must all be worked out without delay. As the forty-second thesis of the 'Philosophy Course for Scientists' puts it: 'The elaboration of these theories is one of the strategic theoretical tasks of our time.'[3]

We might decide at this point to go no further, pleading that such a disembodied 'politics' does not interest us. But that would mean failing to understand that this is in fact politics, and thus the failure to grasp what is at stake in it and the effects it is still capable of producing. The mechanism Althusser set in motion in the 'Philosophy Course for Scientists' is the very same one that governs the *Reply to John Lewis*: 'class struggle in theory'. This mechanism earned the admiration of some readers in 1973, who saw it as a novelty, or as evidence that Althusser, influenced by his reflections on May 68 and the Cultural Revolution, had aligned his thinking more clearly with leftists and thus taken 'a step forward towards the radical break with revisionism'. But the mechanism had already been worked out much earlier, in *Lenin and Philosophy* and in the 'Philosophy Course for Scientists'. Much more than a swing to the left, the rectified Althusserianism we encounter in these texts represents the normalization of Althusser's project, the elaboration of a 'partisan philosophy' conceived as a policing [*police*] of concepts.

The 'rectification' of Althusserianism is first and foremost a displacement of politics. Althusser's 'theoreticist' texts were an answer to an existing political conjuncture: the political and ideological fluctuations which followed in the wake of the Twentieth Congress. They relied for their answer to this conjuncture on the experience of a previous political conjuncture, represented by Zhdanovism and proletarian science. The theoreticist problematic turned on how to apply the lessons drawn from the politico-ideological conjuncture of the Zhdanovian period to the politico-ideological conjuncture of 'de-Stalinization'. 'Partisanship in philosophy', for its part, leaves entirely in the dark the conjuncture of Marxist philosophy at a moment marked both by the Cultural Revolution in China and by the rise of leftist movements in France. This forgetfulness of the present goes hand in hand with a forgetfulness of the past: there is not a single reference to 'proletarian science', either in *Lenin and Philosophy* or in the 'Philosophy Course for Scientists'. Althusser comments at length on Jacques Monod's inaugural lecture at the Collège de France and on the exploitation of biology by religious or moral ideologies.[4] But he never bothers to discuss a more directly political exploitation of biology such as Lysenko's, in spite of the fact that Monod himself is quite vocal about it. It is philosophies, each of which expresses a different conception of the world and all of which link back to class struggle, that 'exploit' the sciences. The schema of this rectified Althusserianism not only reproduces the same absence produced by 'theoreticism' – the absence of power – it also camouflages what, once upon a time, used to designate this absence: Zhdanov and Lysenko, like the banner held high of proletarian science, are out of the picture. The typical exploiter of biology is not Lysenko, but Teilhard de Chardin.[5] Materialist philosophy thus manages without any problems to safeguard its task: to defend scientific practice against those out to exploit it, and particularly against the number one exploiter – spiritualist religious ideology. Partisanship in philosophy places itself from the start at the heart of a perennial combat, for science, and against religion. The intervention demanded of philosophy in 1968 is still the same that had led Lenin to take on Bogdanov in 1908: to fight against the philosophical exploitation of 'crises' in the sciences. Philosophy becomes politics by repeating the atemporal gesture that pits materialism against idealism.

*Lenin and Philosophy* shows this displacement of politics quite well. Althusser there revisits the dispute between Lenin and Bogdanov, but without ever letting go of the theoretical problem that preoccupies him: the fight against leftism, against the relativization of theory. However, he introduces a twist that displaces the stakes of the dispute. It is no longer a question of the relationship between the time of theory and the time of politics, of an understanding of history and an understanding of practice, of a theory of truth and a theory of organization. All of these political stakes are erased to clear the way for the one truly important task: the defence of scientific activity against the spiritualist philosophies that exploit it. After reminding his readers of what textbooks call the 'circumstances' of the dispute (the fight against the Otzovists), Althusser proceeds as if the political relevance of Lenin's intervention were confined to the service it rendered to scientific practice. While Lenin probes a scientific question in order to find arguments to refute Bogdanov, Althusser acts as if Lenin refutes Bogdanov to help the sciences. Similarly, Dominique Lecourt's book, *Une crise et son enjeu*, singles out (outside of a handful of cavalier lines about the bourgeoisie's return to Kant after 1848) as the political effect of *Materialism and Empirio-Criticism* the help it brought to scientists who believed not only in the material existence of their objects, but also in the capacity of the sciences to know those objects.[6] Neither Althusser nor Lecourt seem interested in examining what real political effects might have been produced by the assistance Lenin brought to the sciences – an assistance, it would seem from their books, the sciences could not have done without. Lecourt gives a very good account of how Lenin uses the arguments some scientists had offered against the 'dissolution of matter'. But the truly important question is elsewhere, in the real, not the *likely*, political effects produced by the respective positions Mach and Lenin actually took.[7] If Lenin's had really been an intervention intended to benefit scientists, could it not in fact be accused of addressing a conjuncture that scientists would have considered dated, given that the special theory of relativity is from 1905? Doesn't the discovery of relativity cast doubt on the absolute conception of time and space of classical physics that Lenin is still working with in 1908? And didn't Lenin's materialism serve as the basis for the Soviet campaign to impugn the theory of relativity for being 'bourgeois'? These questions cannot be settled summarily, but we should at least single out the reversal at the heart of Althusser's reading. The sciences were not in need of Lenin's help; it was, rather, Lenin who needed the help of the sciences to work out his philosophical and political refutation of Bogdanov. It is impossible not to pause and wonder at this reading of Lenin, which sees all the political effects of his intervention as confined to the assistance it brought to the sciences, and never asks itself about the reality of these effects. What Althusser develops here is the strange *politics-fiction* that resurfaces in the *Reply to John Lewis* and that – in order to overlay the division between *idealism* and *materialism* onto every politico-ideological conjuncture – is always staging the simple opposition of theses said to aid or hinder knowledge, instead of addressing itself to the complexity of the real political stakes.

The essential question at the heart of the empirio-criticism episode, as of every 'deviation' from that period, is not the question of the effects that a particular philosophy of the sciences produced on the minds and practices of scientists. The crucial question turns, rather, on the political effects that the interpretation of the sciences (and of their 'crises') had on the understanding of socialism, its goals and its forms of action. We should in fact raise a broader question: what is the meaning of the massive use that socialist theorists around 1900 made of idealist philosophies (the Kantianism of the revisionist Bernstein, of course, but also the Bergsonianism of the anarcho-syndicalist Sorel and the empirio-criticism of the Bolshevik Bogdanov)? We can't just say that, after all, it is only natural that the bourgeois intellectuals who rallied to the cause of socialism should have brought with them the philosophical tendencies of their class. The questions they raise concerning the relationship between dialectical materialism and socialist political practice do not stem solely from their class, but from the objective state of socialist movements in Europe around 1900. This is especially clear in Sorel's case. He turns to Bergson in order to answer a problematic raised by a mass political reality, namely, the opposition of anarcho-syndicalism to parliamentary socialism, the existence of a mass strand of workers at once attached to the idea of self-emancipation and hostile to the idea of submitting their autonomy to intellectuals who specialize in politics. That is the basis of Sorel's denunciation of the complicity between the actual functioning of Marxist science and socialism's parliamentary compromise. According to Sorel, making Marxism a science and giving it a truth status that sets it above the struggle is tantamount to founding the double power, ideological and political, of intellectuals. It is to put the proletariat at the service of a fraction of intellectuals whose goal is to take over the machinery of the capitalist state from other intellectuals. Rendering Marxism unto the working class, conversely, means subjecting Marxist science to the jurisdiction of history; it means giving its concepts the function of 'myths' necessary for the organization of the proletariat and its autonomous struggle. Sorel turns to Bergson's theory of 'images' and 'schemes of action' as a response to Kautsky's thesis about bringing consciousness to the working class, a thesis that a mass of militant workers saw as an exploitation and a derailing of their struggle by a fraction of the bourgeoisie.[8] What is really at play behind the recourse to the bourgeois ideology of the 'crises of the sciences' is the relationship between the science of Marxist intellectuals and the autonomy of the working class.

The Bogdanov affair, in other words, is but one episode in the complex political game at work behind the wave of idealism that called into question the meaning of Marxist materialism in the early 1900s. The problem is not just the introduction of bourgeois ideas by petit-bourgeois theoreticians and reformist politicians, but also the questions raised about a certain materialism, a certain Marxist science: that of Plekhanov, Kautsky and Jules Guesde.[9] The results that followed would show that this questioning was in some way justified. Lenin's critique of empirio-criticism, like his critique of Bernstein's revisionism, offers only a partial interpretation and critique of this idealist wave, one that does not distance itself much from Haeckel and Plekhanov theoretically or from Kautsky politically.[10] This restriction is particularly noticeable in *Materialism and Empirio-Criticism*, where the political stakes involved in the interpretation of the sciences are entirely displaced onto the relationship of philosophy to science.

Althusser radicalizes this displacement by making Lenin's polemic the model to be constantly redeployed to protect the sciences from being ideologically exploited by the ruling classes. Althusser's scheme preserves the opposition between science and ideology as its fundamental premise, but modifies its *dispositif*.

What resurfaces in this project for *assisting* the sciences is, in effect, the dominant idea of theoreticism, the Kautskyist idea that producers are incapable of thinking their production. This idea, incidentally, is as old as the class struggle, as old as the opposition between direct producers and non-producers: producers don't know what they do, so they have to be assisted. In the present context, this can be translated as follows: scientists produce knowledges, but they are not fully aware of what it is that they produce. It is philosophy's task to help them become aware.

But the *dispositif* has changed. The 'theoreticist' Althusser saw philosophy as the science of science, a view that – above and beyond its inherent theoretical impasses – had the unfortunate political consequence of situating the authority of philosophy above the authority of the Party. The 'Philosophy Course for Scientists' moves the *dispositif* to the left. To begin with, science does not exist: it is an ideological concept. There are only *sciences*. This pluralization preserves the unity of the concept which gives philosophy its place (how could a unitarian discourse say something about the sciences without passing through the idea of *a* science?), while also masking the political stakes that attach to the concept of science (whose universality designates two things through the same concept: the universality of certain modes of verification and of a certain division of labour). As a result, the relationship of philosophy to science is no longer that of 'exterior consciousness' to spontaneity. The thesis is no longer, simply, '*Scientists don't think their practice*'; it is, instead, '*Scientists are the victims of class exploitation in their thinking of their practice*'. Their spontaneous philosophy is the site of a struggle between a spontaneous materialist tendency originating in their practice and a spontaneous idealist tendency extrinsic to this practice and sourced in the idealist world views and philosophies that exploit the results of scientific activity.[11] This exploitation, of course, prompts the intervention of materialist philosophy.

The text owes its novelty to this theory of a double spontaneity. Its introduction means that philosophy's task is no longer to bring a blind practice to self-consciousness but, more modestly, to bring political aid to a 'good', but oppressed, spontaneity. The excess of Kautsky's theory is corrected here by the theoretical revival of revisionism's practical thesis, which, depending on the needs, can play the card of working-class spontaneity in two ways: as the spontaneity to be corrected (by science and organization) and as an immediately positive class consciousness (against petit-bourgeois students). The theoretical transposition of this thesis into Althusserianism sustains the Althusserian *dispositif* by guaranteeing its two necessary conditions: the neutrality of science and the necessity of philosophy.

Neutrality of science: philosophy represents class struggle in the sciences. But if it needs to be represented, it is, apparently, because class struggle is not already there, for example, in the social function of the scientific institution and in its concomitant modes of selection, in its sources of funding and in the applications of scientific research, in the hierarchy of its organization and in the social image of scientists . . . in sum, in the double relationship scientific activity entertains with power and with the masses. All of this is replaced by a class struggle conceived through the opposition between a materialist element originating in scientific practice and an idealist element extrinsic to it. Scientific practice is thus separated from the places of power where it is carried out and from the power relations it puts into play. The class constraints that weigh on it are reduced to the action of world views that affect, not science, but how it is thought. The site of scientific activity and the site of class struggle are at two extremities of a chain that never links up. Monod is a great scientist, but he happens to have anti-Marxist ideas. The bond between this practice and his ideas is assured, apparently, simply by the identity of their subject.

What resurfaces here is the line of argument we found in Althusser's text about the students. The class struggle does not touch the different forms of scientific activity or the power relations that inform them: the functioning of scientific institutions is not one of the stakes of the class struggle. Class struggle only touches the sciences in the reflection of scientists upon their object, in the struggle, in that reflection, between the idealist and the materialist element. As Althusser's course was ongoing, the status of science was being seriously questioned, in China by the Cultural Revolution and in the West by scientists who wanted to discuss science's enslavement to power, capitalism and war. Althusser, however, pushes all of these questions and discussions to the side. Many scientists at the time talked about a *need for philosophy* – this was their shorthand for the questions they were raising about the political and social function of their science. Althusser replaces it with a substitute: class struggle in the philosophical exploitation of the sciences, the distinction between idealism and materialism. There where the 'need for philosophy' was shorthand for a political demand, Althusser acts as if philosophy itself was the object of the demand, as if philosophy itself was politics.

That was the price to pay to save philosophy. The sciences had to be in need of philosophy. And for that to be the case, some sort of cause had to be attributed to their demand. This could not be a matter of the social status of scientific activity for, were that the real issue, the solution would clearly have to be found elsewhere than in philosophy. Scientists had to be shown that their worries stemmed from the fact that their sciences were being exploited – not by bosses, governments or war hawks, but by philosophies. And against that, of course, the sciences needed *philosophical* weapons. The sciences need philosophy because of the idealists who exploit them by making them believe that they are in crisis when they are doing just fine. The sciences are not protected against that. Why not? Because Element 1 (materialist) is necessarily subordinate to Element 2 (idealist).[12] Repetition is the only proof the text offers for this thesis. Why is it, really, that scientists cannot critique their spontaneous philosophy themselves? Because of the environment they live in? But where do philosophers live? The only argument, in truth, is this: because scientists are here dealing with philosophy, they have no choice but to call upon specialists in the field.

The great wisdom of Althusser's *dispositif* now becomes evident: Element 1 must be inferior to justify the need for philosophical intervention. But it must also always have been there for the philosophical intervention to be seen as a response to a *spontaneous* demand (just as it was necessary for there to have been Bilaks in Czechoslovakia for the Russian intervention to be hailed as a moving instantiation of proletarian internationalism).[13] Hence the strange status of this 'spontaneity': when you point it out to the people concerned, they never recognize it. When philosophers tell physicists that Element 1 of their spontaneous philosophy 'has as its kernel the unity of three terms (object-real/theory/method)', they 'become reticent, they have the impression of hearing not a scandalous language but a language that sounds foreign to them, one that has nothing to do with the content of their own consciousness'.[14] In short, if physicists reject the realist language that Althusser claims is the language of their spontaneous materialism, it is not because of the scientific approach but because of the dominance exerted by the extra-scientific Element 2. Proof: 'A hundred years ago, they employed a totally different language'.[15] Those were the good old days when physicists spoke as they should.

For this is what it is all about. If philosophy can no longer tell the difference between truth and falsehood, then its only function is to distinguish between what should and should not be said, between what is correct and what is deviant or incorrect.[16] Philosophy must ground its political necessity in a dramatization of its relationship to the sciences. The mechanism of this dramatization appears in the two polemics that animate Althusser's 'Course': the one against Desanti's paper in *Porisme* and the one against Monod's inaugural lecture at the Collège de France.[17]

In his paper, Desanti set out to define the possible field of epistemological intervention in the sciences by distinguishing between three types of problems. Problems 'of the first type' are those raised in the language specific to a particular science and solved – albeit with some reworking – in that same language. Problems 'of the second type' are syntactical problems that bear upon the status of certain utterances and upon the conditions of their validity within a theoretical field. Problems 'of the third type' – or epistemological problems – are those that put into play concepts that are effectuable only in semantic fields heterogeneous to the science under consideration. An example of this third type are the questions concerning the *existence* of mathematical objects that arose at a certain moment during the development of set theory. Desanti shows how problems of the third type arise from the introduction into a particular science of presuppositions that belong to other semantic fields, and he suggests that the task of epistemology is to locate and invalidate introductions of this sort. On the face of it, there is nothing in Desanti's argument that might seem threatening to the sciences. As it happens, though, he discusses in his paper an episode in the history of mathematics that had come to be known, well before Desanti, as the 'crisis in set theory'. Althusser anchors his strange reading of Desanti's paper on this. In the problems of the first type he sees 'routine problems'; in those of the second type he sees 'theoretical revolutions'; and in those of the third type he sees 'pseudo-problems' created expressly in order to exploit the sciences through their 'crises'. Desanti invents scientific crises 'in order to kill, phenomenologically, the fatted calf'. But neither the concept nor its problematic is to be found in Desanti. Althusser had to put them there to be able to chase them out while arguing that sciences so dishonestly exploited were in urgent need of a vigilant assistant.

But it is the analysis of Monod's inaugural lecture that stages in full the *dispositif* of *imaginary class struggle* implied by the 'new practice of philosophy'.[18] If there is no class struggle in science, other than the class struggle imported into science's consciousness from the outside, then the question is: how does this happen, according to Althusser? Through the intermediary of certain words, he replies. Thus the notion of 'noosphere', taken from Teilhard de Chardin, reintroduces idealism into Monod's materialist consciousness and to pervert it. But why can this notion insinuate itself so? Because the materialist tendency is always too weak to defend itself alone.

> The idealist tendency against which Monod struggles, with all his strength, in order to make the materialist tendency in *Element 1* triumph, secretly re-enters through the window to triumph in *Element 2*. What is tragic is that it is Monod himself who opens the window. And because we cannot theoretically compare a scientist to a man who willingly opens a window to let the wind of idealism rush in, we say that it is the wind of idealism itself that opens the window. It has all the power necessary.... Which proves that *Element 2* is always stronger than *Element 1*. Which proves that the SPS [spontaneous philosophy of scientists] cannot with its forces alone prevent the window from being opened. And which proves that the SPS needs the support of an external force, allied with *Element 1*, if it is to triumph over *Element 2*.[19]

What is clearest about this avalanche of 'proofs' is that it is entirely directed at proving one thing only: the need for this 'ally'. The demonstration itself, however, merits our attention. How is the game actually laid out? There is a place that is normally innocent of class struggle, and there is the irresistible wind that brings this struggle in from outside: residual elements (words) carry it into the paradise of classless society. There is the inability of the victims of this aggression to defend themselves on their own, and the need of a helping hand to push this intruder back out. A story remarkably similar to that of a Soviet, classless paradise that had to be outfitted with a good police force and better prosecutors to prevent a residual clique of Nazi-Trotskyist saboteurs from exposing the country's defenceless citizens to the evil winds of the surrounding imperialism.

Such is philosophy's fate here: it escapes Zhdanov, only to find itself with Yezhov.[20] But what else are we to expect of an 'instance' entrusted with representing class struggle in a classless society? There is no proletarian science or science of science anymore, but philosophy is still supposed to bring science under its protective wing and lead the class struggle without ever stepping out of the lecture hall. Under such circumstances, what options does it have, other than to become a petty philanthropist that is always but one step away from degenerating into the police? What happens to Althusser's philosophy here is what happens, it seems, to many a Bolshevik when the time of hope and heroism has past: it finds its place. Philosophy becomes an instance of control charged with stopping the words that want to penetrate the spontaneous philosophy of scientists, and more generally of *producers*, with turning away the words that want to corrupt its innocence. It traces a security line around the sciences, like the security lines others were starting to trace around factories.

One will say here that all of this is 'exaggerated', that what Althusser was really trying to do was to promote more discussion between philosophers and scientists, to submit his theses to scientists so that they might correct them, to carry out an empirical survey of philosophy's relationship to the sciences. All of this should be taken into consideration, certainly, if we were trying to judge an individual's intentions. But our goal here is to analyse one way of practicing philosophy. The structure of its problematic – which turns its back to real, politico-ideological options – combined with its compulsion to inject a purely academic philosophical practice with a 'Marxist' political content, could not but yield the very thing we shall find some years later in the *Reply to John Lewis*: 'class struggle in theory', that is to say, the speculative police force of the philosopher–civil servant.[21] After May, this police force was able to give itself a somewhat leftist air and thus nourish that 'Maoist' variation of academic revisionism that 'left-wing' Althusserianism has become today. Many people nowadays pretend to see in class struggle in theory a major leftward turn for Althusserianism, an indication that philosophy, at long last, has recognized the class struggle. But what they recognize in it, actually, is nothing other than their own academic views, which assign class positions based on the correct or incorrect use of words, which treat as revolutionary those who know how to say 'it is the masses which make history' and as reactionary those distracted students who write 'man' where they should write 'the masses'.

Althusser was able to start systematizing the philosophical control of words and utterances elaborated in *Lenin and Philosophy* and in the 'Philosophy Course for Scientists' as early as the start of 1968, in an interview published in *L'Unità* entitled 'Philosophy as a Revolutionary Weapon'. There, Althusser goes from the undeniable fact that words are weapons in the class struggle to the very different notion that certain words belong to certain classes and that it is up to philosophy 'to draw a dividing line' between good and bad words, between those that convey a proletarian world view and those that convey a bourgeois one. He applies this notion in the interview by showing why Marxism rejects being called humanist and why one must not say that 'it is "man" who makes history', but rather the masses.[22] Those who marvel at the novelties of the *Reply to John Lewis* can, it is true, plead that the circumstances were such that they had not had the time to study this text carefully: it appeared in April 1968. The revolution was then in search of other weapons.

Whatever the case may be, it is clear that the machinery was already in working order well before May 68, and it does not seem that the 'events' impacted the Althusserian problematic much. The analysis he gives of the events in one of his letters to Maria Antonietta Macciocchi shows his position to be quite close to Marchais's: the students, petit bourgeois one and all, wanted to give lessons to the working class and teach workers how to make the revolution. But the working class wanted to have nothing to do with the students and their revolution. All the working class was fighting for were better economic conditions, and it won this battle by dint of its own efforts. Even if there were instances of conflict in the relationship between the working class and its syndicalist leaders, 'this second problem, in any event, is its own business and has nothing to do with the students. The students ought to get this simple fact into their heads, even if it is hard for them to understand it.'[23] Instead of going to factories and meddling in what is none of their business, the students would have done better to have invited syndicalist leaders, who could have taught them how to organize an occupation, to the Sorbonne. Having said that, we should be understanding towards the students, distinguish groupuscules from the mass of the educated youth and recognize the fundamentally progressive nature of their movement. We have to be patient and take the time to explain their mistakes to them calmly and deliberately: they imagine that they played a determinant role in May and that their actions led the workers to strike. The source of this illusion is, as always, a bad historical concept: the students confuse *chronological* order (the barricades did, it is true, precede the general strike) with *historical* order. Historically, Althusser explains, the student movement is dependent on the general strike: 'The mass participation of university students, secondary school students, and young intellectual workers in the May events was an extremely important phenomenon, but it was *subordinated* to the economic class struggle of nine million workers.'[24] The notion of subordination allows Althusser to sidestep the issue. Subordination, to be clear, could mean two things: either that the outcome of the May movement depended on the workers, in which case Althusser would not be saying anything different from Geismar or Cohn-Bendit,[25] or that the student movement owed its spark, its nature and its objectives to the general strike, and this, really, would be too Hegelian a history ... Althusser works his way out of this corner by attributing to the students a thesis that very few of them would have accepted ('The mass of the students thinks that they were the *vanguard* in May, leading the workers' actions'[26]), and which he proceeds to refute by turning to the idea, largely accepted by the interested parties, that they were 'detonators'. What must still be explained is why the students are prey to so many illusions. Althusser's answer is ready: just as physicists, beset by the evil winds of idealism, resist the 'spontaneous' language Althusser offers them, so too the students have a hard time understanding that it was the general strike which set off the barricades because the bourgeoisie makes them believe the opposite scenario. The students' reflections on their role in the 'events' are not the fruit of what they did and saw in May, but the fruit of what the bourgeoisie makes them believe. Althusser

69

draws the same conclusion here as in the case of the scientists: students, unable to distinguish between historical and chronological order, need vigilant advisors.

But here is where the problems start. It is not enough for there to have been advisors on hand; the students still had to ask for their advice. As it happens, though, the illness afflicting the students at the time was, precisely, thinking that they were not sick and that they didn't need to be treated. 'Those "concerned", or at any rate *many among them*, fiercely refuse, and will continue to refuse, the "care" that some, assuming they are actually interested in helping out, will offer.'[27] The problem is that a 'gap' had opened up between the PCF and the revolting students. And Althusser was not optimistic about the attempts made to bridge that gap: 'I have reason to fear that the new contacts we are making now are grounded on a certain misunderstanding...'[28] In effect, the PCF's university and cultural policies at the time were not likely to attract anti-authoritarian students to the Party, since the 'communist' flag at the university then consisted of re-establishing order within the university and of defending knowledge and mandarins. It was important to 'hold on to the May victories' (Faure Law and the experimental university at Vincennes).[29] This policy meant an open confrontation between the PCF and the entire student left. In June 1969, following the boycott of university elections at Vincennes, the Party had to send in its forces of order to impose Faurist participation and to defend the 'May victories', neither of which held any interest for May militants.

This declared politics of order put Althusserianism in a compromising position. These were the times when many a professor, frightened by May, turned to the PCF as if to the last rampart of academic order. And the Althusserian discourse on science and ideology invested this meeting with a measure of theoretical honour. The classical Althusserianism of 'Student Problems' or of 'Marxism and Humanism' was the designated orthodoxy of 'left-wing' young Turks who were hoping to carve out a place commensurate with their talents within the reformed university (that is what the 'May victories' meant to many people: more places for epistemologists and semiologists). At Vincennes, the student–professors responsible for the theoretical formation of the young men and women of the UEC advised them to read Althusser, Balibar and Bachelard as antidotes to 'Foucault and the leftists'. The intellectuals of *La Nouvelle Critique* – the 'in' ones, who were Althusserians through and through –

put themselves at the forefront of the 'theoretical' offensive against leftism. A bit of Althusser, a bit of Bourdieu-Passeron, a lot of Kautsky (preferably extracted from Lenin's texts), and the sauce was ready. The students simmered in it, prisoners, in their spontaneity, of bourgeois ideology. Their very condition locked them into a playful activity in which they mimicked class struggle. From this pot we were served Michel Verret's 'Mai étudiant ou les substitutions' and Claude Prévost's book *Les Étudiants et le gauchisme*.[30] Not so long before this, Althusserianism had attracted militant students formed in the struggle against the Algerian War; now it was attracting budding mandarins scared by the anti-authoritarian struggle. This was also the time of the alliance between *La Nouvelle Critique* and *Tel Quel*, of the great inroads of young communist intellectuals into the crème of Paris's theory circles. This could all have been the pretext for a few conferences and for launching the careers of some impatient go-getters. But Althusser was the sort to see further ahead. The PCF could not without risks come to be seen at the university as the party of scared mandarins or of young careerist intellectuals. Similarly, it could not come to be seen at the factory as the party of foremen and accountants. Politically, Althusser agreed with the return to order; indeed, he had even contributed a little bit to it.[31] But he had no intention of being its theorist. Orthodoxy was as distasteful to him as rupture. Moreover, he saw the future dangers of this politics: the Party had to find a way to attract the revolting youth being produced by the university and the factory as soon as possible. It was imperative to preserve the future on the left.

This explains the difference in tone between the letter addressed to Maria Antonietta Macciocchi and intended for a foreign audience, in which Althusser expresses rather bluntly his adherence to the Party's official theses, and the tone of the article against Michel Verret. In the prose of this overly zealous defender of 'science' (Verret), Althusser undoubtedly saw the dangers, a threat to him as well, of being confined to a simple philosophy of order. His answer to Verret highlights the problems still to be solved and the dubious character of certain solutions. This double attitude takes up anew the old game of strategy and tactics, but in something of an inverted form. In texts like 'Student Problems', the unconditional support for the positions of the Party actually camouflaged some subversive propositions. There was heterodoxy hiding behind orthodoxy. The point, back then, was to effect a gentle regeneration of the Party's politics through Marxist theory. The situation inverted after May 68; the forces Althusser could perhaps rely on at first were essentially outside the PCF, and it was no longer the Party that had to be moved, but leftists – the point was to bring a Maoist fringe to the Party. Althusser's texts, consequently, became readily contentious: bitter reflections on the shortcomings of the Party (the article against Michel Verret), mockery of the Party's academic policy ('Ideology and Ideological State Apparatuses'), an unofficial version of Stalinism (*Reply to John Lewis*). The tactics of Althusserianism were now aimed at leftists. Differently put: heterodoxy now hid orthodoxy.[32] And while his colleagues were trying to defeat ideology with science, Althusser kept in reserve the new theoretical weapon that could seal the alliance between progressive revisionist intellectuals and a fringe of moderate 'leftist' intellectuals: class struggle in theory.

This alliance had become possible because May traced not a single but a double dividing line between Marxist intellectuals. A first dividing line had separated 'leftists' from all those who were determined to preserve the authority of their knowledge (*savoir*) while they pursued their peaceful careers as mandarins *and* communists ('I am in the PCF', one of them once explained to his students, 'because it is the only organization that does not oblige me to be militant'). The leftist camp, however, had been divided from within. May 68 and the Cultural Revolution could in fact be interpreted in two ways. The left saw it as follows: bourgeois ideological domination is first and foremost the work of a set of institutions, against which one must wage a material political combat. Intellectuals are welcome to participate in this combat, as long as they are willing to strike down the foundations that support this system: the power of 'science', the separation of intellectual and manual labour, the separation of intellectuals and the masses. Today, the ideological combat of revolutionary intellectuals has nothing to do with refuting reactionary books with revolutionary books; it has to do, instead, with abandoning their specific roles as intellectuals and joining the masses, with helping the masses themselves to speak up and with fighting all the apparatuses – from unions to the police – that stand in the way of this free expression. Such was the view of the intellectuals who gathered around the Gauche prolétarienne and the Secours rouge.[33] The 'leftist right', however, had a completely different view of things. What had the Cultural Revolution shown? That class struggle was everywhere, and, since it was everywhere, there was no need to bother. 'What's the use', an eminent left-wing Althusserian used to ask us, 'of going to factories to talk to the same three workers every day?' There was no need 'to take philosophy out of the lecture halls', for class struggle was in those halls. No need to abandon book and pencil case, for class struggle was in the text and in the commentaries on the texts. No need to go see what was happening behind the walls of factories, prisons and homes. Suddenly, an immense battlefield opened up: one could fight revisionism in theory, defend science against its exploiters, preserve the materiality of writing.

Some 'anti-revisionist' intellectuals thus found themselves engaging in the same activities as PCF intellectuals. That is to say, through 'class struggle in theory' they found themselves waging the struggle of academic Marxism against the 'petit-bourgeois' voices of revolt. But things were not so simple for the vast majority of intellectuals in this camp. The efforts to shatter the status of intellectuals didn't settle the question of the function of theoretical activity. For many, class struggle in theory could seem like the complement to militant, anti-revisionist action. This double consciousness was reproduced in the duality: militant action and academic practice. But even those who wanted to do away with the old forms of the division of labour in their practice had not, for all that, destroyed such divisions within their own organization. The preservation of traditional power within Marxist-Leninist or Maoist organizations meant that the mechanism of imaginary class struggles was always being reproduced: every difficulty, every objective contradiction, every resistance to the direction of the organization's leadership was immediately represented as the struggle between petit-bourgeois ideology and proletarian ideology, as the fight against egoism and so forth. Chinese slogans, divorced from the material confrontations of the Chinese Revolution, sustained this mechanism. 'Class struggle in theory' might thus have seemed to some to be a product of the Cultural Revolution. Before May, academic ideology and revisionist ideology had joined hands to produce the struggle of Science (revolutionary) against ideology (bourgeois). After May, revisionist academic ideology could join hands with the authoritarian ideology of leftism to produce 'class struggle in theory'.

The conjuncture defined by this double division allows us to gain a better understanding of the strange status Althusser gives to the problematic of ideological state apparatuses. The fundamental theoretical lesson that the mass movement of May 68 had brought to everyone's

attention, and that the leftist critique of Althusser had started to systematize, was this: the bourgeoisie's ideological domination was not the
result of a social imaginary wherein individuals spontaneously reflected
their relations to the conditions of their existence. It was, instead, the
result of the system of material power relations reproduced by different
apparatuses. Ideological domination was not exerted on students primarily through the content of the courses themselves, or through their
spontaneous ideas, but through the concatenation of the forms of selection, transmission, control and use of knowledges (*connaissances*). The
question of ideology was not the question of the subject's relationship to
truth, but of the masses' relationship to power and knowledge (*savoir*).
In a text from 1969 on the theory of ideology,[34] I undertook to criticize
Althusser's conception of knowledge (*savoir*) by showing that, more than
a simple form of knowing (*forme d'une connaissance*), knowledge (*savoir*)
is an apparatus of power. The problematic of *ideological apparatuses* meant
a political rupture both with the opposition – science/ideology – and
with the notion of 'class struggle in theory'. It manifested the point of
view of those who saw ideological struggle as the struggle against the
apparatuses that produce the bourgeoisie's ideological domination.

This means that the concept, a theoretical product of the May movement, of ideological state apparatuses was fundamentally critical of the
Althusserian problematic of ideology. Taken seriously – in other words,
taken to mean a *political* rupture – the concept was useless for a philosopher of the PCF because it could not be separated from a practice of
struggle. Of what practical political use could this be for a Party whose
solution to the crisis in education was to increase the number of professors and their salaries, and whose solution to uprisings in prisons was,
likewise, to increase the number of guards and their salaries?

The only way for Althusser to be able to introduce this notion into his
problematic was to cancel out, purely and simply, the *political* conditions
of its production. Althusser pretends to have discovered this problematic,
one raised by a mass movement, when he embarked upon a path 'indicated' by the classics of Marxist theory, particularly Gramsci.[35] The
notion, already touched on, of theoretical heroism here takes on its most
outrageous form: *May 68 did not exist.* It is instead the solitary researcher
Althusser who discovers – as he treads the arduous path of his research –
the idea, which he presents as a stunning hypothesis ('This is why I
believe that I am justified...', '[T]his thesis may seem paradoxical...')

but which no one following the May movement could have doubted, of the dominant character of the academic apparatus.[36] Here, Althusser moves beyond pitting 'historical' against chronological order. It is only by denying the existence of May 68 and of the anti-authoritarian revolt that Althusser is able to credit the heroic investigations of the solitary theoretician with the distinction of having discovered, amid the general blindness and deafness of the population, the political role of the school: 'In this concert, one ideological State apparatus certainly has the dominant role, although hardly anyone lends an ear to its music: it is so silent! This is the School.'[37] Yes, the music of the dominant ideology is indeed quite 'silent' for those who do not want to hear the noises of revolt, for those whose theory depends on the theoretical suppression of that noise, for those who find – in this theoretical need – the principle for their membership in an organization committed to putting an end to this noise in practice.[38] Althusser's theory of ideology remains a theory of the necessary domination of bourgeois ideology, a theory of ideological normality that must be shored up by the reality of its normalization. 'It is so silent.' Meaning: thank heaven that it is so silent, that no noise disturbs the theoreticians of this silence.

The Althusserian project of the 1960s unfolded against the real silence of the masses. Now that this silence didn't exist anymore, Althusserian theory had to announce it so as to be able to claim that only the heroes could pick out the low music, inaudible to coarse ears, of class domination:

I ask the pardon of those teachers who, in dreadful conditions, attempt to turn the few weapons they can find in the history and learning they 'teach' against the ideology, the system and the practices in which they are trapped. They are a kind of hero.[39]

The heroes are, of course, teachers. In Althusser's 'anti-historicist' history, no student has been able to pick out the low music of or turn any weapons against the system. The fundamental thesis has not changed: the masses live in illusion. Ideology 'interpellates individuals as subjects'. And these subjects, of course, *work*.

[C]aught in this quadruple system of interpellation as subjects, of subjection to the Subject, of universal recognition and of absolute guarantee, the subjects 'work', they 'work by themselves' in the vast majority of cases, with the exception of the 'bad subjects' who on occasion provoke the intervention of one of the detachments of the (repressive) State apparatus.[40]

There are some bad subjects, but they are rare. And anyway, the riot police can always take care of them. Here is the price Althusser must pay to be able to introduce the notion of ideological state apparatuses into his problematic: he has to make it coexist comfortably with his old theory of the imaginary, the notion of interpellation serving as the tenuous link between the two. The problematic of ideological state apparatuses is placed alongside an analysis of the eternal structure of all ideology. Instead of an analysis of the functioning of the religious ideological apparatus, what we find is an extraordinary, and atemporal, analysis of religious ideology as the 'interpellation' of the subject, a sort of new 'essence of Christianity' which gives religion no other reality than that of dogma. What does this teach us about the actual functioning of existing churches, about the contradictions that inhabit them, about the way in which Christians live their faith in our societies, about the political role churches play in such or such a place? Does Althusser really want to teach us how the God of Abraham, Isaac and Jacob 'interpellates' his subjects? But what we want to know is how the God of Irish or Basque revolutionaries, of peasant syndicalists in the West of France and of proletarian syndicalists at the Lip factory functions.

Class struggle in the domain of ideology remains unthinkable so long as we remain bound to a theory of ideology as a theory of illusion, one confined to the relationship between three terms: subject, illusion and truth. How does ideology think class domination? As the production of an enslaving illusion. Such a theory can think an *enslaving* mechanism, in general, as the instrument of ideological domination by one class. But it does not allow us to think either the struggle pitched around a state apparatus like the school, nor the functioning of the concepts, 'ideas' and slogans that classes deploy in their struggles. The notion of ideological state apparatuses offers – it is true – a certain representation of bourgeois domination. But there is something missing from the picture it paints: the class that is dominated. This is class domination without a class to dominate (assuming that we understand class through the opposition of one practice to another, without which there is only the relation of power to individuals). The remark Althusser added later indicates the need to think the matter through the class struggle.[41] But such repentance does not yield a different theory, or a different politics. The notion of ideological apparatuses only makes sense from within a political rupture that Althusser rejects. This rejection explains why he can only think the notion here through the theory of universal illusion: the representation of an enormous, despotic machine that subjects every individual to its functioning. The very weapons we thought we had to fight against it (unions and parties) are themselves only cogs in the machine. 'Ultra-left-Platonism' would be an appropriate name for this strange theoretical figure. The double truth of Althusserianism after May 68 finds itself split between two poles: the speculative leftism of omnipotent ideological apparatuses and the speculative Zhdanovism of class struggle in theory, which cross-examines every word to make it confess its class. Althusserian philosophy tilts decidedly towards this second pole when it becomes 'partisan'. Thus it is that, in the *Reply to John Lewis*, ideological state apparatuses serve no function at all; all that is left is the fight of good against bad concepts, of the norm against deviations from it.

The contradiction here is resolved in irony. It may be that some militant Party members raised their eyebrows when they read, in the pages of *La Pensée*, that parties and unions are ideological apparatuses of the bourgeois state. But the list was so long and the indication so discreet that it was possible for them not to pay too much attention to it. No doubt Georges Cogniot's faithful followers, used to celebrating the Langevin-Wallon plan and the academic work of defunct republics, might have had some questions about the silent music of ideological state apparatuses. But they probably also thought that all of this was only theory, nothing to get too worked up about. Had there been something subversive in it, it would certainly have been denounced. What mattered, anyway, was that Althusser continued to write for the communist press.

There we have the only thing of political importance: the words didn't have to be orthodox, they just had to be printed in the right publication.


## APPENDIX: ON CLASS STRUGGLE IN TEXTS

Althusserianism, when it was the science of science, accorded a certain status to the epistemological break in Marx. The break served as the exemplary demonstration of the transition from ideology to science:

before 1845, the young, ideological Marx; after 1845, the scientific Marx. When we came across passages in the mature texts that were too similar to those of the young Marx, we said that the similarity was in the words only and that the concepts themselves were different, but that Marx, unfortunately, was still using a vocabulary that predated the break because he himself had not thought out the concept of the break all the way through.[42]

Class struggle in theory naturally steps in to rectify this *dispositif*. If philosophy is not a science, then the scientific *break* has to be distinguished from the philosophical *revolution*. The philosophical revolution directs the break, and politics directs the philosophical revolution. If Marx was able to define proletarian class positions in theory and found the science of history, it is because he adopted proletarian positions in politics.[43]

There is no better evidence for the real path traced by Althusser since writing 'On the Young Marx' than the pages he devotes to this very problem in the *Reply to John Lewis*. Nothing remains in them of the ambitious project Althusser had outlined in 1961: to draw attention to the actual terms of the debates that had given shape to Marx's thought, to the links between the transformations in his thought and political confrontations, to the effects his discourse produced on the labour movements and to the class struggles of his day. All we have now are the very same ghosts Althusser denounced in Soviet Marxologues. The evolution of the young Marx is summed up thus:

> He was to pass from radical bourgeois liberalism (1841–42) to petty-bourgeois communism (1843–44), then to proletarian communism (1844–45). These are incontestable facts.[44]

One wonders what Althusser in 1961 would have made of these 'incontestable facts', their language so reminiscent of the language of CGT representatives who have to present to their comrades the latest elucubrations of the Party as incontestable evidence: 'These are facts, comrades'. Is the passage from 'petit-bourgeois communism' to 'proletarian communism' a fact? What petite bourgeoisie and what proletariat are being discussed here? What do the qualifications—'petit-bourgeois communism' and 'proletarian communism'—mean in Paris in 1844, in the context of the debates that were then occupying the minds of communist groups, and of the members of the League of the Just in particular? What modifications do these qualifications imply in the sphere of political practice? Was the break of 1845 really the result of the fact that Marx adopted 'proletarian class positions in theory'? Doesn't this explanation ultimately amount to nothing more than coupling a tautology (Marx created Marxist science because he adopted Marxist theoretical positions) to a norm (proletarian is the one consecrated as such by the Marxist tradition)?

Althusser gives us the choice: either nothing happened at all around 1845, as John Lewis (providential John Lewis...) says, or there is *the* break. Now, many things did happen. Proudhon was praised to the skies in 1844, and then given a hiding in 1847: 'So something irreversible really does start in 1845'.[45] Let us note in passing that the irreversible something that starts in 1845 does not concern Proudhon, who in 1846 receives a still very deferential letter from Marx and Engels inviting him to be part of an international correspondence among socialists.[46] But that is not the crux of the matter. The main problem lies in the theoretical notion Althusser uses to make sense of the history of Marx's thought: the *philosophical revolution*. This notion contains in itself the solution to the problems posed by the survival, in the mature Marx, of categories from the young Marx. Whoever says revolution, says sleeping counter-revolution. Marx occupies proletarian class positions in theory. But with the ruling classes waging a fierce battle against proletarian class positions in theory, the old concepts return. If Marx, in *Capital*, speaks of alienation and of the negation of the negation, it is because the bourgeoisie, as with Monod, has blown open the window and penetrated his discourse.

> In practice, when the state of the class struggle enables it to put on enough pressure, bourgeois ideology can penetrate Marxism itself. The class struggle in the field of theory is not just a phrase: it is a reality, a terrible reality.[47]

Class struggle in theory here gives itself its Golden Legend: class struggle in Marx's texts.[48] When Marx says 'process', it is the proletariat that is speaking through him. But when he says 'alienation', it's because the bourgeoisie has penetrated his discourse. Naturally, these class struggles are all in 'close and constant relation to the class struggle in the wider sense'.[49] But as Althusser cannot very well show how the strong presence of alienation in books 3 and 4 of *Capital* is tied to a bourgeois offensive, or how the proletarian response to this offensive developed, what he does is establish a *parallel* between the swirls of theory and the whole of Marx's militant life. Marx was 'a leader of the labour movement for thirty-five years. He always did his thinking and his "investigating" in and through the struggle.'[50]

Althusser tips his hat in tribute to the workers's movement, only the better to wash his hands of empirical workers. Marx, who was less prone to blowing his own horn than Althusser, and who knew well enough that merely stressing a word (leader) was not enough to give a matter substance, recognized on different occasions that he was not the leader of much. He also holed up for many long years in the British Museum, thinking that this was probably the greatest service he could render to the revolution. Althusser's grandiloquence is there only to make us swallow an unverified and unverifiable thesis: when the concepts and schemas of the young Marx resurface in the old Marx, it is because of the pressure exerted by the bourgeois class.

The only way to get out of this phantasmagoria is through the serious study of the problems that prompt each and every reintroduction of the old concepts, or of concepts that 'resemble' them. What is the discursive function of each reintroduction? And what are the real political stakes? We cannot simply answer by saying that they 'tendentiously' disappear as Marx's thought matures and ripens. The concepts in question are brutally discarded for a short period (1845–47), during which Marx makes systematic use of an empiricist language, and during which he works to reduce every philosophical concept to an empirical reality (which means, among other things, that the concepts formally discarded are, often enough, simply disguised; hence the strange theoretical figure of *The German Ideology*). They reappear after the Revolution of 1848, but with different functions. Marx borrows the categories and schemas of his critique of religion to think the political phantasmagoria of the Revolution of 1848; he relies heavily on Hegelian and anthropological categories when he resumes the critique of political economy (the *Grundrisse*); he turns to Hegelian logic for the elaboration of *Capital*. The most interesting examples are, undoubtedly, those in which Marx uses anthropological schemes to echo the struggles and aspirations of workers. It would not be difficult for Althusser, who gently reminds John Lewis that 'he can always try' to find alienation in Marx's political texts,[51] to find, in the first draft of *The Civil War in France*, considerations – about the state and society and about the need for the people to reclaim 'its social life' – whose origins cannot be doubted.[52] These considerations are at the very heart of the reflection on that 'scientific' concept, the state apparatus. And behind the concept of fetishism, which must be expelled, it seems, from a properly 'scientific' *Capital*, we also find the aspirations of the working class. The point from which it becomes possible to think the mystification of merchandise and understand the functioning of the capitalist system is that of the aspirations which fuel the workers's struggle: the association of 'free producers', of 'freely associated men' whose social relations and whose relations to their objects will one day be 'perfectly simple and intelligible'.[53] An idea of the social stamp of work on objects which mirrors the contemporaneous dream of bronze workers on strike in Paris, the dream of a civilization of 'men who can breathe freely, and who stamp upon their work the indelible character of the social life they breathe'.[54]

These brief indications are intended simply to suggest that maybe there isn't *a* Marxist conceptuality which must be saved from ideological doom and bourgeois invasions. There is not one logic in *Capital*, but many logics; it contains different discursive strategies, each of which corresponds to different problems and each of which echoes, in many different ways, the discourses through which classes think themselves or confront an opposing discourse, be it the science of classical economists or the protests of workers, the discourse of philosophers or the reports of factory inspectors, and so on. The plurality of these conceptualities is also a manifestation, not of 'class struggle in theory', but of the effects that class struggle and its discursive forms have had on the discourse of theoreticians. Those who pretend to isolate the 'scientificity' of Marxist discourse from every non-scientific element are far from being at the end of their pains. And those who want to draw a dividing line between 'petit-bourgeois' and 'proletarian' concepts have only touched the surface of their discontent.

# CHAPTER FOUR
## A Lesson in History: The Damages of Humanism

*Every measure the courts have taken against the*
*freedom of the press and political associations*
*would be lost if one could, every day, portray to*
*workers their position compared to that of a higher*
*class of men, by reminding them that they are*
*also men, and thus have the right to the same benefits.*

Persil, State Prosecutor

*As their ideology is freed from bourgeois and petit-bourgeois*
*notions, the masses stop recognizing themselves in 'men'*
*and claiming their 'human dignity'.*

Saül Karsz, Théorie et politique: Louis Althusser

*It is possible: we produce, we sell, we pay our ourselves.*

Lip workers

Philosophy ventures into new territory with the *Reply to John Lewis*. Class struggle in theory no longer limits itself to closing the windows that let the wind of idealism penetrate the spontaneous philosophy of scientists. Henceforward, it will speak about the questions 'burning to be expressed',[1] it will deal with politics in the everyday sense of the term, that is, the politics of workers and the bourgeoisie, of Soviets and Czechs.

We may be surprised to discover that this new intervention is essentially a continuation of Althusser's age-old battle, which pits Marxism against theoretical humanism. But that would be to forget the relationship between philosophy and politics prescribed by the Althusserian rectification: philosophy is *political* intervention only insofar as it is eternal, only insofar as it is the indefinite repetition of the same battle. Philosophy must indefinitely remind scientists that they are right to believe in the reality of their object, just as it must constantly remind the masses or, rather, their (political and philosophical) avant-garde, that Marxism is not humanism, that humanism is nothing other than the political figure assumed by bourgeois idealism. We should not ask Althusserian philosophy to say anything else, for it has nothing else to say. The only novelty it can muster comes from saying the same thing, but about new objects. Consequently, in this chapter we look at how it says what it says and at the place outlined in that utterance for philosophy, politics and the masses.

Why is the problem of humanism the cross of Althusserian philosophy? The answer is easy. On the one hand, 'M-L is formal': Marxism is not humanism. 'Man', with a capital 'M', is an ideological myth of the bourgeoisie that allows exploitation by masking it. On the other hand, Marxist theorists and leaders, from Marx to Mao, speak a bit more than they should about man, his alienation, his history-making and about the need to change what is deepest in him. Workers are even worse. Much as Marxist anti-humanism is their 'class theoretical position',[2] they are always talking about man, always insisting that they are men and not dogs, always singing that 'the earth belongs to men'[3] or calling for a more humane society. As Althusser's book was entering France's theoretical market, workers at the Lip factory were challenging the bourgeois order with the following principle: 'The economy should serve man, not man the economy.' Are these workers perhaps still living in 1844? What is the relationship between the 'man' being chased from universities and the one being invoked in factories?

Philosophy assures us that, in suppressing 'man', it does not suppress 'real men'.[4] The precaution is unnecessary, since we've known for some time now that philosophy's crimes are always only speculative. What interests us is the relationship between philosophy's battle against humanism and the battles over words waged in the class struggle. Two answers are open to philosophy here. One is to say that philosophy speaks about *philosophy*, that its object is not the cries of indignation or generous words that invoke man, but man as a philosophical concept with a theoretical function; it examines whether or not man can pretend to provide the *theoretical* starting point of Marxist science. This allows philosophy to avoid all ambiguity, but at the price of rendering it incapable of saying anything other than generalities accepted by everyone. Man is not the *theoretical* starting point of *Capital*? But who would argue with that? Even within Althusser's party, where the appeal to the humanist tradition is widespread, nobody defends the thesis that man is the theoretical starting point of *Capital*. History does not have a subject? And who takes the trouble to give it one? John Lewis, you say? And who gives a second thought to John Lewis? If you had to cast so far in order to find a partner, is that not because, inside your own party, where no one is shy about saying all manner of things, you cannot find anyone who defends the formidable thesis that man is the subject of history? The battle against theoretical humanism and the philosophy of the subject is an important class struggle in philosophy today? Just look around. *On this issue*, French universities are as calm in 1973 as Soviet society was in 1936. The death of man and the annihilation of the subject are on everyone's lips. Invoking Marx or Freud, Nietzsche or Heidegger, the 'process without a subject' or the 'deconstruction of metaphysics', big and small mandarins are everywhere, tracking down the subject and expelling it from science with as much zeal as Aunt Betsy puts into chasing donkeys from her grass in *David Copperfield*.[5] The only disagreement among our academic philosophers concerns what sauce to eat 'the subject' with. As for 'man', any *hypokhâgneux*[6] would blush to invoke him in a paper. The only ones who dare speak of man without provisos or precautions are, in fact, workers.

Hence the question: what exactly does philosophy fight against? The interview Althusser gave to *L'Unità* in 1968 assigned it a certain role. If philosophy draws dividing lines between concepts, and if it is so attentive to correcting words, it is because 'in political, ideological and philosophical struggle, words are also weapons, explosives, tranquillizers, or poisons. Occasionally, the whole class struggle can be summed up in the struggle for one word against another.'[7] It seems that man plays every role in political and ideological struggle, except for the role of subject of history. But if philosophy refuses to consider the stakes in that, if it says that the sphere where words produce effects ('the abolition of man's exploitation of his fellow men', 'the insurgent, his real name is man', 'socialism with a human face') is not its problem – since there one is no longer dealing with the *concepts* of proletarian theory, but only with angry, indignant or generous *words* – then philosophy establishes a division that undermines its pretentions to politics. On one side of that line is the realm of the intelligible, of the 'proletarian class positions in theory'[8] that discard man as a bourgeois myth; on the other is the realm of the sensible, whose actors do not have 'the same choice of words'.[9] What this means is that the words of these actors cannot be taken literally, but have to be explained by particular circumstances and referred back to what they designate (the poor also have their 'index concepts'). The man Althusser denounces in John Lewis has nothing at all to do with the man that the bourgeoisie and proletariat fight over on a daily basis. Philosophy is thus confined to attending only to theses whose political effects never leave the classroom.

If philosophy is unwilling to accept this predicament, then it must be willing to speak not just about the subject of history, but also about humanism as a practical political ideology; not only about the philosophical concept of 'absolute origin', but also about the roles 'man' plays in the ideological class struggle. It must explain, for example, why, in the struggle between employers and workers, 'man' is on the side of the employers.

On the face of it, it seems the whole thing can be easily demonstrated: the market relations generalized by capitalism have the sanction of bourgeois law. The law that declares the bourgeoisie free to exploit the work of others and the worker free to sell his labour power also produces a juridical ideology: an ideology of freedom, of the legal subject, of the rights of man. This juridical ideology produces the category of the subject, in the philosophical realm, and, in the political realm, the category of man and humanism. With all its talk about man, with its assurances to the proletariat that all men are free and equal, in sum, with its 'humanist song', the bourgeoisie keeps the proletariat from seeing the reality of the class struggle. It persuades them that they are free subjects and all-powerful as men. What Marxism must do is deliver workers from this illusion. A loyal commentator of Althusser gives us the following, idyllic vision of this liberation: 'As their ideology is freed from bourgeois and petit-bourgeois notions, the masses stop recognizing themselves in "men" and claiming their "human dignity".'[10] These masses cannot but be happy. Finally freed from their 'bourgeois' claims to 'human dignity', they are no longer prey to the ills that befall millions of workers in the four corners of the globe, who are being shot or deported for having filled their heads with such silly ideas. But happier still are the leaders who so deftly administered the scientific education that freed the masses from all such bourgeois notions.

What do these analyses presuppose? That only the bourgeoisie think and that – so long as workers have not learned the science of intellectuals – the man, the laws and the freedom that workers talk about are, at best, the inverse expression of the relations of domination they endure. 'The ideology of freedom is imposed on workers, and they spontaneously include it in their representation of society and of their place in it.'[11] What freedom is being discussed here, and what does 'impose' mean? The bourgeoisie can always impose its freedom – the freedom that it wrote into law with the passing of the Le Chapelier Law in June 1791 – on workers by force.[12] But this does not change the fact that the worker's idea of freedom has always been antagonistic to the master's idea of it. For the bourgeoisie, freedom means being able to hire and fire workers on the basis of a free agreement between two individuals. For workers, freedom means being able to work where they want to work, to sell their labour only at its 'right price' and to walk out on the workshop as a group when they are refused the right price for their labour. The masters have a name for this freedom: the despotism of the workers . . .[13] And the freedom of the masters is, likewise, tyranny for the workers. The master's freedom is the freedom to be able always to deal only with individuals. That of the workers, conversely, is the freedom to stick together, to negotiate collectively, to abandon the workshop as one group. The entire history of the workers' struggles over the course of the nineteenth century to secure the establishment and enforcement of a basic rate of pay shows that 'the freedom to sell one's labour power' cannot not be translated into the freedom of each worker. The only contract that is valid is a contract with the collectivity of workers; if two workers in a workshop agree to work for less than the basic rate, the entire guild rebels against this violation of its rights. The 'economic' struggle for a basic rate is in fact, and above all, the battle of proletarian legality against bourgeois law. It took the concerted and centuries-old effort of the police, the judicial system and the penitentiary apparatus – not to mention intense fighting inside trade unions – to render the bourgeois notion of 'the liberty of labour' acceptable. And our daily experiences show that the bourgeoisie is still far from having fully succeeded.

Bourgeois law may very well be a source of philosophical illusions about the subject and its freedom. But things are a bit different for workers. The problem is that when it speaks about masters and workers, the beautiful image of equality among peoples and the elimination of the couple, person/thing, is shattered. When bourgeois law effaces class differences, it is not through natural dissimulation, or simply as a result of an evolution in relations of production: it is because workers have forced it to do so. What the workers instructed by the battles for a basic rate and for controlling the hiring process saw in the Napoleonic Code was not individual freedom, but the legal differences between employers and workers. And they fought for more than half a century against the articles that materialized that difference: articles 414 and 416 of the penal code and article 1781 of the civil code. The former two not only prescribe different punishments to be meted out to 'associations' of employers and to workers' 'associations', they also specify a category exclusive to the latter – that of 'chiefs' or 'movers'. (Implicated in this additional category, beyond the sheer severity of the punishment – up to five years imprisonment, followed by up to five years of close monitoring by the high police – is an entire ideology about the workers's struggle). Article 1781 of the civil code, for its part, states that the master's word concerning the sums paid is to be believed. If these articles are no longer part of our legal codes, it is because of the struggles workers waged against this denial of *their* legal rights. It is because they fought to be 'people' with the same status as the masters, to be recognized as 'men' and not as workers.[14]

Paradoxical as this demand might seem, it does in fact represent an answer to a certain discourse of the bourgeoisie. After all, the 'humanist song' the bourgeoisie sings to the working classes has always been rather peculiar. Consider, for example, the bourgeoisie that rose to power in 1830 and found itself, a year later, under death threat from rebelling silk workers in Lyons. What did the bourgeoisie sing to the workers then? That we are all men, all equal, all brothers under the sun? Not at all. It said the opposite: there is a class struggle, a battle of the have-nots against the haves, of barbarians against civilized people. What one must not do, above all, is grant to the barbarians at the heart of civilized societies the title or the prerogatives of *man*. Immediately following the uprising in Lyons, the *Journal des Débats* printed the following warning: 'The sedition in Lyons has revealed an important secret, the intestinal struggle that rages in society between the owning class and the labouring class. Our commercial society, like every other, has its scourge, and this scourge is the workers. There cannot be factories without workers. . . . And with the steady increase of an always needy population of workers, there can be no rest for society. Each manufacturer lives in his shop like a plantation owner among slaves in the colonies, one against a hundred . . . . The barbarians threatening society are not in the Caucasus, or in the Steppes of Tartary. They are in the suburbs of our industrial cities.'[15] Hence the conclusion: we must not give weapons or rights to these barbarians who have nothing to defend. Here, the opinion of the owning class coincides with the opinion of the state apparatus, as expressed by Persil, a state prosecutor who would go on to become minister of justice, during the trial of a public crier in 1833: 'Every measure the courts have taken against the freedom of the press and political associations would be lost if one could, every day, portray to *workers* their position compared to that of a higher class of men, by reminding them that *they are also men*, and thus have the right to the same benefits.'[16]

There is class struggle, declares the bourgeoisie, and telling workers that they are men, like the members of the bourgeoisie, is out of the question. The workers' paradoxical reply to this is: people are not *either* barbarian *or* civilized; there are no class distinctions – we are men, like you.

The print-worker Barraud replies to the piece in the *Journal des Débats*:

Workers are not slaves. In France, workers still enjoy the title of citizens, and they see themselves, without pride or vanity, as being every inch as free as their employers. . . . What, may I ask, have my PROLETARIAN colleagues done to you, that you hurl at us so many furious imprecations, all of them worthy of the days when great lords thought proper to cut off the ears of marauding commoners who dared commit the *heinous crime* of passing before their noble person without taking off their hats?[17]

Apparently, all Barraud does is hold up to the frightened bourgeois the official ideology of his class: am I not a free citizen, like you? This democratic illusion rests, supposedly, on the contempt the labour elite has for 'slaves'. But the use of words requires a bit more attention. The well-read bourgeois, in his terror, spins out a metaphor: scourge, slaves, plantation ... The proletarian refuses the metaphor. This referral to the letter is also a referral to practice. For those who endure the hardships of the workshop, words have a different measure of reality. To refer to us as slaves is to treat us as slaves. The one who says, 'We are surrounded by slaves', is not simply voicing his contempt for workers: he is also strengthening the chains of capitalist domination. And what does he want to prove with his language? That workers are not to be given weapons. The use of words incurs the use of weapons. And it is the workers' right to weapons that Barraud defends when he says that workers, like their bourgeois counterparts, are men. The language tempered by respectability of these workers initiates the chain that leads to the language of insurgent workers. Barraud says: it is not just owners who are men. We are also free citizens. Give us weapons, then. Pottier: 'The insurgent, his real name is man.' Man, that is to say, producers, for *only* producers are men: 'The idle have to go live elsewhere.'[18]

The tailor Grignon replies to Persil: if the government 'does not allow workers to be taught that they are men', it is because it 'regards us as instruments for the pleasures of the idle rich'.[19] The qualification the government denies to workers is made up for by the qualification the masters grant them, but which the workers uniformly reject: 'They dare accuse us of *revolt*. Are we their Negroes, then? . . . These gentlemen all want to recognize that the vast majority of tailors are both honest and SUSCEPTIBLE to good sentiments. . . . It is not becoming for men who have emerged from our ranks, and can one day rejoin them, to declare us SUSCEPTIBLE to good sentiments.'[20] The revindication of the quality – man – is the rejection of the power to qualify workers that masters grant themselves. The latter power is nothing other than the expression, materialized in the letter of their *Manifesto*, of the property rights they claim to have over their workers: 'Let these gentlemen stop thinking they can claim property rights over us, and we shall be able to find an agreement.'[21] There is the decisive word. Workers claim for themselves the quality of 'man', but the man they claim is not the ghost produced by the freedom and equality of trade relations. It is, rather, the image wherein is affirmed the resistance to those relations, the rejection of the tendency immanent to them to transform workers and not just their labour power into

**89**

merchandise over which the masters claim property rights and which they would like to market like other goods. Workers denounce this tendency towards *slavery* as inherent to capitalism. In the fall of 1833, the tailor-workers pointed the way out of capitalist slavery: workers must appropriate the instruments of production. To be able to provide for themselves during their strike, and in order to show that *men* don't need *masters*, the tailor-workers created a national workshop, where they made and sold their products on their own.[22] The meaning of such an initiative was not lost on the bourgeoisie:

In their delirium, they went so far as to publish a text in which they say that there will be no more masters, that they would make clothes by relying solely on the infrastructure of the associations, without credit or liability, and with men who are all equal, who do not take orders from anyone, and who carry out their tasks as they see fit.[23]

This is the role the 'man' claimed by the tailor–workers plays. As there are only men beneath classes, it is possible, in the end, for workers to do without masters. Man is not the mask that derails the struggle, but the rallying call that effects the transition from labour practices that grant control over the labour process to the appropriation of the means of production – the passage from labour *independence* to the *autonomy* of producers. The new chain that is initiated there leads straight to our present. Lip 1973: workers are not people one can separate and displace however one pleases. A weapon to remember this by: 'It is possible: we produce, we sell, we pay ourselves.' A future is outlined there: an 'economy that serves man'.

*It is possible*: the whole ideological struggle between the bourgeoisie and the proletariat is played out there. The only song the bourgeoisie has ever sung to workers is the song of their impotence, of the impossibility for things to be different than they are or – in any case – of the workers' inability to change them. From the day cares the liberal bourgeoisie created around 1840 – it is never too early to start inuring working-class children to resignation – to the CETs[24] we all know, the bourgeoisie has only had one lesson to teach to the children of the proletariat, and it is not the lesson that man is all-powerful, but the lesson of order, obedience and individual promotion. Even if it proclaims all men free and equal before the law, the bourgeoisie has never forgotten to add that men are not all free and equal in fact and that the inequality between men is inscribed into the very nature of things, much as the couple – domination/servility – is inscribed into human nature itself. This is the lesson Montfalcon teaches workers in 1835, and it has not changed much since:

> The wealthy aristocracy is perhaps an evil, but an inevitable one. Land, money, homes, riches of every sort – give everything to the poor class, apply agrarian law, level out the conditions so that no one today has more than another and, tomorrow already, all the vices inseparable from our nature – negligence, profusion, incapacity – will have re-established the inequality you abhor.[25]

The 'free' subject of the bourgeoisie is a determined nature, one determined, precisely, to inequality. The 'man' of bourgeois discourse is always double; it posits the inevitability of the couple, dominant/dominated. Humanism, if we want, but no discourse about man-as-God, only a discourse that says to proletarians that they cannot do anything on their own.

> In spite of the means used to confine us to bare needs, they know better than we do that we are all the strength, all the power, because we are the source of all wealth. . . . Thus, to hold us captive, they work to fill our heads with notions that chain us down. They dare say that we could not live without speculators, because they are the ones who give us work.[26]

Such are the considerations through which the bourgeoisie enchains workers: there are necessary laws, and these imply a necessary dependence – employers *give* work.[27]

That is how the bourgeoisie expresses its great wisdom to the workers who reject lay-offs: you want full employment? Well, there cannot be full employment without a good economic market, and there cannot be a good economic market without capital, and there is no capital without a guaranteed return on investments, and there is no guaranteed return on investments without the freedom to hire and fire workers. There you have the circle. We cannot change it. The alternative is the USSR. No unemployment there. But also no possibility of working where you would like. On the contrary: workers are assigned to a workplace by the authority of the state, populations are displaced and forced labour is exercised on a large scale. The choice is yours. But you will not get out of the circle. There will always be a minority – whether owners or simply managers – who, either through the free play of the market or the constraint of the state apparatus, assigns workers to the places where their labour will be most profitable.

Lip workers reply:

> They want to convince all workers that lay-offs are normal, that they regulate the economy just as rain and good weather regulate the earth's water supplies. But that is false. This regulator is inherent to the capitalist regime, but it is not at all necessary to an economy designed to serve man.[28]

The bourgeoisie proclaims, You want to stay together? That is very fine; it's perfectly 'human'. But the economy has its laws. The man workers mobilize in their discourse to combat this idea plays the same role 'history' plays in Marx: both denounce the 'nature' that justifies capitalist domination, both transform the bourgeois claim (it is impossible for the economy to function otherwise) into the revolutionary claim that another economy is possible.

This practical claim about what is possible can, with no mystification, be conveyed in the demand for rights: the right to work, the right to access company information (*droit de regard sur l'entreprise*). To insist on the right to work is not tantamount to falling into the juridical illusion of the 'legal subject'; it is, on the contrary, to use the judiciary to show that economics is in fact politics, that such economic necessities as lay-offs and the dismantling of companies are nothing more than strategies used by employers to suppress the rights acquired by workers and to destroy the community that is the source of their strength. What is at stake here, more than just turning bourgeois juridical ideology against employers' practices, is the opposition between two ideas of rights. The right to *indemnification*, intones the bourgeoisie: workers are 'super-preferential creditors'. The right to *work*, reply the workers. This is the continuation of an old ideological struggle between *bourgeois philanthropy*, which helps workers out of the tight spots they might fall into as a result of the natural constraints of the economy and the fallible nature of employers, and *labour autonomy*, which insists on the workers' right to collective organization. It is the same struggle that, in 1848, found workers and employers locked in battle over the right to work and the right to assistance. Ultimately, this battle over rights is a battle between *powers*: between the institutions through which the state and employers exercise control and the institutions through which labour exercises control – the forms of the labour community.

At the end of the day, it is a battle between two factories. 'There where the men are, that's where the factory is.' This sentence by Piaget, beyond the specific circumstances of the Palente occupation,[29] gives the struggle its meaning: it is an answer to the capitalist factory, its despotism, its hierarchical organization and its commercial secrecy – an answer to the top-down measures by which it lays off and indemnifies workers. Set over and against this is the factory founded on the labour community, which imposes its own rhythm on the work, its non-hierarchical organization and its non-secretive commercial practices. What the appeal to man denounces here is what the Althusserian *dispositif* (economism/humanism) masks of the reality of capitalism: factory despotism, the power apparatuses that guarantee its reproduction and the ideologies of assistance these apparatuses reproduce, whose only line, repeated to workers as if on a loop, is that it is impossible for things to be otherwise. This is a despotic system whose every effort, from the very beginning, has been directed at breaking the labour community, its autonomous institutions, its collective practices and its collectivist ideology. The capitalist factory is not, *first and foremost*, the development of productive forces, but the broken labour community. At the factory that is 'there where the men are', conversely, the labour process is founded on the labour community, as it has been perpetuated or reconquered through resistance. The road is always the same: what begins from the basic demand for full employment issues in the struggle for another world, a world made 'for men', that is to say, in no uncertain terms, a world made for and by the labour community.

What is involved in the struggle, consequently, are not just words, but class discourses. At one level, the distinctions are clearly marked: freedom, which is either of employers or of workers, and man, who is either owner or producer. But the distinctions do not affect the words themselves (man on the right, classes on the left); they are, rather, vehicled in and through words, in and through their turns, twists and slips. A savage dialectics in which even the theoreticians of the revolution sometimes get lost – understandably, since the rupture is never simple. The man, rights, justice or morals that Parisian Internationalists demanded under Marx's watchful eye never stop sliding from one end of the pole to the other: from Tolain, the doctrinal accountant who would become a Versaillais, to Varlin,[30] the revolutionary who did not want to rise through the ranks and out of his class; from bourgeois integration to proletarian autonomy. The 'empty' words of these workers (who Marx, in 1870, was delighted to see behind bars) become, in March 1871, the slogans of the revolt of the producers who 'storm the heavens'.[31] This was more than simply the transmission, through the intermediary of the young Hegelian Grün and the 'petit bourgeois' Proudhon, of the old lesson of Berlin-style philosophy to these self-taught brains. It was also the slogan of a new world. This duality in the evaluation of the political situation is reflected in Marx's theoretical discourse, in the first chapter of *Capital*, for example, where the reveries about the association of free producers and transparent social relations interrupt the beautiful rigour of Marx's analysis of the commodity. The very terms of these passages not only echo the contemporaneous declarations of bronze workers in Paris, they also bind the possibility of science to the ideal brought forward by fighting proletarians: the association of free producers.[32] Everything splits in two. If *fetishism* is not the new face of alienation, it is because the freedom of Paris workers is different than that of the Freemen in Berlin,[33] because the 'man' whose dignity bronze workers plead against the manoeuvres of their bosses is not Feuerbach's *man*. That explains why man, the free producer, although not the starting point of Marx's 'analytical method', nevertheless has a role to play in Marx's *theoretical* discourse. And his role is not that of rhetorical ornament or philosophical remainder: he is the point that makes the very design of science possible. This theoretical role, founded on labour practices and discourses, could not, of course, be that of a philosophical 'foundation' of science. In other words, the effort to identify what man political and philosophical discourses are talking about, and what role he is made to play in those discourses, is not unfounded. As it happens, though, such an effort is unthinkable within the *dispositif* of Althusserian theory, for the latter replaces a real discursive division with a double, speculative division between science and ideology, between concepts and words. Althusser brings the class discourse in which man, his rights and his freedom are discussed under a single unifying concept, *humanism*, and proceeds from there to organize his entire discourse on a double theses: (1) Marxism is an anti-humanism; (2) but it does not condemn 'socialism with a human face' or 'the abolition of man's exploitation of his fellow men' – these are words, not concepts.

What is lost in this separation is the very thing Althusserian philosophy had set out to think: *the power of words*. Ultimately, Althusserianism only manages to think that power from within a theory of *representation*: the word 'man' is an image that reflects and masks the conditions of bourgeois domination. The bourgeoisie's ideological power is thus described as the superposition of systems of representation: the system of juridical inscription transcribes trade relations; juridical ideology is reflected in the discourse of 'man' and 'subject'. The efficiency of power in ideology is nothing other than the efficiency of a representation of the conditions for the existence of that power.

The theory of ideological state apparatuses vanishes here. All that remains, in fact, is the interplay between essence and appearance that leads Althusser back to the very spot he had wanted to leave behind: that of the young Marx. 'Behind Man, it is Bentham who comes out the victor.'[34] In other words, behind the universality of the free citizen is the egoism of private interest; behind humanism are trade relations. But Bentham is not about private interest or trade relations hiding behind the beautiful universality of the rights of man. Bentham stands for the ideology and practice of assistance and surveillance that take root in the despotism of the factory as a result of the need to guarantee the ability of the minority to exercise control over the majority. The formation of men necessary for the reproduction of bourgeois relations depends much less on the play of illusions produced by the text or by juridical practices than on the practical and discursive effects of an entire system of disciplines: the workshop, the school, the prison, and so on. The *political* decision not to take into account what Marx identifies as the very heart of bourgeois ideological oppression – the separation between the worker and the 'intellectual powers of production' – means that Althusser remains hostage to an old metaphysical notion according to which 'ideological' power is exercised through the subversion of vision. Words, for him, are not the elements of discursive practices that are, in turn, articulated to different social practices. They are representations of existing conditions. As a result, they only allow the following division: on the one side are the words that represent bourgeois domination (man, rights, freedom), and on the other are the words forged *elsewhere*, that is, in scientific knowledge (masses, classes, process, and so on). This division gives to philosophers the power to be the word-keepers. But it also confines that power to being the power of *censure*, which philosophy can exercise over workers and intellectuals, whether in Paris, Moscow or Prague, passing through Besançon, where workers insist on using the words of the bourgeoisie.

As we have seen, philosophy only escapes its role of censor by introducing yet another division, which divorces the order of truth from that of the empirical and which distinguishes between theoretical utterances (man, concept of 'absolute origin') and practical utterances (man, cry of indignation or rage). Do not confuse what must not be confused, philosophy tells us: Garaudy's man and the Czechs's socialism with a human face are not the same thing. What the Czech people were demanding was not theoretical humanism (though I doubt a cop has ever seen a protester demand a subject of history), but socialism in the national independence: they wanted 'a socialism whose face (not the body – the body does not figure in the formula) would not be disfigured by practices unworthy both of itself (the Czech people: a people of a high political culture) and of socialism'.[35]

The combatants for Czech socialism and Soviet protesters have the right to speak about man and about socialism with a human face because they are caught in a practice that does not afford them 'the same choice of words' as here. Armchair Marxists in the West, on the other hand, are not to be forgiven: they have the 'choice of words', and they should use only rigorous concepts. Differently put, the correction of words is only politically important there where words are 'freely' chosen. But the freedom of word choice exists only there where words have lost their importance: in philosophy journals. Yes, certainly Garaudy could have carried on a discourse about integral humanism on the pages of the Party journal his entire life, without anyone taking offense.[36] The Garaudy problem, however, was born precisely because his words, spoken in the Party apparatus, echoed what was happening in Czechoslovakia and in the USSR: they established a relationship between the present as it was unfolding there and the future as it was being projected here. And that is exactly what the apparatus of the PCF rejects. According to it, what happens there has nothing to do with what happens here. Czechoslovakia? We condemn the invasion, but there is nothing to fear here: our political freedom and national independence are guaranteed. Solzhenitsyn? It's unfortunate. But look at the common programme: everybody is free to publish whatever they want, provided they can find a publisher, of course.[37] Truly, it is difficult to see what relationship there can possibly be between these affairs and the functioning of our political apparatus.

This separation intensifies the Althusserian distinction between what counts *there*, in practice, and what counts *here*, in theory. The distinctions in the *Reply to John Lewis* find their sense in Althusser's speech at the Fête de l'Humanité[38] in 1973: Pierre Daix is perfectly free to raise questions about Solzhenitsyn. But here, the discussion of the Solzhenitsyn affair can only be scientific. And a scientific discussion among communists can only take place in the Party press. Pierre Daix, in other words, is wrong to discuss it in the pages of *Le Nouvel Observateur*.What happens elsewhere should not lead us to change our rules here. We should support the Czech movement, but that does not mean that we have to import into our philosophy what is only valid for their practice. What happens there does not raise questions about the functioning of the communist political apparatus here (the Czech movement is a *national* movement).

This sidestepping of the question of 'communist' political apparatuses is at the heart of Althusser's analysis of the 'Stalinist deviation', an analysis that many critics welcomed as the great novelty of the *Reply to John Lewis*, though without pinpointing exactly what is so *new* about it.[39]

Evidently, the novelty does not reside in the way the book lays bare the 'economist' character of Stalinist politics, that is to say, the primacy that politics accords to the unbridled development of productive forces at the expense of effecting a revolution in the relations of production. Nor is it to be found in the way it goes about explaining the superstructure through the discussion of relations of production and the class struggle. These theses were already quite well known. If analyses to that effect – Castoriadis's,[40] for example – had remained confidential, it is because no political mass movement would have endorsed them. But things had changed with the Cultural Revolution in China and the appearance of the leftist movement in the West. The Cultural Revolution amplified certain already-existing traits of Chinese communism: an economy walking on two legs, the refusal to sacrifice farmland to the development of heavy industry, the primacy of collectivization over mechanization, the fight against hierarchy and rigidity in the division of labour, the appeal to the initiative of workers themselves and the struggle against material incentives. In all these traits we saw a reversal of the priorities that characterized economic development in the USSR: the primacy of heavy industry, accumulation at the expense of farmland, the development of Stakhanovism,[41] material incentives, salary hierarchy, the omnipotence of cadres and top-down management. Moreover, we saw the political choices underwriting each mode of development, as well as the political effects of each: in the Cultural Revolution, we saw the mass solution to the problems that Stalinist power had entrusted to the care of the police and to the judicial and penitentiary systems. All of this was well known, and traces of it could be found a bit everywhere: in Bettelheim's books and in the works around it, in books about China (Macciocchi, Jacoviello, Karol, etc.), in the political texts published in *Manifesto*, as well as in innumerable university courses.[42] The novelty of the *Reply* actually lies elsewhere: in the political displacement of these theses, in the theoretical treatment this displacement imposes.

The political gesture of the *Reply to John Lewis* is the annexation to 'communist' orthodoxy of a series of theses that had till then been the patrimony of leftism. The gesture of referring the superstructure to the relations of production, much like the questions levelled at the Stalinist model of economic development, were not new in themselves, but they were new to the Party. The task here, as with the theory of ideological State apparatuses, is to import leftism into the orthodoxy. As we have already seen, carrying out this task presupposes a mechanism of political and theoretical cancellation, one that separates a theoretical problematic from its political base and singularizes discovery (the 'risky hypotheses' in which the solitary scholar 'takes the risk' of advancing ideas that are already running the streets). Thus, May 68 could only be introduced at the price of being immediately suppressed. Importing leftism into ortho-doxy is an operation that demands a speculative mechanism quite simi-lar to the one whose functioning Marx lays bare in his discussion of Stirner: the transformation of the elements of a political practice into manifestations of an essence. Every manifestation of class struggle that makes its way into Stirner's philosophy of the unique is transformed into a predicate of the sacred: the state, politics and the demands of workers were all, quite simply, manifestations of the sacred. For the 'Maoist' critique of Stalin to gain entrance to the patrimony of the PCF, Stalinist politics had to be treated as a predicate of economism; it had to be a historical form that rendered manifest the ideological couple, econ-omism/humanism.

The *theoretical* novelty of the book is there. It is not in the determination of Stalinist 'economism', but in the application of the old Althusserian schema to the Stalinist object: bourgeois ideology is constituted by the joint forces of a technicist/economist ideology and a moral/humanist ideology.[43] The entire effort, here as elsewhere, is directed at fitting the new to the old, at seeing in a new object the repetition of the timeless rupture through which materialist philosophy repudiates its perennial antagonist: political idealism as represented by the couple, economism/humanism.

The novelty of the book is in its intensification of the notion of economism, and in the concept that enables this intensification: *deviation*. The cause for Stalin's 'economist' politics is the efficiency of *the* economist deviation. Now, the existence of *the* economist deviation is widely recognized (in the canonical texts), and there is no doubt as to who its parents are (the Second International).[44] And the rest explains itself: provided we keep 'things *well in proportion*', the Stalinist deviation can be seen as a '*form* . . . of the *posthumous revenge of the Second International*'.[45] This brings us to the promised land: from Kautsky's 'economism' to Bernstein's 'humanism', from Bernstein's neo-Kantian humanism to John Lewis's Sartrean humanism, the circle is closed – the struggle against humanism is indeed the make-or-break struggle of the century.

Posthumous revenge? A history of ghosts? Not at all, Althusser says, what we have here is an application of the Leninist method.

> If some readers are disconcerted by the comparison between the economism of the Second International and that of the 'Stalinian deviation', I will *first* of all reply: you must look and see what is the first principle of analysis recommended and used by Lenin at the beginning of Chapter 7 of *The Collapse of the Second International* to help understand a *deviation* in the history of the Labour Movement. The first thing you have to do is to see if this deviation is not 'linked *with some former current of socialism*'.[46]

The metaphysics of the Same is here establishing its credentials: read Lenin's books, and you will see that this is what *they* say. Lenin's approach, however, has nothing of the metaphysical about it. Lenin tries to determine the origins of the positions that various fractions of Europe's socialist parties adopted in reaction to the imperialist war through an examination of their past political behaviour, and he concludes that the divisions supposedly precipitated by differences over the war essentially reproduced, a bit everywhere, the divisions that had earlier pit opportunists against revolutionaries. The *currents* Lenin invokes represented real political fractions, they represented tendencies *at once* operative inside a single party and in the context of a single economic (imperialism) and political system (parliamentary democracy), *and* based on the social forces nourished by these systems: a labour aristocracy – the product of imperialism – and a professional petite bourgeoisie – the product of the parliamentary system.

Is the 'Stalinist deviation' not linked to some 'former current of socialism'?[47] In vulgar, 'historicist' history, such a remark would spark the search for this former current, not in Germany's social democracy, but in *Russia's*. Why doesn't Althusser undertake this search? Clearly, it is because this would oblige him to determine the 'deviation' in relation to the Leninist 'norm'. And the problem is that, on the question of the development of productive forces, this deviation is by no means self-evident.

Is it not the case that all the traits of Stalinist and post-Stalinist 'economism' find their support in Lenin's texts and in the practical measures he adopted? The theory of state capitalism as the antechamber of socialism, the valuing of capitalism's 'rational' organization of labour and of Taylorism in particular, the need for iron discipline and absolute managerial power in factories, the deference to specialists, the material incentives for labour – Lenin affirmed all these in his theory and implemented them in his practice. People will no doubt say that Lenin – unlike Stalin – was a dialectician, that zigzags and rectifications were his way of functioning, that he always tried to reconcile the development at any price of productive forces and the establishment of *concrete* forms of control by the masses over the conditions of their existence, that the solutions he championed were always provisional and determined by the analysis of the current moment. If he recommends the Taylor system in 1918, it is not out of an abstract predilection for its rationalizing virtues. Like Pouget,[48] Lenin had immediately thought, upon first reading Taylor, that his system was tantamount to slavery. If he backtracks in light of the challenge launched in December 1917 (we can do without bourgeois specialists), it is because the delays and the difficulties involved in organizing popular control of production oblige him to take a step back.[49] Many a time, Lenin qualifies as a *setback* choices that Stalin will treat as necessary to the development of socialism. It is no less true, however, that if Lenin downplayed the effects of these setbacks and the length of the provisional, it was in light of a certain understanding of the struggle against the restoration of capitalism. As he saw it, the ideological transformation of the large masses – peasants in particular – depended entirely on industrialization (especially electrification). The main struggle was fought on the economic level, and Lenin saw this struggle, essentially, as the struggle of large-scale against small-scale production. The latter is responsible for constantly recreating the capitalist market and its ideological habits (egoism, anarchy). The victory of socialism is the victory of large industry over small production. This victory is only possible, however, if one adopts the most advanced forms of the capitalist division of labour, and with it the forms of power this division implies at the level of labour processes (managerial omnipotence). This is a strategy for forces of production that regards them as susceptible of only one form of development. Lenin does not think that capitalist forms of the division of labour are neutral, but he does see them as an unavoidable step in the development of socialist forces of production. There is an understanding of power implicated in this: the political power of the proletariat is not the power of factory workers. Socialism is composed of two halves: state capitalism – which entails the subjection of workers to the iron fist of directors and the repression of their 'petit-bourgeois' tendencies – and the power of the proletariat centrally defined at the level of the state apparatus.[50]

Stalin's 'economism' can claim this as its norm. What becomes clear now is that the question covered over by the indeterminacy of the concept of economism is the question of *power*. It is not a matter of the influence bourgeois ideology exerts on the 'labour movement' through 'economist tendencies', but of the relationship between *proletarian power* and *factory despotism*. The ideological power of the bourgeoisie is not the power of economism and humanism. It is the power to dispossess workers of their intelligence, to mutilate their capacities, to confront them with a science that has been moved entirely to the side of 'powers of production'.[51] And the problem posed by the theory of the 'two halves' is the problem of the compatibility between the absence of power at the level of labour processes, and power at the level of the state. It is the problem of the *localization* of power. The essential insight yielded by the Chinese Revolution, and by the Cultural Revolution in particular, is that a class cannot guarantee its power within a state unless it has power over all of it.

The heart of the problem is the relationship between the question of the development of forces of production and the question of power. And it is clear that, at that level, the relationship of the 'economist deviation' of the Second International to the 'Stalinist' deviation passes through the Leninist 'norm'. In other words, social democrats in Russia and Germany do share some ideas, chief among these being the idea that there is a necessary order of succession to modes of production. Lenin refuses to wait for the development of forces of production within the framework of bourgeois power to bring about the material conditions for socialism. He affirms, instead, the need to break this power. But he also thinks that the development of socialism within the framework of proletarian power must pass through the capitalist development of productive forces. He believes in the necessary, and progressive, character of capitalist technique and of capitalist forms of the division of labour. This idea is echoed in the way Lenin conceives the Party, and in the theory of the 'school of capitalism' that underwrites it: the discipline that befits a revolutionary organization is the discipline capitalism teaches in the school of the factory.[52] The 'former tendency', the one that in 1918 characterized the Leninist understanding of economic organization (let us all enroll in the school of corporations), is the one that had characterized the organization of the Party in 1902: it was a certain idea of the capitalist school. Every party organized for the takeover of power anticipates, in the forms of the division of labour and in the distribution of power and knowledge that define it, a certain organization of the society to come. The organization Lenin imposed on his Party was based on a German social democratic model. No need for Kautsky to haunt the nights of Stalinism; the Leninist problematic can do that well enough on its own.

By following Lenin's remark, it becomes possible to outline a less speculative filiation from Kautsky to Stalin than the one we find in Althusser. Such a filiation remains nevertheless quite abstract, and, in trying to extract the traits of Stalinist society from *What is to be Done?*, one will have to nourish a passably metaphysical anti-Leninism. We cannot isolate Bolshevik understanding from the conditions of the class struggle through which Russian social democracy was formed. And the phenomena that characterize Stalinism (the strengthening of hierarchical structures and of workers' discipline; the constitution of new, privileged layers; the massive recourse to police, judicial and penitentiary repression) cannot be deduced from the 'tendencies' borne by Bolshevik ideology and organization. These tendencies were only able to play a role at all because they combined with objective factors such as the fights led by the formerly exploiting – or intermediary – classes, the class struggle in the countryside and the tensions between urban and rural areas, the spontaneous forms of the re-establishment of the power of experts, capitalist relations and the repressive practices of Tsarist apparatuses.[53] But this does not make the question disappear: what specific role did Soviet state apparatuses, and particularly the first head of the Bolshevik party apparatus, play in the reconstitution of capitalist forms of the division of labour and the reappearance of privileged layers that oppress the majority of the population? How much responsibility, exactly, can be attributed to the Bolshevik understanding of power, of its takeover, of the organization that has to control it, of the places and forms of its exercise? This may seem an 'abstract' question for a materialist history of the class struggles in the USSR – one trapped by the idealism of retrospective reconstitutions, and lined by the platitudes of bourgeois anti-communism – but it cannot really be dismissed, for it is a question about the forms of power that constitute the 'dictatorship of the proletariat', about the specific class effects produced by the functioning of 'proletarian' state apparatuses. It is at this level that the effects of 'bourgeois ideology' do their work: not in the relationship between 'humanism' and the 'labour movement', but in the relationship between the instruments of the ideological power of the dominant classes – factory discipline, the school, the army (fear of the police, secrecy of the administration, solemnity of the trial, penitentiary 'education') – and the instruments given to the people to take, and exercise, its power. These questions resound, and oblige us to ask ourselves what socialist future our 'communist' and 'proletarian' organizations have in store for us. They oblige, for example, the communist Althusser to ask himself what future is being prepared for us by a communist party in which the leaders do politics, intellectuals debate their points of view at conferences, and rank and file militants walk the streets putting up posters. They oblige him to ask himself what real power relations represent the present and forecast the future of its 'democratic centralism', and what forms of the division of labour and power can be expected there where the apparatus of his party holds power, that is, within its own organization, as well as in the districts and boards it controls. The question must also be asked of those organizations that pretend to have broken with the 'revisionism' of the PCF: what society is prefigured in their organizations and in their forms of the division of labour, of the exercise of power and of the distribution of knowledge?

That is why there cannot be a serious analysis of the Stalinist period that does not go through an analysis of Leninism. What that means is that there is no Stalinist deviation that breaks with the Leninist norm, no division between an orthodox Marxism and its deviations. What Marx's theory must produce is not emblazoned on its forehead. The forms of appropriation of Marxism exist within specific class struggles and within specific apparatuses of power.

The possibility of Althusser's discourse, however, is entirely dependant on the concept of deviation. That explains why Lenin appears only to ensure his own disappearance, upon which is premised the return to the abstraction of a deviation and to the subject that has been the designated medium for every deviation: the Second International. It is not possible simply to smile at this *'posthumous revenge'*. We must, on the contrary, recognize in it a perfectly calibrated theoretical mechanism. The Second International is, in fact, one of those strange objects that shores up – in Althusser as well as in others – the mechanism of speculation: it is a theoretical operator whose task is to produce an illusion of *reality*, to make one believe that 'Marxist' philosophy speaks of real events and historical filiations, when in fact it speaks only of such speculative ghosts as economism and humanism. These operators, in a very Hegelian fashion, transform the empirical into the speculative and the speculative into the empirical; they reduce historical phenomena like Stalinism to meagre abstractions like economism; they embody concepts like 'humanism' in the empirical existence of particular individuals. Bernstein? A 'declared' neo-Kantian and humanist.[54] But why a *declared* humanist? The basis of Bernstein's approach and analysis is not a theory of man, but the examination of the economic evolution of capitalism and the political evolution of social democracy. In light of the evolution of capitalism (it is not rushing headlong towards catastrophe), he enjoins social democracy to elaborate a theory of its (reformist) practice, and to do so by applying Kant's critical philosophy to Marxism. In Althusser's discourse, however, Bernstein is an operator who serves no other purpose than to underwrite the categories of *economism* and *humanism*, than to make it possible for Althusser to replace the reality of class struggles and political confrontations with the timeless tendencies of the *Labour Movement*.

That is a basic requirement of 'class struggle in theory': it only works by reducing the actual to the eternal, the other to the same. It postulates that history is discontinuous, only to reinsert strange continuities into it, like this 'labour movement' that has the Second International and Stalinist politics as so many of its manifestations. How does Althusser ground such concepts as 'revival' and 'posthumous revenge'?

> Not because of some vulgar 'historicism', but because there exists a continuity, in the history of the Labour Movement, of its difficulties, its problems, its *contradictions*, of correct solutions and therefore *also of its deviations*, because of the continuity of a single class struggle against the bourgeoisie, and of a single class struggle (economic, political *and ideological-theoretical*) of the bourgeoisie against the Labour Movement. The possibility of cases of 'posthumous revenge', of 'revivals', is based on this continuity.[55]

An exemplary passage: the minute class struggle intervenes, the entire *system of heterogeneities* – the theory of history as discontinuous and of the 'current situation' – vanishes. All that remains is the transhistorical unity of a subject and its predicates. What must this prove? That the tendencies at work in German social democracy in 1900 played a role in Soviet Russia in the 1930s. The whole answer trades on the unity of one subject: the Labour Movement. And why can we speak of a self-same subject? Because it leads the *same* class struggle. That is how philosophers used to prove the eternity of the soul before Kant: the soul is eternal because eternity is one of its predicates. That is how Althusser's 'process without a subject' comes to be populated by strange subjects: *the* Labour Movement, which gathers within it the Moscow trials and the PCF's electoral success; the Paris Commune as well as the invasion of Czechoslovakia; *the* working class, a subject nine-million strong during the strike of May 68; *the* M-L that refutes John Lewis. The mechanism behind this repopulation is easily understood. Althusser is in the same situation as Feuerbach, who wanted predicates, but no subject, religion, but no God. Althusser wants a discontinuous history, 'without a subject or goal(s)'.[56] But he also wants a philosophy able, with each object and each circumstance, to distinguish the *idealist* from the *materialist*, the *proletarian* from the *bourgeois*, the *correct* from the *deviant*. And so he must organize a procession of all these subjects whose empirical reality is the incarnation of a concept: the Labour Movement, the Party, the Working Class, Marxism-Leninism . . .

The political advantage of this speculative operation is that it masks, behind the tendencies and deviations of the 'Labour Movement', the question of the class nature of 'proletarian' political apparatuses. The decisive question covered over by Stalin's 'humanism' and his 'economism' is the question of the class nature of Stalinist power. It is not a matter of determining whether Stalinist politics was contaminated by bourgeois ideology, but of determining what real social forces found expression in it and what power relations it actually established, both at the level of the state apparatus and at the level of the labour process. To say that post-Stalinist Russia is still afflicted by the effects of economism is in fact to brush a series of uncomfortable questions under the carpet. What is the nature of Soviet power? What class holds power in the USSR? The answer of Chinese communists to these questions is that the USSR is a social-fascist state where a bourgeois minority oppresses the people. Althusser, for his part, wants to make philosophy out of this, that is to say, he wants to displace 'the position of the problem'.[57] We must return from the superstructure to the fundamental problem: the economist line. This is where Mao enters the picture – only to help Althusser avoid the questions Mao raises. What Althusser retains from the Cultural Revolution is the idea that class struggles are essentially 'line struggles', and that these struggles are eternal. Something is not working in the USSR; the same is true about the PCF, certainly. But this means we have to go back to the roots: if something is not working in the USSR or in the PCF, it is because both are afflicted by the economist line. Now, the contamination will continue to exist for as long as there is even one bourgeois on the face of the earth. In light of this fact, the best thing to do is fortify, with philosophy's help, the anti-economist and anti-humanist proletarian line. And if we can use Mao for that, it is because he, too, is part of the Labour Movement. Everything happens inside the same subject: Brezhnev and Mao, Scheidemann and Rosa Luxembourg, Georges Marchais and Pierre Overney are all different figures of the same labour movement.[58]

Althusser's explanation not only has the merit of sidestepping the really challenging questions, it also outlines the face of a new orthodoxy: the time when official spokespersons were tasked with justifying everything at any price is over. That system invariably resulted in the spokespersons asking themselves too many questions and raising problems. Pierre Daix denied the existence of labour camps in the Soviet Union; he never convinced anybody, and we all know where he stands today.[59] Althusser proposes something else. He does not deny repression. What he does, rather, is sound the alarm against dangerous theoretical forms that could serve to protest repression. That is not what is important, he says. It is not important to determine whether or not there are labour camps in the USSR, or whether dissidents are sent to psychiatric asylums ('even supposing that the Soviet people are now protected from all violations of *legality* – it does not follow that either they or we have completely overcome the 'Stalinist' deviation'[60]). What really matters is that humanist protests keep us from hearing clearly the silent music of the economist line:

> One is even justified in supposing that, behind the talk about the different varieties of 'humanism', whether restrained or not, this 'line' continues to pursue an honourable career, in a peculiar kind of silence, a sometimes talkative and sometimes mute silence, which is now and again broken by the noise of an explosion or a split.[61]

By 'the talk about the different varieties of "humanism", *whether restrained or not'*, we should understand the following: the discourse of the intellectuals who are locked up in psychiatric hospitals and the discourse of the officials who locked them up are the same thing. The discourse of power or the discourse that denounces power: it's all the same 'talk'. To speak out for human rights in the USSR amounts to strengthening the dominant humanism, to masking the dominance of the 'economist' line.[62] We can forgive them: they don't have free choice in their words. But we should protect ourselves from contamination. A new discourse for the justification of power: 'Enough talk; the evil comes from elsewhere, make room for analyses.'

True, we must analyse. But the problem is always the same: *who* analyses? True, Althusser is right to remind us that he has always asked the same question about de-Stalinization. But the problem has not changed: where can he raise this question from? Althusser has learned already that there is no place in his party for a philosophy that says what should be done, but only for a philosophy that justifies what is.[63] The discourse of a 'communist' intellectual can only have two statuses: it is either political justification of the Party or free cultural chit-chat. Althusser wants to do something else. He wants to open a discussion about Stalin and post-Stalinism. But he must have this discussion without raising, even for a moment, either of these questions: who holds power in the USSR? What is the class nature of the PCF? He takes his self-censuring so far as to claim not to know whether or not there are 'legal' violations in the USSR today ('even *supposing* that the Soviet people are now protected from all violations of *legality*' [first italics added]).[64] If there is one thing we all know for certain about the USSR today, it is that such violations do indeed exist. What are they, then? Mere blunders of Soviet democracy? A manifestation of Soviet bureaucracy? A sign of class oppression? We can discuss these. What we cannot do, however, is pretend not to know what even PCF authorities recognize.

On such a basis, the 'leftist' explanation can only be the confirmation of what is: Althusser refers the superstructural manifestations of Soviet society to the reality of the class struggle, but then refers class struggle to the efficiency of the 'deviations'. It is always the same notions that enable this sidestepping, always 'humanism' that makes it possible to forget the real relationships of domination and drown out the voices of revolt. In 1964, Althusser asked: What is the status of Soviet humanism? And he answered: Soviet humanism is the ideology of a nation being apprenticed into classless society. Today, humanism leads back to the class struggle, but this class struggle, when all is said and done, is the struggle of humanism and economism to contaminate the labour movement.

Philosophy, Althusser tells us, displaces the position of the problems. No 'idealist' philosopher would take issue with this definition. More bluntly, Marx says that philosophy is the art of transforming real chains into ideal ones. Hence Marx's conviction that a real displacement would only be possible by stepping out of philosophy. The 'displacement' Althusser operates here amounts to extracting the problem from the terms that give it meaning to millions of people, and inscribing it in the debates of academic Marxists. The question of 'economism', if it is posed in its real terms, is the question of the organization of labour processes, of hierarchy, of the possibility for large industry to avoid the despotism of the capitalist factory. The serious political question that a 'communist' militant could ask of his party in the wake of the Cultural Revolution is not the question of 'economism' or of the 'scientific and technical revolution', but the question of hierarchy. Séguy declares that workers will never be able to do without foremen; René Le Guen (leader of the CGT's federation of cadres) explains that salary hierarchy is a form of class struggle because it reduces employers' profits. Isn't it there that the important problems lie? Is it not there that words have impact and that today's practices can be seen grappling with the 'socialist' future we have been promised? Behind 'economism', there are always power practices at work. The 'evil wind of economism' that blew through China in 1966 was not a wayward tendency of the 'labour movement', but the distribution of bribes to a working-class aristocracy. The question of economism is the question of the power workers tomorrow might have over the labour process, and that question is in turn tied to the question of the power they may have over their struggle today. That is what Piaget's 'economy that serves man' puts into play for workers, and that is what the critique of economism and humanism covers over.

But you are really being disingenuous, the 'left-wing' Althusserian will say. Is it possible you don't see that Althusser is alluding to all of that? He knows as well as you do that it is not ghosts who make history. He is trying to open a discussion inside the PCF. And he cannot, of course, say everything so bluntly, and all at once. You are taking advantage of that to make fun of his ghost stories, but you know perfectly well what lies behind them.

True, we do know the formula, now a ritual in the discourse of Althusserians: 'Greetings, crafty reader.' Althusser speaks to the clever, to those who can see further than obtuse bureaucrats and know how to decipher his discourse. It is in this, precisely, that his discourse is akin to that of bureaucrats, that his 'leftist' discourse serves as a conduit for the power of specialists. 'Class struggle in theory', the power to decree, from the height of his armchair, that these utterances are bourgeois and those proletarian – but also to speak between the lines to 'crafty readers', that is, to Marxist mandarins – is also, like salary hierarchies, a form of 'class struggle'. At this point, though, the double truth cancels itself out. The professor's 'Maoism' says the same thing as the cadre's economism or the manager's humanism: it defends the privilege of competent people, of the people who know which demands, which forms of action and which words are proletarian, and which bourgeois. It is a discourse in which specialists of the class struggle defend their power.

Philosophy's power is that it can designate mistaken tendencies and deviations. This power to refer the fact to the tendency speculatively reproduces the discursive practices of 'proletarian' power: the discourse of Stalinist prosecutors, who took objective contradictions as indexes for the evil tendencies of those in charge, who saw in incorrect words the presence of an enemy class and in a machine that breaks down the bourgeois tendencies of the Industry Commissioner. What does philosophy tell us here? That Stalin's crimes are founded on the existence of a Stalinist deviation. What is most remarkable is that this explanation is solemnly and seriously received. If things didn't work, it is because the norms were not respected. In 'Marxist' heads, this reasoning is rock solid. We saw it in practice at the end of 1968. The power of 'class struggle in theory' stems from its reliance on the modes of reasoning favoured by the discursive practices of Marxism turned *raison d'état*.

Class struggle in theory: the union of the discourse of impotence and the discourse of power – the impotence to change the world, the power to reproduce the power of specialists. It is certain that Althusser will never introduce Maoism into the programme of his Party, but, then again, his Maoism is essentially the privilege of Marxist intellectuals, the privilege of seizing *their* truth – slightly different from the truth of the apparatus – and of making it the principle of their power.

Achilles, we used to say, will never catch up to the turtle. But that is the source of his philosophical dignity.

# CHAPTER FIVE
## A Discourse in Its Place

The great ambition of Althusser's project was to think Marx in his historical context to allow us to implement Marxism in ours. He wanted to rediscover, against the keepers of the doctrine, the *singularity* that could make the letter of Marxism something other than a justifying discourse or fodder for cultural chit-chat, namely: the cutting edge, in the conflicts of our times, of what Lenin called Marxism's living soul, the revolutionary dialectic. We should look at what has become of this ambitious project today.

In 1961, Althusser wanted to lead us to the living history of Marx's thought. In 1973, he gives us a paranoid fairy tale in which the evil words of the bourgeoisie attack proletarian class positions in philosophy. In 1963, he tried to find in Lenin and Mao the singularity of a dialectic that was not the science of the *fait accompli*, but a weapon to change the world with. In 1973, he gives us the trite formula for all our evils, past, present and future: the couple economism/humanism.

What remains of Althusser's ambitious project today is a philosophy reduced to its own caricature: an endless chit-chat that holds forth on all things – from Feuerbach to Stalin and from bourgeois law and rights to the labour movement – with the approximative discourse of academic (that is, obscurantist) knowledge for the sole purpose of producing the self-justification of 'class struggle in theory' and of elevating the churning over of ever more contrived truths to the dignity of an actual struggle to save the revolution; an endless repetition of the same, a normative discourse committed to denouncing the concepts that have infiltrated Marxist theory as others denounce in their leaflets the 'bourgeois provocateurs' who have infiltrated the factory, and to teaching its readers what they should and should not say if they want to be good Marxists.

This lesson in Marxism is, to be sure, a little different than the lessons taught in the schools of the Party, where future cadres learn the new gospel: the scientific and technical revolution – science has become a direct productive force. The transistor is an example: it was but a few years between its scientific discovery and its industrial exploitation. Proof of the great changes of our times and of the fact that our great hopes can be realized, if only we join hands with engineers and cadres against monopolies.

At Althusser's school, conversely, we learn to mock the ideology of productive forces and of the scientific and technical revolution. That's nonsense fit only for bureaucrats. We know Marx's true doctrine, and that is why we can be so bold in our texts as to wax ironic – after taking a few precautions, to be sure – about the nonsense the Party teaches. It's a way of showing that our total freedom remains intact.

The fact is that Althusser is perfectly free to propose all the theses he wants. All his 'subversive' theses, however, share the following interesting peculiarity: they never entail any disruptive practices. He is free to put forward the concept of ideological state apparatuses, and free to use this concept to mock, however gently, the reformist illusions of communist teachers. But when a teacher in a communist district is barred from teaching secondary school because he tried to disrupt the framework of the school apparatus, and when district authorities rally to the aid of academic inspectors to denounce the troublemaker, it is obviously none of Althusser's business. He is free to criticize the 'ideology of productive forces', provided he does not meddle in the politics of the Party; free to cite Mao in the prefaces to Latin American editions of his work, provided he keeps quiet when Marchais spits on the corpse of Pierre Overney;[1] free to proclaim the primacy of class struggle, provided he does not bother himself with any of the class struggles happening today. This is a well-known kind of freedom, the very kind the bourgeoisie reserves for intellectuals: the freedom to say anything and everything at the university, where intellectuals can be Marxists, Leninists, even Maoists, provided they perpetuate its functioning; the freedom to wax ironic about the power that channels the intellectual's attachment to order. That is one bourgeois lesson the leaders of the Communist Party have finally learned. They have stopped asking their intellectuals to come up with crazy theories to support their politics. It is much better just to let intellectuals say whatever they want, in the places where their discourse is sure to merge into the hum of cultural chit-chat. There was a time when intellectuals were hesitant to join the Party, when being a member meant having to deny their own demands and possible conflicts within their milieu, where they might be accused by their 'peers' of being 'merely politicians'.[2] Today, conversely, the membership of communist intellectuals is compatible with the defence of academic elitism and with the justification of their practice. Indeed, it is their practice as academics that authorizes their heterodoxy in relation to the official theses of their party. There are the official members, who develop academic policies, oversee the schools of the Party and write books that the PCF can endorse. And there are the informal, marginal members, whose heterodoxy attests to the freedom communist intellectuals enjoy at present. In post-1968 France, this element of disorder was a prerequisite for the orderly functioning of every institution. The apparatus matches Althusser's irony with its own. Who, of all people, wound up writing the review in *France nouvelle* of the book where Althusser denounces 'economism'?[3] None other than Joë Metzger, the representative of the engineers and cadres in thrall to the 'scientific and technical revolution'. And what does he say about the book? In broad strokes, he accuses Althusser of saying a lot of nonsense and of not having read enough Georges Marchais, but, and that is what matters, Althusser's book shows that members of the Party can say whatever they want. The fox can always be outfoxed. The effrontery of his Maoism earns Althusser an invitation to the Fête de l'Humanité, where he can add his voice to the chorus against Pierre Daix's 'revisionism'.[4] He wants to be the wolf in the flock, but the Party turns to him when it needs to scare its black sheep. He pretends to raise embarrassing questions, but the Party shows him that it understands his words for what they are: a discourse of order.

Such is the inevitable fate of a discourse that pretends to ignore the place where it is held. Althusser wanted to find the rationality of politics outside politics, the revolutionary dialectics outside the systematization of existing ideas and practices of revolt. A university professor and a philosopher of the Communist Party, he believed that it was possible, from the place appointed to him by these two powers, to find anew the weapon of the revolution. But the purpose of academic discourse is the formation of students, and a communist philosopher is not in the position to give his superiors the forgotten weapon of dialectics. Althusser must have confronted early on the problem, which every specialist of Marxist theory must face, of the relationship between the stated power of theory and the real power relations wherein the discourse of the theoretician is produced. This limitation does not condemn the words of the intellectual to impotence or servility, but it does oblige the intellectual to take into account the place where his discourse is produced and to inscribe this discourse in a practice directed at transforming the power relations that make him or her *nothing other* than an intellectual. Althusser, however, has devoted all his energies to routing from his discourse the power effects that constrained it. At the end of 1963, Althusser was being questioned from both sides: the authorities of his party were questioning him about the relationship between his theory and Chinese politics, and student unions were questioning him about the relationship between the discipline of science and university discipline. He answered them by neutralizing the place of his discourse. He made the power of the professor the power of science, and he reduced the question of his place within the PCF to a *tactical* matter (what terms must we adopt so as to be acceptable to Party leaders?). He pretended to speak, not from within the university, but from within theory; not from within the PCF, but from within the labour movement. These 'neutral' places were supposedly not affected by the rifts that were starting to divide Marxists and university students alike. Even after the fights broke out inside the university and the PCF – leaving the 'Marxist' camp effectively split in two – Althusser continued to speak from this doubly neutral place: from Marxism-Leninism (that of Brezhnev and Mao) and from the labour movement (that of the worker Marchais and of the worker Pierre Overney). When it came to political practice, of course, he was obliged to choose. And he chose, not *the* labour movement, but a certain labour movement, namely the one that has Brezhnev as its leader and that sent tanks into Prague and rained bullets on the workers of Gdansk, the one whose representatives at Renault-Billancourt denounced Pierre Overney to their bosses before insulting his corpse. But, because he speaks from *within theory*, Althusser acts as if he could speak for everybody (for leftists as well as for the PCF), as if he could use the experience of every labour movement – Mao's included. He could, after all, explain why – given his Maoism – he is a member of the PCF; he could justify his position, as Régis Debray does when he says that we should be realistic, that the millions of PCF and PS voters are something of a different order of importance from all these little groups of intellectuals longing for a bit of adventure, that we must be reformists in our tactics in order to be revolutionary in our strategies. But the position of Althusser's discourse makes it impossible for him to justify his political position. He must act as if the question could not even be raised; he must speak from the side of order as if it were the side of revolt, from the ENS as if it were the revolutionary university of Yenan. That done, the effects follow on their own: the more this discourse wants to be political, the more it is academic; the more it believes itself to be in synchrony with history, the deeper it sinks into the atemporal; the more leftist it wants to be, the more normalizing it becomes. He pretends to be pursuing free research, but he gives us the discourse of a state prosecutor. All there is in the words 'class struggle', 'the masses', and 'revolution' is a long litany of order. This discourse claims that it is 'the masses which make history', but it does so only the better to cement the power of the ones who say so, the ones who decree from their armchairs that these words are bourgeois, those proletarian. It borrows the discourse of leftists and of the Cultural Revolution only to repress the words of revolt and to boost the confidence of the doctors of Marxism-Leninism.

The inversion here gives us the key to this Maoism. It is the simple figure for the slight but necessary difference that enables Marxist philosophy to play its part in repressing or diverting ideas of revolt. Far from stemming from an intellectual's pious desire to reconcile his philosophical ideas with his militant loyalties, this Maoism is a cog in the revisionist machinery. It is a specific form of repression that grants to professors the power to represent, not the universality of classical bourgeois discourse, but the union of the universality of science and the positivity of the proletariat.

Such, in fact, is the function now guaranteed to Marxist political discourse within the bourgeois ideological order. The time is gone when Marx denounced a philosophy that enshrined the division of labour in the power of ideas, in self-consciousness and in the critique of critique. Today, much to the contrary, Marxism serves the cause of enshrining these divisions. 'Class struggle in theory' represents philosophy's latest attempt to cement, once and for all, the division of labour that guarantees it its place. We might then conclude that it poses no greater threat in Paris in 1973 than the critique of critique posed in Berlin in 1844, that 'class struggle in theory' is only a new figure for that old philosophical function: to interpret the world so as not to have to change it. But that would be to forget that the development of Marxism and of its forms of political appropriation have changed the status of the intellectual and of interpretation. Since Marxism became *raison d'état* in the USSR, interpretation has given another power to a category of intellectuals: more than just transforming real into ideal chains, intellectuals are now able to impose real chains in the name of the proletariat and of class struggle. Atop the repression of intellectuals we've seen rise the power of the intelligentsia: the power to speak in the name of the masses, to represent the consciousness or ideology of the proletarian, and to interpret – in light of this representation – the actions of individuals and the movement of the masses. The functioning of this mechanism reaches its paroxysm in staged scenes such as the Moscow Trials, but every level of the hierarchy is an apprenticeship in the mechanism. To transform a militant worker into a political or union cadre is to impart to him the power of interpretation: the power to recognize the provocateur lurking beneath the worker, or to distinguish the true from the false cause.[5]

Philosophy enrolled in the school of this new power when it became 'class struggle in theory'. It wields its power to 'represent' the proletariat against 'petit-bourgeois intellectuals': to teach them to recognize the true cause of their dissatisfaction or of their revolt, to show them who their true enemies are and how inadequate and feeble their resources are against such enemies, to bring scientists grappling with the question of their relationship to power to see that their true enemy is idealism and revolting intellectuals to see that the first thing they must do is protect themselves against contamination from humanism. At a moment when the urgent question being asked is, 'how can we determine what, in our Marxism, constitutes the weapons of Chinese peasants and workers, and what the discourse of Soviet *raison d'état*?', philosophy is there to tell us that the real threats to Marxism are humanism and the ideology of human rights and liberty. At a moment when it is vital for every form of anti-capitalist and anti-state subversion to give free rein to its autonomous expression, philosophy is there to remind everyone how one should and should not speak. This is idealism hiding behind the mask of a critique of the subject and of exhortations to class struggle and proletarian ideology; it is a call to order in the language of leftism – of Maoism even, when necessary.

This discourse of order composed in the vocabulary of subversion is a cog in the machinery of modern revisionism, that graduate from the school of Soviet *raison d'état* now being pit against new forms of anti-capitalist revolt. The twists and turns of academic Marxist discourse are directly correlated to the system of practices – discursive and otherwise – of our communist apparatuses. True, their leaders abandoned long ago the Marxist idea of worker self-emancipation and the goals of destroying state power and abolishing the despotism of the factory and of wage labour.[6] The problem, though, is that their aspirations to work within the structures of capitalism must above all not be expressed in the language of reformism. The era of Bernstein is gone. It is no longer a question of whether to abandon or correct a Marxism that has demonstrated its capacity to capture and subjugate ideas of revolt. Or of saying that the time for revolution has passed, that capitalism can overcome its crises and that it might just be better to live with a government capable of implementing a few reforms to improve the quality of life of workers. Try to maintain Party discipline with such a discourse. Try using this bit of wisdom to attract the revolting youth produced by capitalist factories and schools. Only the language of class struggle can serve the double function of normalization and recuperation that defines the relationship of revisionism to revolt. When its own power is threatened, revisionism puts this language at the service of the simple cause of order. That is what happened in 1969, when the fight against 'provocations' moved into the foreground. Today, though, when the PCF needs to win more than the votes of the left,[7] it can no longer recruit on the basis of this discourse of order. The young people who turn to the JC want something else. There was a time when leftists cried, 'Revolution, the only solution', and we replied, 'The only solution, a common programme'. But young communists today have hit upon a synthesis: 'Revolution, the only solution; the only means, a common programme'. The language of Marxism today is no longer obliged to celebrate the calmness and the dignity of labour organizations while cursing the anarchists and provocateurs who play the game of the bourgeoisie.[8] The time is gone when Mr André Gissel-brecht could write, in one or another of his anti-leftist diatribes, that 'taking power' is a petit-bourgeois concept which must be discarded in favour of that scientific notion, the 'phase of transition'. Today, JC members occupy the Chilean Embassy like vulgar leftist provocateurs.[9] And theory must follow in lockstep. There is space, *alongside* the official discourse about state monopoly capitalism, for a leftist discourse that invests revisionism with a theoretical, Maoist soul, just as there is space for leftist methods and slogans to be introduced to the practice of young communists. There is space for a philosophy of recuperation.[10]

This was not possible in 1969, when PCF leaders feared for their hegemony, but it is possible today. By the time Althusser's book appeared in France, their fears had been appeased, and those who had once vituperated against the provocateurs were now calmly and serenely commenting on the 'death of leftism'. Maoists had abandoned their dream of being the sinews of a new popular unity; Trotskyists were bringing up the rear of left-wing parades; and the old combatants of May 22 were singing about the libido and about desiring machines. But the historical decline of leftism is by no means evidence that the anti-capitalist and anti-authoritarian aspirations it once represented have vanished. Everywhere, these ideas and aspirations are finding new forms of expression; everywhere, communities of struggle are being formed against the bourgeois order; everywhere there are workers who refuse capitalist restructuring, peasants who refuse to give their land to the army, immigrant workers who refuse serfdom, young people who refuse academic and military barracking, women, national minorities... This expansion multiplies the places where the question of power is being raised and thus renders absurd the efforts of classical leftism to unify these struggles and bring them under its hegemony. The Lip affair showed how deeply subversive the practices and thoughts of workers and employees who were supposedly so respectful can be. And it also showed the radical impotence of leftist movements to spread this subversion and make it the principle of new forms for organizing revolt. This was no doubt the birth of a new figure of subversion, but it was also quite clearly the end of leftism's grand and totalizing discourse. The end, we might say, of the opposition of small communist worlds to the big one. Now that the time for competition has passed, the postponed project of recuperation can get underway. The spread of revolt, the end of organized leftism . . . doesn't all this prove that the old apparatuses, so much maligned, are actually the only unifying factors? The PCF and the PS are fighting it out to recruit the forces that leftism was able to set in motion, but unable to unify.

This conjuncture restores the ecumenical discourse of armchair Marxists to a place that had been imperilled by May 68. It would hardly have been possible, in the wake of the May events, to pretend that one's discourse was *the* discourse of Marxist philosophy, to say, ingenuously: 'Marxism-Leninism teaches that...'. A too-recent experience had shown that every 'Marxist' discourse has to be put through the test of practice and declare its real nature – as a discourse of order or of subversion. The pretensions of philosophers to systematize the practice of others had been rendered unacceptable. There were, to be sure, 'leftist' professors who explained that to have a revolutionary strategy one first had to develop a theory of modes of production, of class and of class alliances. There was an audience for this sort of thing, but it didn't fool many. To young intellectuals – the potential clients of Marxist philosophy – it seemed quite clear that the ability to systematize class struggles was held by those who actually fought them. In what concerned Marxism, the universalizing function no longer belonged to theoreticians, but to political organizations. What this means is that the discourse of these organizations managed to satisfy a basic need for generalization and systematization. Leftism countered the totalizing discourse of revisionism with its own totalizing discourse. Such was the discourse of the Gauche prolétarienne, for example. For as much as we might critique it, call it crazy or confront it with tons of Marxist literature, its discourse did not fail to function as something of a universal against which Marxist intellectuals could pit their experiences and their culture. In 1970, Emmanuel Terray pit Marxist and Leninist theories not against 'economism' and 'humanism', but against the theses of the Gauche prolétarienne.[11] Today, the splintering in the movements of revolt marks the end of the great political syntheses of leftist discourse. In 1969, it was still possible for leftists to encompass the anti-authoritarian uprising of France's youth and the proletarian struggles with their unifying discourse. But is it possible, today, to think the unity between the struggles of peasants, labourers, students, women and immigrants without resorting to the most blatant generalities? It is not just that these struggles, which attack power in its varied and sometimes contradictory manifestations, present us with a multiplicity that makes achieving a synthesis more complicated. It is, more importantly, that they are themselves a multiplication of the discourses of struggle. 'When the prisoners began to speak', Foucault says, 'they possessed an individual theory of prisons, the penal system, and justice.'[12] It will be pointed out, certainly, that prisoners are in a privileged position to theorize their condition, and that if their uprisings have been deeply felt by the bourgeois order, their discourse has made no inroads at all into the political discourse. In Besançon, however, when Lip workers began to speak, what they put forward was a coherent discourse about their practices. There were none of the words, cries of indignation or formulaic sentences that leftist practice cuts from the discourse of revolt and pastes onto the discourse of the spokesperson for the universal proletarian. What they gave us, instead, was a veritable theory about what they were doing, a theory where the ideas of May 68 joined hands with the syndicalist tradition, but also one where we recognized a new kind of 'fusion': that of the experience of the workers' struggle with a Christian ideology that yearns, it seems, to be something other than 'the sigh of the oppressed creature'.[13] This is not a unique and isolated surprise. In the face of a Marxist discourse that has become a discourse of order, what we are finding in many places are subversive practices that rely on 'idealist' theories. The impossibility of mastering the multiplication and reversals of the discourse of revolt or of thinking the unity in today's anti-capitalist and anti-authoritarian struggles gives back to the discourse of Marxist philosophy a place that can no longer be occupied by the grand syntheses of leftism. True, it does not meet the demand for an overall reflection about today's struggles, but it does install itself in the void created by the very impossibility of such a reflection – the void of the universal, the void of the book.

The return of the old parties to recapture a revolt breaking away in every direction is accompanied by a return of armchair Marxists, who pick up anew the discourse about the universal proletarian that leftist politicians can no longer expound. In the wake of revisionism's attempt to recuperate leftism, the ecumenical dogmatism of professors of Marxism arrives to efface the rift between ideas of order and ideas of revolt while saying the rosary of the certainties that are everyone's common property: that it is the masses which make history; that they must be led by the party of the working class; that this party must have a correct political course, apply a mass line, and provide an accurate analysis of the intermediary classes in order to forge solid class alliances and thus be properly armed for the assault on power (which, thank God, is not for tomorrow). This discourse soothes the troubled conscience of the Marxist with its solid certitude. It assures him that one can speak, quite simply, of *the* proletariat, of *Marxism-Leninism* and of the labour movement, that there is indeed a distinction, among the ideas at the basis of revolt, between those that are bourgeois and those that are proletarian, and that the guardians of Marxist knowledge are always in a position to tell which is which. Althusser invests this enterprise of restoring dogmatism – its monuments are accumulating fast – with a philosophical principle: the 'critique of the subject' and the theorization of the 'process without a subject' are the trick that allow dogmatism to speak once again in the name of the universal proletarian without having to ask itself anything about the place it speaks from or who it speaks to. The only price to pay is this simple split, which represses 'petit-bourgeois' conscience and thus guarantees dogmatism its place in the discourse of proletarian ideology.[14]

The return of a philosophy we had thought dead and buried in May 68 reveals the limit that the subversion of that month of May was unable to breach: it did not destroy the theoretical and political machine of *representation*. Leftism was able to continue speaking from within the discourse of representation, the discourse of the universal held in the name of the masses. The renewal of Althusserian philosophy, and of armchair Marxism more generally, attests today to the continuing inability, since May 68, of radicalized intellectual spheres to think *positively* the specificity of their revolt, that is, the place of their revolt in the space of the revolution. The student revolts against bourgeois knowledge, the split that led a whole fraction of intellectuals (understood not as the representatives of culture, but as the intellectual agents of the reproduction of bourgeois relations) to revolt: these ruptures did not succeed in fully releasing their positivity. The fact is that a mass uprising of a fraction of intellectuals against the whole of bourgeois power raised a totally new political problem, and this novelty was threatened by traditional, and complementary, political figures: the humiliated petite bourgeoisie and the avant-garde intelligentsia. Still, there was an idea that, through May, we inherited from the Cultural Revolution: to abolish the division of labour that separated intellectual from manual labour. The Gauche prolétarienne, in particular, undertook to carry out this project. But the abstraction of the project yielded only a simple negation. We decreed the death of the book, and with it the futility of those struggles that stayed within the apparatuses of bourgeois ideology. Intellectuals transformed themselves into manual labourers or professional revolutionaries. They decided to become proletarians (*se prolétariser*). At this point, though, the new idea (to abolish bourgeois forms of the division of labour) suddenly found itself trapped by the old idea (to repress the base uprising). This prompted a reversal effect: to transform the uprising of one class into the uprising of another class, to make intellectuals speak in the name of the proletarian. The mechanism of representation was restored, and reduplicated at the level of the relations between organizational powers. A number of intellectuals, to be sure, appointed themselves the representatives of the 'proletarian ideology' that the 'petite bourgeoisie' would have to submit to. But for the 'petite bourgeoisie' to become proletarian, it had to be split in half, and one intellectual faction had to repress the other in the name of the proletarian.

In this way, the various attempts to transform the function of intellectuals and to unite their struggles with popular struggles were always being more or less undermined by the discourse of representation. The repression of the determinant objective contradictions of the revolt of one social strata and of the forms and aspirations proper to this specific uprising authorized a group of intellectuals to speak, once again, in the name of the proletarian and thus to reintroduce, against the stated intentions of this very group, the substitutive discourse of revisionism. This mechanism is not the product of ignorance or of the arrogance of petit-bourgeois 'spontaneity', but of the Marxism learned in the classrooms of universities and 'working class organizations'. A discourse that allows one to speak for others, that cancels out the place and subject of its own speech: such is the mechanism that has found its paradigmatic form in Althusserian discourse, founded as it is on the denial of the place from which it speaks, of what it speaks about, and of who it speaks to. We might find it amusing that it should reappear today for the encore performance Hegel and Marx warn us about, but we should also see its reappearance as an indication of the limit that every attempt since May 68 to transform intellectual practice has consistently failed to breach. This failure not only explains the inability to think the place of that practice in any way other than through the split between the plebeian 'petite bourgeoisie' and the chivalrous 'proletarians', but also the pretension to speak of a universal invested in proletarian positivity. Leftism's only answer to this discourse, inherited from the machineries of Stalinism and revisionism, was the accusatory, and merely reactive, discourse of 'desire'.

It is obvious that no decree can free the discourse of revolt from the mechanism of representation. Some today are urging us to forget Marxism, but this does not change the fact that the class struggle will continue to exist and that Marxism itself will continue to serve the ambiguous role it serves nowadays – that of a system of multiple identifications, of the place where discourses of revolt meet and where the discourse of subversion is perennially being transformed into the discourse of order. Others are trying to find, beyond the Leninist discourse of representation, a new way back to Marx – the Marx who denounces factory despotism, who theorizes workers' practice of association and who announces a world of free producers. But this effort does not change the fact that there is no pure Marxism, that Marxist discourse has always been inflected by social practices, inflected by discourses and practices of revolt – whether of workers in Paris in 1871, workers in Moscow and Petrograd in 1905 and 1917 or peasants in Hunan in 1926 – and inflected by the disciplines and discourses of power. Still today, only mass struggles can shake up the theoretical and political apparatus of representation that blocks the autonomous expression of revolt.

It goes without saying that the present discourse does not pretend to situate itself somewhere outside this circle. By what right do we refer to the 'masses' and invoke the practices of workers in Paris and peasants in Tatchai in order to shore up our discourse? What exactly is demonstrated by confronting the philosophical discourse Althusser holds in Paris in 1972 with the old rough draft of the 'Theses on Feuerbach', or by turning for help to bits and pieces of the discourse of workers from long ago and prosecutors from the reign of Louis Philippe? Undoubtedly, we have not proved much, and realists would not be wrong to say that after destroying so much it might not be a bad thing to have something to build – assuming, of course, that all of this is something more than a scholarly pastime tailor made to swell the existing ranks of Marxist and para-Marxist literature.

The only answer we can give to these questions is that this discourse does not pretend to deny its encompassing circle, and that it tries instead to reveal the closure that dogmatism is constantly trying to efface. It tries to shed some light on the power that allows professors to ground the universality of their discourse on the claim that it speaks in the name of the masses. That was the purpose of the double operation performed here upon an exemplary discourse of this sort: to re-inscribe it in its history, that is, in the system of practical and discursive constraints that allowed it to be uttered at all; and to surprise its articulations by forcing it to answer other questions than those posed by the complacent partners it had picked out for itself, and by reinserting its argumentation into the concatenation of words used, now as in the past, to articulate both the inevitability of oppression and the hopes for liberation. This was not a refutation – it is useless to refute dogmatism – but a staging designed to jam the functioning of one of the many academic Marxist discourses currently occupying our theoretical space so as to reveal how that discourse cloaks its consecration of the existing order in the language of revolution. In so doing, we wanted to echo the expressions through which the struggles and questions of our present seek to give voice to a new freedom.

January–May 1974

# APPENDIX
On the Theory of Ideology: Althusser's Politics[1]

## INTRODUCTORY NOTE

The origin of this appendix is a course I taught during the first semester of 1969 at the Université de Paris VIII/Vincennes. This university, created from scratch in the summer of 1968, was supposed to give rebelling students the novelty they were hoping for. It was a nursery of young academics marked by their Marxist convictions and by the theoretical novelties of the time: structuralist linguists and anthropologists, Althusserian philosophers, Lacanian psychoanalysts, sociologists trained by Bourdieu and literature professors instructed by Roland Barthes's semiology and by the 'literary theory' of the *Tel Quel* group. The whole thing had the looks of what we called at the time a 'recuperation' of the May movement, and it seemed bound to dissolve that movement's political potential into academic and cultural novelties. The Marxist professors who had concentrated there soon split into violently opposed camps. One rejected the 'recuperation' and tried to use this out-of-the-box university as a base to continue the fight against the institution of the university as such. The other embraced the thesis of the PCF, which said that Vincennes was a 'victory' of the May movement, one that had to be consolidated and defended against leftist 'provocateurs' intent on sabotaging it. Althusserianism became, as a matter of course, the theoretical weapon of this second camp, and it drew to its side new recruits who were no longer attracted by subversion but by the desire to put an end to it. In this context, my course, which had been intended primarily to comment on Marx's texts on ideology, quite quickly became the instrument for a reflection on the situation of this university, on the return to order it was then undergoing in the name of Althusserian Marxism and on what seemed to me to be the heart of the project – the Althusserian theory of the battle of science against ideology. At the end of the semester, Saül Karsz, who had attended the course, asked me to write an article based on it for a collection of essays on Althusser to be published in Argentina. It is quite likely that he showed my piece to Althusser and possible also that it might have played a part in Althusser's introduction of the notion of ideological state apparatuses to his thought. Be that as it may, the text was published in Argentina in 1970 and only appeared in France in 1973. The editor of *L'Homme et la societé*, Serge Jonas, had heard about it and asked me to publish it. I thought it necessary then to indicate my reservations concerning that part of its argument – the substantialization of 'proletarian ideology' as the ideology of the proletariat, the identification with Marxist-Leninist theory and the tendency to explain every theoretical and political position criticized as stemming from its author's membership in the 'petite bourgeoisie', which fact doomed him, by his 'class position', to oscillate forever between a bourgeois ideological past and a proletarian scientific future – that relied most heavily on what is most questionable in the Marxist tradition. As a result, for its publication in *L'Homme et la societé* and, a year later, in the concluding section of this book, I added a series of notes in which I distanced myself from that rhetoric. It seems to me today that the book from 1974 provides, on its own, the critique of its appendix, and so the text is being presented here as it was written in 1969.

*Jacques Rancière*
*June 2010*

*Certainly it is an interesting event we are dealing
with: the putrescence of absolute spirit.*

*Karl Marx*, The German Ideology

'All mysteries which lead theory to mysticism find their rational solution in human practice and in the comprehension of this practice.'[2] For a long time, we looked upon this sentence as upon the deepest of mysteries. And the solution we gave it was itself not without a hint of mysticism: like the young theologians in the seminary at Tübingen, who rummaged through the undergrowth in search of new 'powers', we multiplied 'practices' and endowed each of them with their own laws. Theoretical practice contained its own norms of verification, and it was, of course, at the top. And so the matter was settled, especially since the opponents to our solution could only challenge it with a practice, called 'praxis', which had been reduced to nothing more than its invocation.

In May 1968, however, everything was suddenly and brutally clarified. As the class struggle broke out openly inside the university, the status of the 'theoretical' was thrown into doubt, though not by the perennial blabber about praxis and the concrete, but by the reality of a mass ideological revolt. Thenceforward, Marxist discourse would no longer be able to rest its entire case on the affirmation of its own rigour. The class struggle made the bourgeois system of knowledge an open question because it raised, for everyone, the problem of knowledge's ultimate political meaning, of its revolutionary or counter-revolutionary character.

This conjuncture revealed the political meaning of Althusserianism to be entirely different from what we had thought it to be. The problem wasn't just that the theoretical presuppositions of Althusserianism had kept us from understanding the political meaning of the student uprising; it was, more importantly, that in the course of the year following the uprising, we saw the hacks of revisionism relying on Althusserianism for the theoretical justification of their offensive and their defence of academic knowledge. Suddenly, what we had until then tried to ignore became clear: the link between the Althusserian reading of Marx and political revisionism was not just a case of equivocal coexistence – it was an effective theoretical and political solidarity.

The remarks that follow are an attempt to single out the precise point at which the Althusserian reading forges this solidarity: the theory of ideology.

*

What is distinctive about Althusser's theory of ideology can be summed up in two fundamental theses:

1. The primary and commonly shared function of ideology in every society, whether or not it is divided into classes, is to ensure the cohesion of the social whole by regulating the relations of individuals to their tasks.
2. Ideology is the opposite of science.

The critical function of the first thesis is clear. It is directed at ideologies of disalienation, according to which the end of capitalist alienation would herald the end of the mystification of consciousness and the advent of a world where man's relation to nature and to each other would be perfectly transparent.[3] The transition is akin to St Paul's, from seeing reflections in a mirror to looking at them face to face.[4] Althusser confronts these ideologies of transparency with the fact that every social structure is necessarily opaque to its agents. Ideology is not only present in every social totality – because the totality is determined by its structure – it is also invested with a general function, namely, to provide the system of representations that allows agents of the social totality to carry out the tasks determined by the structure.

> In a classless society, as in a class society, ideology has the function of assuring the *bond* among people in the totality of the forms of their existence, the *relation* of individuals to their tasks assigned by the social structure.[5]

Althusser thus gives a general definition of the concept of ideology prior to the intervention of the concept of class struggle. And the appearance of the concept of class struggle will to some extent 'overdetermine'[6] ideology's primary function.

In one particularly explicit passage, we see how Althusser grounds the first thesis and links it to the second:

> In class societies, ideology is a representation of the real, but necessarily distorted, because necessarily biased and tendentious – tendentious

because its aim is not to provide men with *objective knowledge* of the social system in which they live but, on the contrary, to give them a mystified representation of this social system in order to keep them in their 'place' in the system of class exploitation. Of course, it would also be necessary to pose the problem of the function of ideology in a classless society – and it would be resolved by showing that the deformation of ideology is socially necessary as a function of the nature of the social whole itself, as a function (to be more precise) of *its determination by its structure,* which renders it – as a social whole – opaque to the individuals who occupy a place in society determined by this structure. The opacity of the social structure necessarily renders *mythic* that representation of the world which is indispensable for social cohesion. In class societies this first function of ideology remains, but is dominated by the new social function imposed by the *existence of class division,* which takes ideology far from the former function.

If we want to be exhaustive, if we want to take account of these two principles of necessary deformation, we must say that in a class society, ideology is necessarily deforming and mystifying, both because it is produced as deforming by the opacity of the determination of society by its structure and because it is produced as deforming by the existence of class division.[7]

The first problem for us is the nature of the concepts introduced to account for the general function of ideology. The notion of 'social cohesion' echoes the formula in the passage cited earlier, 'the *bond* among people in the totality of the forms of their existence'. 'Bond' or 'cohesion' of the 'social whole': is this really the realm of Marxist analysis? After declaring that the entire history of humanity is the history of class struggle, how can Marxism define functions like *ensuring social cohesion in general*? Is it not precisely because Marxist theory has nothing to say on that subject that we have moved over to another field, to a sociology of the Comtian or Durkheimian sort which actually does concern itself with the systems of representation that ensure or disrupt the cohesion of the social group? And is it not the shadow of this 'social group' that Althusser's analysis outlines here? We see an index of this displacement in the status Althusser accords to religion:

From primitive societies – where classes did not exist – onwards, the existence of this *bond* can be observed, and it is not by chance that the first form of this ideology, the reality of this bond, is to be found in *religion* ('bond' is one of the possible etymologies of the word *religion*).[8]

We can, if we invert the analysis, ask the following question: to define ideology in general, before defining the class struggle, is that not to define it on the model of the traditional analysis of religion, that is, on the model of a sociology that is heir to the metaphysical discourse on society? The *superimposition* of two functions of ideology (the preservation of social cohesion in general and the exercise of class domination) could then mean, for us, the *coexistence* of two heterogeneous conceptual systems: historical materialism and Durkheimian bourgeois sociology. What is distinctive about Althusser is that he transforms this coexistence into an actual union. The move implies a double subversion:

1. Ideology is not initially defined from within the realm of Marxism, but from within the realm of a general sociology (theory of the social whole in general). Marxist theory is then superimposed on this *sociological* theory of ideology as the theory of overdetermination specific to class societies. Thus, the concepts that define ideology in a class society will depend upon the concepts of this general sociology.

2. But the level of this general sociology is said to be one level of the Marxist theory of ideology, even though the latter has nothing to say about it. This explains why the operation works backwards, with the projected analysis of the general function of ideology being carried out with the concepts and analyses through which Marxist theory understands the function of ideology in class societies. Hence the use of the Marxist concepts that define class societies to define society in general.

The mechanism of this subversion is clearly visible when Althusser lays bare the double determination of ideology in class societies:

[I]n a class society, ideology is necessarily deforming and mystifying, both because it is produced as deforming by the opacity of the determination of society by its structure and because it is produced as deforming by the existence of class division.[9]

But what is this 'structure', whose level Althusser distinguishes here from that of class division? Translated into Marxist terms, the determination of a social totality by its structure is the social totality's determination by the *relations of production* that characterize a dominant mode of production. But what we understand by 'relations of production' are the social forms of appropriation of the means of production, and these are in fact class forms of appropriation. Capitalist relations of production show the class opposition between those who possess the means of production and those who sell their labour power. The distinction between the two overlooks the fact that the level of the 'structure' is, strictly speaking, the level of a class relation.[10]

The analysis of fetishism demonstrates this point quite well. It is not enough, in fact, to say that fetishism is the manifestation-dissimulation of relations of production (as I did in *Reading Capital*).[11] What fetishism conceals, quite specifically, is the *antagonistic* character of relations of production: the opposition between capital and labour disappears in the juxtaposition of sources of revenue. The structure is not concealed just because it likes to hide, like nature in Heraclitus. What it conceals is its *contradictory* nature, and this contradiction is a class contradiction. In other words, the manifestation-dissimulation of the structure does not mean the opacity of the 'social structure in general', but the efficiency of relations of production, that is, of the opposition between working and non-working classes which marks every class society. Stretched beyond class societies, this efficiency of the structure becomes a perfectly undetermined concept – or one determined as the substitute for a figure from traditional metaphysics: the evil genius or the cunning of reason.[12]

The distinction between levels of ideological dissimulation is thus highly problematic. It clearly functions by *analogy* with the Marxist analysis of the double nature of every process of production (the labour process in general, and the socially determined process of production). But the analogy is also clearly illegitimate. By transferring the law of 'the last instance'[13] to the superstructures and by making the effects reproduce the law of the cause, the analogy posits the social whole as a totality of levels, each of which expresses the same law. It is easy to see the absurdities that would follow from the application of this same principle to an analysis of the political superstructure. The principle would allow us not only to say that 'the social totality in general' requires the existence of a political superstructure, but also to define the general functions of a state prior to any consideration of the class struggle. This approximation is not just a joke: ideology could very well have in Althusser the same status that classical metaphysics assigns to the state. Indeed, his analysis could very well be a renewal of the myth of an ideological state of nature, a myth whose theoretical and political significance we must now explain.

This requires, first of all, spelling out the irreversible consequence of the distinction between two levels: ideology is not posited, at the outset, as the site of a struggle. Instead of being related to two antagonists, it is related to a totality, of which it forms a natural element:

> It is as if human societies could not survive without these *specific formations*, these systems of representations (of various levels) which are ideologies. Human societies secrete ideology as the very element and atmosphere indispensable to their historical respiration and life.[14]

Placing myths of origin (or of ends) under the restrictive form of the 'as if' is a classical gesture of philosophical modesty, one Kant perfected. Indeed, this is not the only time we shall run into Althusser's Kantianism. The investigation of origins, under the 'as if' mode, retains its political function: to mask division. Thus, ideology will not be posited as the site of a division, but as a totality unified through its relationship to its referent (the social whole). Similarly, the analysis of the second level will not be the analysis of ideological forms of the class struggle, but of the 'overdetermination' of ideology (in the singular) by class division. We will then speak about the ideology of a class society, and not about class ideologies. It is only at the end of the analysis that Althusser divides ideology into 'tendencies'.[15] But at that late moment of the analysis the introduction of this division is useless: ideology, which was not posited at the outset as the field of a struggle, has in the course of the argument surreptitiously become *one of the participants in the struggle*. The class struggle in ideology, forgotten at first, reappears in an eerie, fetishized form as the class struggle between ideology (weapon of the dominant class) and science (weapon of the dominated class).

Before commenting on them, let us spell out the stages of this logic of forgetfulness:

1. Ideology is a system of representations that governs, in all societies, the relations of individuals to the tasks fixed by the structure of the social whole. This system of representations is thus not a system of knowledge. It is, on the contrary, the system of illusions necessary to historical subjects.

2. In class societies, ideology acquires a supplementary function: to keep individuals in the place determined by class domination.

3. Thus, the principle capable of subverting this domination belongs to the opposite of ideology, that is, to science.

The crucial strategic move of this demonstration is that by which it articulates the function of ideology to the domination of a class:

> In class societies, ideology is a representation of the real, but it is necessarily distorted, because it is necessarily biased and tendentious – tendentious because its aim is not to provide men with *objective knowledge* of the social system in which they live but, on the contrary, to give them a mystified representation of this social system in order to keep them in their 'place' in the system of class exploitation.[16]

By articulating two theses (ideology is the opposite of knowledge, ideology is at the service of a class) that he had to this point only juxtaposed, Althusser reveals the mechanism that, at a deeper level, binds one to the other: ideology is a false representation because it yields no knowledge. And it yields no knowledge because it is at the service of the dominant class. But what ideology is involved here? Would the function of the ideology of the dominated class be to keep the exploited 'in their place' in the system of class exploitation? What is defined here as the function of ideology is, in fact, the function of the *dominant* ideology. To be able to think the general function of ideology, Althusser must posit the domination of *one* ideology as the domination of *ideology*. Now the die are cast: the general function of ideology will be said to work for the benefit of class domination, and the task of undermining this domination will be entrusted to the Other of Ideology, that is, to Science. The initial exclusion of class struggle prompts a particularly interesting game of theoretical hide-and-seek. The ideology/science couple will reintroduce the class struggle, and the class struggle, in its turn, will come to the aid of the opposition, science/ideology. Ideology had at first been posited only as something *other than science*. But, in its articulation to class domination, to the radical opposition between dominant and dominated classes, this *other than science* becomes the Other of Science. Difference has become contradiction.

What has happened here, if not the very operation through which metaphysics laid its foundations, and which it has incessantly repeated in the course of its history? The operation that answers the old problem raised in the *Sophist*: how to think, in the figure of the Other, difference as contradiction?[17] We shall have to return to the fact that Marxism here serves to accomplish this necessary but impossible task of philosophy. For now, it is enough to point out the significance of the displacement that has taken place in the understanding of ideology. Ideology is first of all an instance of the social whole. As such, it is *articulated* to other instances, but it is not confronted with an opposite. The oppositions which concern it are determined entirely from within it; the most important of these is that which opposes the ideology of one class to that of another. But how, then, can the couple, ideology/science, become the relevant opposition with which to think ideology? Through an operation that detaches ideology from the system of instances and erases the axiomatic division of the ideological field to constitute, in Marxist theory, a space jointly shared by science and ideology. The ideology/science opposition presupposes the re-establishment of a space homologous to the space the metaphysical tradition as a whole conceives so as to be able to pit science against its other and thus posit the closure of a discursive universe that it has split into the realms of true and false, into the world of science and its other (opinion, error, illusion, etc.). When ideology is no longer thought as being, fundamentally, the site of a struggle – a class struggle – it falls into the spot determined by the history of metaphysics: that of the Other of Science.

*

So far, we have only shown the general form of this displacement. We must now show how the science/ideology couple that displacement constitutes actually functions in a *political* analysis. To that end, we have two texts by Althusser: the article 'Student Problems', and the text 'Marxism and Humanism', both of which are devoted to drawing out the political consequences of the theory of ideology.

'Student Problems' cut into a conflict that had broken out between the PCF's position on the university and the position then dominant at the UNEF. The UNEF opposed the purely 'quantitative' demands of the Party (more campuses, professors, etc.) with a qualitative questioning of the pedagogical relation, which it saw, through the concept of alienation, as analogous to a class relation. Althusser's intervention aimed to trace the real lines of demarcation that would serve as the basis for the political and syndicalist action of the student movement. 'Student Problems', in other words, is not an occasional article commenting on an issue of the time, but a text that draws out the strict consequences of the Althusserian theory of ideology. These have since provided the framework, whether stated or not, for the revisionist discourse about the university.

The key to the argument is the displacement of the dividing class line from the professor/student relation, where the theoreticians of the UNEF had traced it, to the content of knowledge itself. In other words, the dividing line does not cut across the transmission of knowledge between professor and student, but across the very content of knowledge – across science and ideology. For his demonstration, Althusser engages a whole system of implications that we must spell out here.

Althusser makes the distinction between the technical and the social division of labour the basis of his argument:

> What are the theoretical principles of Marxism which should and can come into play in the scientific analysis of the university milieu . . . ? Essentially, the Marxist concepts of the *technical* and the *social* division of labour. Marx applied these principles in the analysis of capitalist society, and they are valid for the analysis of every human society (understood as a social formation based on a determined mode of production). These principles are valid *a fortiori* for a particular social reality such as the university, which, for obvious reasons, belongs to every modern society, be it capitalist, socialist, or communist.[18]

We recognize already on a first reading the same mechanism that was at work in Althusser's analysis of ideology: the elimination of class struggle and its replacement by the generality of a function necessary to the social whole. But the concepts here call for special attention: Althusser says that what he will do is *apply* the Marxist concepts of technical and social division of labour. But these concepts are not given as such in Marx's analysis. What Marx reveals, rather, is the double character of every process of production, which can be treated either as the labour process in general, or as a socially defined process of production that reproduces the relations of production that determine it. While it is possible to deduce the distinction between the 'technical' and the 'social' division of labour from this analysis, it is not a real distinction, but merely a *formal distinction* corresponding to two ways of conceptualizing the same process.

Technical division and social division are two aspects of the *same division*. The functions that ensure the technical reproduction of the process are the same ones that determine its social production.

Althusser treats the distinction as a real distinction between places and functions, and he correlates each to one or the other division. Thus, the 'technical division of labour corresponds to every job "post" whose existence is exclusively justified by the *technical* necessities that define the mode of production at a given moment of its development in a given society', while the function of the social division is 'to ensure the labour process of the society in question in the very forms of class division and domination'.[19]

Thus formulated, the distinction is enigmatic: how can one define the exclusively technical necessities of a mode of production? These would have to be independent of its social goals, that is, of the reproduction of the social relations of production that determine it. And, conversely, doesn't the functioning of the process of production already imply the reproduction of relations of production, and hence of the forms of class division and domination?

To solve the puzzle, we have, once again, to read the argument backwards: the technical division of labour is supposed to shed light on the function of the university. But it is in fact the status accorded to the university that will enlighten us about the function of the concept of 'technical division of labour'. Althusser tells us that the university, 'for obvious reasons, belongs to every modern society, be it capitalist, socialist, or communist'. Thus, the division of labour that seemed at first to correspond to the demands of a defined mode of production turns out to correspond instead to the technical necessities of a society – in Marxist terms, this means a society that has reached a certain level in the development of its productive forces. And now the distinction is clear: the technical division of labour corresponds to a given level of development of productive forces, and the social division corresponds to the reproduction of the relations of production of a determinate mode of production.

It is 'as if' it were possible to define a certain number of necessary places and functions of a modern society in general solely in light of the level of development of productive forces. A conclusion that should not fail to surprise Althusser's readers. Hasn't Althusser, after all, devoted so much energy to extracting the Marxist theory of history from every ideology that thinks history in terms of evolution and linear develop-ment? But doesn't the 'modernity' advanced here entirely contradict this attempt? We have to examine what is at stake here politically to under-stand the meaning of this contradiction. The motivation for this backslid-ing is anyway quite clear: if we follow it, we end up attributing to the technical division of labour – that is, to the objective demands of science or of rationality – that which belongs to the social forms of the capitalist mode of production.[20]

The concept of the technical division of labour appears then as the simple justification for revisionist slogans founded on such notions as 'the nation's real needs', 'the real needs of the economy', 'modernization' and so on. We know that the PCF has replaced Marxist dialectics with a Proudhonian electism that distinguishes the good and the bad side of things. The PCF reduces a revolutionary need – to destroy bourgeois relations of production in order to free productive forces – to the task of suppressing bad bourgeois relations (the domination of monopo-lies) while preserving and perfecting good ones (the forms of the divi-sion of labour that correspond to the needs of every society). But what we have learned from Marx is that a society's 'real' needs always serve to mask the interests of a class. In this instance, they mask the inter-ests of the class that the PCF has increasingly come to represent: the labour aristocracy and intellectual cadres. The concept – 'technical division of labour' – is deployed here in such a way as to justify the two complementary aspects of revisionist ideology: the theory of 'real needs' and the defence of a 'skills' hierarchy.

We can now explain the backsliding and the contradiction we noted earlier. Althusser has simply moved from the realm of Marxist theory to its opposite, that is, to the realm of revisionism's opportunistic ideology. We have seen this displacement of Marxist analysis onto the electism of good and bad sides before: it describes the very same movement by which the theory of ideology is displaced onto the dual relation meta-physics establishes between Science and its Other. The core of Althus-serianism lies without a doubt in the articulation of the spontaneous discourse of metaphysics to revisionist ideology, an articulation that becomes clearly visible in the way Althusser goes on to develop his argu-ment. The distinction between the technical and the social division of labour is expressed in the university as the distinction between science and ideology. In other words, the theory of ideology, whose foundation had seemed problematic, is now founded on the theory of the double division of labour. As the latter is only a scholarly justification for revisionism, we can say that the theory of ideology has here revealed its political foundation. Marxist theory was at first instrumental in solving a problem internal to the metaphysical tradition, and this problematic is in its turn put at the service of revisionist ideology. The analysis of knowledge makes this movement explicit:

> Through the knowledge taught at universities passes the permanent dividing line between technical and social divisions of labour, the most constant and profound of class divisions.[21]

All the pieces of the game are perfectly arranged here: the science/ideology distinction is what allows the technical/social distinction to pass itself off for a line of class division. In other words, in Althusser's discourse, metaphysics orchestrates the promotion of revisionist ideology to the rank of Marxist theory. This *dispositif* is the condition of possibility for the 'evidence' of Althusser's thesis, a thesis that depends, in fact, upon a double distortion. The first, which we have already noted, concerns the status of ideology; the second concerns the efficiency of science, which is said to be, as science, on the side of revolution.

> It is not by chance that a reactionary or 'technocratic' bourgeois government prefers half-knowledge in everything, and that, conversely, the *revolutionary* cause is always indissolubly tied to knowledge, that is, to *science*.[22]

For our part, we can say that it is not by chance that Althusser's thesis appears here in an inverted form. It is both necessary for Althusser's argument and impossible, without revealing what underlies it, to state directly the thesis that scientific knowledge is, by its very nature, subversive of bourgeois domination. The only way for a thesis as problematic as that to make sense is through a process that extends Marx's theses on scientific socialism beyond their proper field so as to make them say that the emancipation of the proletariat is impossible without a theory of the conditions of this liberation, that is to say, without the Marxist science of social formations. Here, what guarantees the link between the revolutionary effort and scientific knowledge is the object they share in common. But we cannot infer the revolutionary nature of science in general from this. Indeed, it is enough to apply this thesis to the reality of scientific instruction to see its inanity. There is little doubt that the content of the vast majority of science courses in medical and other schools is perfectly valid scientifically. If science courses have a clear-cut reactionary function, it is not because they are positivist in the way they teach science, but because of the very structures within which these courses take place: type of institution, selection mechanisms, relation between students and professors, who not only possess a certain knowledge, but who also belong to a social hierarchy (consider, in medicine, the role of consultants). The domination of the bourgeoisie and its ideology is not expressed in the content of knowledge, but in the configuration of the structures where knowledge is transmitted. The scientific character of knowledge does not affect the class content of the instruction in any way. Science is not the Other of ideology. Rather, it exists within institutions and forms of transmission that manifest the bourgeoisie's ideological domination.

Some might say that at least the second element of the thesis is sound: ideology does strengthen the power of the bourgeoisie – just think of the role played by the human sciences. But that is a bad way to frame the problem. These disciplines owe their role to the fact that, in the system of knowledge, they constitute the place where the confrontations of the class struggle are reflected most directly. Accordingly, the problem is not that their nature is more or less 'ideological'; the problem is the nature of the ideology transmitted through them. If psychology, sociology, law and political economy – as taught at our universities – have a reactionary function, it is not because they lack scientificity, wholly or in part, but because the ideology of the bourgeoisie spreads through them. Their being 'ideological' is not the issue; the issue is whether their ideology is *bourgeois*. The task of revolutionaries is not to confront them with requirements of scientificity, or to exhort these pseudosciences to raise their standard of success to the ideal scientificity of mathematics or physics. It is to oppose bourgeois ideologies with the proletarian ideology of Marxism-Leninism.

Even an elementary concrete analysis of the university institution shows the metaphysical character of Althusser's division. The science/ideology pair is not to be found in the analysis of the university, because what that analysis is concerned with is not 'ideology', but the ideology of the dominant class. And the latter is not simply – we might even say, not essentially – expressed in this or that content of knowledge, but in the very division of knowledge, in the forms of its appropriation, and in the university institution as such. Bourgeois ideology is not contained in the discourse of one or another ideologue, or in the spontaneous system of representation of the students, but in the division between disciplines, in the examination system and in the organization of departments – all of which realize the bourgeois hierarchy of knowledge. Ideology, in fact, is not simply a collection of discourses or a system of representations. It is not what Althusser calls – the word choice is important – an 'atmosphere'. The dominant ideology is a *power* organized in a collection of institutions (the system of knowledge, information, etc.). Althusser misses this point completely because he thinks in the classical metaphysical terms of the theory of the *imaginary* (understood as the system of representations that separate the *subject* from the *truth*). That explains why ideological struggle is completely turned around, its function now being to put science there where ideology used to be. What Althusser does is counter bourgeois academic discourse with Marxist academic discourse; concretely, that means countering the 'spontaneous' and 'petit-bourgeois' ideology of the students with the scientific rigour of Marxism as embodied in the wisdom of the Central Committee. The struggle of science against ideology actually benefits bourgeois ideology because it strengthens two of its crucial bastions: the system of knowledge and revisionist ideology.

There is not, at the university, an ideology that would be the Other of science. Nor is there, indeed, a science that would be the Other of ideology. What the university teaches is not 'science', in the mythical purity of its essence, but a selection of scientific knowledges that have been articulated into *objects of knowledge*. The transmission of scientific knowledge does not emanate directly from the concept of science. It is inscribed, instead, into the *forms of appropriation* of scientific knowledge, and these are *class* forms of appropriation. The transmission of scientific knowledges passes through a system of discourses, traditions and institutions that are the very existence of bourgeois ideology. In other words, the relation of science to ideology is not one of rupture but of articulation. Dominant ideology is not the shady Other to Science's pure light; it is, rather, the space where scientific knowledges come to be inscribed, the space where they are articulated to the elements of knowledge constitutive of a social formation. It is in the forms of dominant ideology that a scientific knowledge (*connaissance*) becomes an object of knowledge (*savoir*).

In effect, the concept of knowledge (*savoir*) is not just that of content that can be either science or ideology. Knowledge (*savoir*) is a system whose 'contents' cannot be conceived outside their forms of appropriation (acquisition, transmission, control, use). This system is the system of ideological dominance of a class. It is not 'science' or 'ideology'. Rather, the class appropriation of science and the ideology of the dominant class are articulated in this system. The science/ideology division hides a node which itself expresses the ideological dominance of a class. There is no more class division in knowledge (*savoir*) than there is in the state; knowledge has institutional existence only as an instrument of class rule. It is not that knowledge (*savoir*) is internally affected by a division that reproduces the division between classes; it is, rather, that its configuration is determined by the dominance of a class. The system of knowledge, like state power, is an object of the class struggle and must, like state power itself, be destroyed. The university is not the site of a class division, but the target of a proletarian struggle. To transform this target into the neutral site of division is in effect to mask the class struggle. Just because we have finally laid to rest the notion that there is a bourgeois and a proletarian science does not mean that we can infer that science is inherently proletarian – or, at the very least, the site of a peaceful coexistence. Science as such, its arguments or demonstrations, cannot be bourgeois or proletarian; conversely, the constitution of scientific knowledges into objects of knowledge, together with the mode of their social appropriation, can be. There is not a bourgeois and a proletarian science; there is only bourgeois knowledge and proletarian knowledge.

The soul of Marxism is the concrete analysis of a concrete situation. It is clear, though, that the science/ideology opposition is unsuited to such an analysis. Consequently, in lieu of a concrete analysis, what we find is the lonely repetition of a classical division of metaphysics, brought in to trace an imaginary class division that serves no other purpose than to make it possible to turn a blind eye to the real sites of class struggle.[23] This initial elision explains Althusser's misconception of the function of knowledge and of the struggle that trains its sights on it. Althusser misses the site of politics at the outset, and so, when politics reappears, it is not in its place. It appears dissimulated in the supposed neutrality of the technical division of labour, or displaced into the hypothetically revolutionary function of science. We have already seen the implications of the 'technical division of labour'. It remains for us to take a close look at the concept of science and at what gives it the specific function of masking the class struggle.

To that end, we must look at the second central thesis of Althusser's argument, which defines the pedagogic function:

> The pedagogic function has as its object the transmission of a determinate knowledge to subjects who do not possess it. Therefore, the pedagogic situation is based on the absolute condition of an *inequality between knowledge and a lack of knowledge*.[24]

We see the logic that ties this thesis to the previous one. While the first thesis indicated the real line of class division (science/ideology), the second denounces the false line of class division (professor/student). The function of the pedagogic relation is to transmit knowledge to those who do not possess it. Thus, it is founded only on the technical division of labour. The two theses complement but also absolutely contradict one another. For while the first posits that knowledge is *determined* by the difference between science and ideology, the second wipes the board of every determination, save for determination through the opposition between knowledge and the lack of knowledge, plenitude and emptiness. The line of division that had been traced between the concepts 'science' and 'technology' is effaced the instant the reality of the pedagogic function comes into play. Thus, Althusser declares that students 'often risk alienating the good will of their professors by unfairly regarding their pedagogic activities with suspicion and by thinking the validity of their knowledge superfluous'.[25] But doesn't the science/ideology distinction imply that a deep and radical suspicion of the knowledge of professors is in fact entirely justified? To lift this suspicion, knowledge has to be given the status of science. This requires bringing the relation of science to non-science to intervene a second time, though not under the figure of error (science/ideology) but of ignorance (knowledge/lack of knowledge). The concept of science now appears in its true colours: the whole function of the science/ideology distinction, it turns out, was to justify the pure being of knowledge (*savoir*) – or, more precisely, to justify the eminent dignity of the possessors of knowledge. Those interested in understanding this reversal of quality into quantity have to listen, once again, for the voice of the revisionist prompter: we need an education 'of quality', 'of a high cultural level'. As for professors, they are, in their double quality as scholars and wage labourers, objective allies of the working class. And who would be interested in criticizing them, if not provocateurs bankrolled by the bourgeoisie? It is not by chance that . . . and so on and so forth.

We would be mistaken, however, to see in Althusser's discourse simply a hackneyed argument in the service of revisionism. What is interesting about it, on the contrary, is that it reproduces the spontaneous discourse of metaphysics, the traditional position of philosophy in relation to knowledge. Althusser designates, and hides, this position with the following definition of philosophy: 'Philosophy represents politics in the domain of theory, or to be more precise: *with the sciences* – and, *vice versa*, philosophy represents scientificity in politics, with the classes engaged in the class struggle.'[26]

Althusser's thesis fails to see that this double representation – of scientificity in politics and of politics in the sciences – already exists, precisely in *knowledge*. Knowledge (*savoir*) constitutes the system of appropriation of scientific knowledges (*connaissances*) for the profit of a class. It is indeed remarkable to note that philosophy was established and developed in a particular relation to knowledge, but that it never recognized its class nature. When Plato attacks the Sophists and Descartes the Scholastics, their critiques function as a critique of knowledge (*savoir*), that is to say, as a critique not only of a false discourse but of a certain political and social power.[27] But even when they themselves grasp the properly political dimension of this knowledge (Plato), they cannot perceive the cause, that is, the articulation of knowledge to class domination. Unable to see knowledge as the system of ideological dominance of a class, all they can do is criticize the effects of this system. Thus, philosophy develops as a critique of false knowledge in the name of true knowledge (Science), or of the empirical diversity of knowledges in the name of the unity of science. This critique of knowledge, having failed to recognize knowledge's class function, is carried out in the name of the Ideal of Science, through a discourse that separates the realm of science from the realm of false knowledge (opinion, illusion, etc.). The function of the opposition of Science and its Other is to ignore the class nature of knowledge. And metaphysical discourse ignores this every time it posits itself as a discourse on science, that is, as a discourse guided by the question: what accounts for the scientificity of science? The typical gesture of modesty in the 'epistemological' tradition Althusser takes up is to suggest that this question is produced by the demands of science itself. Thus, for Althusser, a new science (Greek mathematics, Galilean physics, etc.) would require a discourse that could account for the forms of its scientificity (Plato, Descartes, etc.). But isn't that simply to accept the game proposed by the question? And, in truth, could it not be that the question is there only to keep *another question from being posed*: what is the foundation of knowledge? This would mean that the question is not produced by the demands of science (even if these are part of it), but by knowledge's self-concealment.[28]

Traditionally, what philosophy does is offer a critique of knowledge which is, at the same time, a denegation of knowledge (i.e. of the class struggle). Its position in relation to knowledge can be described as ironical, since it puts knowledge in question, but never touches its foundations. In philosophy, the questioning of knowledge invariably ends with its restoration, a movement that great philosophers are always laying bare in the work of their peers. Hegel's critique of Cartesian doubt is that it ends up restoring the authority of everything it had pretended to reject. Feuerbach pinpoints the same pretension in Hegel's 'path to despair'. 'The Idea's lack of self-knowledge in the beginning is . . . only an ironical lack of knowledge.'[29] This irony is what resurfaces in Althusser: the line of division is traced, only to be immediately erased. The doubt about knowledge was only there to better establish the authority of a knowledge elevated, in the end, to the rank of science.

Althusser, in repeating this movement, sheds light on its political import by revealing what is at stake in it: the status of the possessors of knowledge. The radical doubt that initially affected the content of knowledge vanishes when the question of its subject is raised, and when the very existence of a group possessing knowledge is at stake. Here again there is an evident homology with the classical philosophical gesture exemplarily illustrated by Descartes' *cogito*: to question the object of knowledge only to confirm its subject. The doubt cast on the object of knowledge only guarantees the certainty of its subject. This contradiction is the very contradiction that gives philosophy its status: it rises up against the power of the false possessors of knowledge or, more precisely, against the possessors of false knowledge (Sophists, theologians, etc.). But it cannot bring itself to question the existence of knowledge itself as a class instrument. When confronted with the object of false knowledge, philosophy appeals to the subject of true knowledge. In the last instance, this guarantees the grounds for domination by the possessors of (true) knowledge and, in so doing, justifies class domination. The movement that leads philosophy back from the object of false knowledge to the subject of true knowledge would thus correspond to the political demand of a class excluded from power, a demand that philosophy would stamp with the form of universality (Cartesian 'good sense'). The movement, in the end, has no other function than to better safeguard the privilege of the possessors of knowledge – a form of class domination.

This is the very same movement described by the Althusserian theory of ideology, and we see now how that theory articulates the spontaneous discourse of metaphysics to revisionist ideology. All that is needed, to seal the operation, is one more mediation, supplied by Althusser's *academic ideology*, which entrusts to the spontaneous discourse of metaphysics the task of justifying the instructors, the possessors and the dispensers of bourgeois knowledge (to which academic Marxism also belongs). Althusser, speaking for the possessors of knowledge (defending their authority), naturally aligns himself with the class position expressed by revisionist ideology, that of the labour aristocracy and of cadres. The spontaneous discourse of metaphysics is the necessary mediation that allows Althusser to recognize his own class position in the class position expressed by revisionism. The site of this convergence is the question of knowledge and the defence of academic authority; within that space, Althusserian ideology functions as the theory of an imaginary class struggle that benefits an actual collaboration with a real class, that of revisionism. And thus the unravelling of Marxism into opportunism is complete.

\*

This covering over of class struggle reveals its most radical effects in the analysis of humanist ideology.[30] This analysis was intended as an answer to the question: what is the function of the humanist ideology currently embraced in the Soviet Union? As an answer to this question – that is to say, as a way *to avoid raising the question at all*. For there is only one way of raising the question, and that is to inquire into its class meaning. This question, however, is subsumed under another, more general question, for which the answer is ready-made: as the USSR *is* a classless society, all one needs to do is apply the theory of ideology to it, minus those elements that apply to the exercise of class domination. What remains after this subtraction, as we all know too well, is the claim that ideology is not science and that it allows men to live their relations to the conditions of their existence. 'Socialist humanism', in other words, designates a whole set of new problems, without thereby yielding any knowledge of them. And what are these problems? They are, precisely, the problems of a classless society:

> In fact, the themes of socialist humanism designate the existence of real problems: *new* historical, economic, political and ideological problems that the Stalinist period kept in the shade, but still produced while producing socialism – problems of the forms of economic, political and cultural *organization* that correspond to the level of development attained by socialism's productive forces; problems of the new form of *individual development* for a new period of history in which the State will no longer take charge, *coercively*, of the leadership or control of the destiny of each individual, in which from now on each man will *objectively* have *the choice*, that is, *the difficult task* of becoming by himself what he is. The themes of socialist humanism (free development of the individual, respect for socialist legality, dignity of the person, etc.) are the way the Soviets and other socialists are *living* the relation between themselves and these problems, that is, the *conditions* in which they are posed.[31]

There are three elements in this text. First, there is a series of very general statements about the passage from a class society to a classless society, a passage said to raise a number of problems – political, economic, ideological, and so on. Secondly, there are general statements we know very well about the function of ideology. And, finally, there is the absence, in the hide-and-seek game of these generalities, of the object to be analysed – the realities in the Soviet Union. The absence of this reality means a massive presence of its image. What is, in fact, this 'new' reality that according to Althusser explains the return to an old ideology? It is nothing other than the self-image projected by Soviet society. That is to say, it is nothing other than the self-image its governing class projects: 'a new of history in which the State will no longer take charge, *coercively*, of the leadership or control of the destiny of each individual', a 'world without economic exploitation, without violence, without discrimination', and so on.[32] The 'explanation' of humanist Soviet ideology is nothing other than its reduplication. The whole ruse of the theory of ideology results in this naïveté, which paralyses every analysis of ideology at its roots by treating an ideological discourse as the adequate expression of what it is supposed to convey, by taking at its word the discourse that claims to have originated in a classless society. It is clear that this reduplication is not an empty operation, as it strengthens the effect this discourse is designed to produce: to mask class struggle through the affirmation of having surpassed it.

The circularity of the analysis closes the circle of the Althusserian theory of ideology, which here returns to its starting point. We must understand this return in a double sense: on the one hand, the 'concrete' analysis of the ideology of a classless society takes us back to the generalities touching upon the function of ideology in general. The repetition of the theory passes itself off for the analysis of its object. On the other hand, the political significance of the theory is illuminated by its meeting the object that it does not want to think – indeed, that it is expressly designed to avoid. Revisionism is not just the object that Althusserian discourse misses or hesitates to think; it is, strictly speaking, *its unthought*, the political condition of its theoretical functioning. Althusser pretends to be explaining Soviet ideology, when in fact it seems rather that it is revisionism which both explains and grounds Althusserian ideology. A theory that posits, even independently of the existence of classes, that there must be a function for ideology – is that not the very expression, the very interpretation, of a politics that pretends to have moved beyond classes?

If the Althusserian theory of ideology ends on such a theoretical suicide, it is precisely because of the ban that keeps it from thinking ideological discourses as discourses of the class struggle and allows it, instead, only to refer them to their 'social functions' and to their lack of scientificity. The critique of humanism, consequently, leaves its object intact, as it can only think that object in reference to a scientificity from which it is excluded. In that critique, the concept of man is that of a false subject of history, a new figure of the old idealist subject (spirit, consciousness, cogito or absolute knowledge). Such a critique leaves aside the main question: what does humanism represent politically? What does the concept – man – designate? Experience allows us to reply that the function of humanist theory has always been to uphold, under cover of universality, the privilege of one particular category of men. *Man* is the Prince or the Bourgeoisie; it can also be the cadre or party leader. But it can also be, according to an essential law of ideology, the concept in which is affirmed the opposition and the desires of those who revolt against the power of the Prince, the Bourgeoisie, and so on. Humanism always functions as the discourse of a class in struggle. This is the case with the various forms of humanist ideology that have been embraced in the Soviet Union. Stalin himself can point us in the right direction: isn't the famous formula, 'man is the most precious capital', only the flip side of the slogan that proclaims that 'cadres decide everything'? And can we think the present humanism of the person[33] in any other way than through the reference to the restoration of capitalism? Is it not the equivalent, in ideology, of what the famous 'State of all the people' is in the realm of politics?[34] The recent history of the USSR and of 'popular democracies' shows to what extent humanism functions both as the discourse of the new dominant class, which denies the existence of classes in these societies, and as the expression of the uprising of the classes and peoples oppressed by revisionism. It is remarkable, in fact, that Althusser refers ideological forms of humanism, not to the reality of a struggle or of a division, but to the unity of a *problem* addressed to the unity of a *group*: 'What need do the Soviets have for an *idea of man*, that is, an idea of themselves, *to help them live their history*?'[35]

The answer to this question turns on the relationship between the *tasks* to be accomplished (those pertaining to the passage to communism) and the *conditions* under which they must be accomplished ('difficulties due to the period of the *"cult of personality"*, *but also* the mark of the more distant difficulties characteristic of the *"construction of socialism in one country"*, and in addition in a country economically and culturally "backward"').[36] Problems men must resolve, objective conditions, backwardness, pathological phenomena: these are the game pieces. But there is one thing Althusser absolutely refuses to think: contradiction. It is as a result of this that he passes from the domain of Marxism to that of bourgeois sociology. We pointed out this displacement initially, and now we know its political function.

A theoretical platitude that is the correlate of political naïveté: such is the inevitable end of every theory of ideology that does not begin with the class struggle.

In order to understand this initial omission, we must revisit the original goal of Althusserian theory: to offer a critique of theories of transparency and disalienation. To challenge these, he had to show that the world is never transparent to consciousness, that there is 'ideology' even in classless societies. We suspected at this point that the demonstration might very well have a totally different end, and that its opponent had perhaps been determined only by the needs of the cause. But, in truth, the relationship cuts both ways. If the Althusserian discourse on ideology is governed by the need to justify revisionism, it is also the case that it is *because* Althusser remains captive to a classical philosophical problematic that he finds himself in the camp of revisionist ideology. Althusser's battle against the ideologies of alienation places him at the heart of the transparency (idealist) and opacity (materialist) dilemma, and this leads him to fight on the opponent's turf. The characteristic gesture of the para-Marxist theories he criticizes (Lukácsian, existentialist or other) is to identify the Marxist theory of ideologies with a theory of the subject. Althusser does not untie this knot between Marxist theory and the idealist philosophical tradition. He limits himself to criticizing one quite specific aspect of it: the interpretation of Marxist theory as a theory of consciousness. The critique establishes the status of ideology according to two fundamental determinations. On the one hand, the theory of ideology is a theory of the illusion of consciousness; on the other, ideology is not just 'false consciousness', but must also be invested with an objective status. Thus, ideology is a system of representations (images, signs, cultural objects) that surpasses the realm of consciousness and possesses an objective social reality. This correction, however, leaves out what is specific to the Marxist theory of ideologies: the 'ideological forms' Marx talks about in the 'Preface' to *A Contribution to the Critique of Political Economy* are not simply social forms of representation, *they are the forms in which a struggle is fought out*.[37] The realm of ideology is not just the realm of subjective illusion in general, of the necessarily inadequate representations men form of their practices. The only way to give objective status to ideologies is to think them through the class struggle. This means that ideology does not exist only in discourse or only in systems, images, signs and so on. In the analysis of the university, we saw that the ideology of a class exists primarily in institutions, in what we might call *ideological apparatuses*, to echo the way Marxist theory speaks about state apparatuses. Because of his starting point, Althusser can only give ideological forms the latent objectivity of systems of 'signs', of 'cultural objects' and so on. In other words, he fuses a metaphysical theory of the subject (under the form of a theory of illusion) with a sociology of 'systems of representation'. We have seen how these two are articulated in a theory of ideology that is entirely metaphysical, in the strict sense: it cannot think contradiction. This alone, however, would enable it to step out of the metaphysical turf on which its opponent stands.

The *political* problem posed by the 'end of ideologies' vanishes under Althusser's wand. 'Only an ideological world outlook could have imagined societies *without ideology* and accepted the utopian idea of a world in which ideology (not just one of its historical forms) would disappear without trace, to be replaced by *science*.'[38] This passage poses the problem exactly in the terms favoured by the theories being criticized: it identifies the end of ideologies with the reign of science, that is to say, with the end of subjective illusion in general. And, at that point, it becomes easy to show that the world of transparency will never exist and that classless societies will never be free of ideology, as Althusser defines it. We have already seen how, in practice, this critique of utopia betrays a most radical naïveté. Nor should that be surprising, since the way the problem is posed means that the object to be thought – the waging and the end of class struggle in ideology – is hidden from view at the outset. It is impossible to understand the problem and to produce any sort of concrete analysis of it if *ideology* is treated as illusion; stressing the 'social' necessity of that illusion does not change the situation. To understand it, one must think *ideologies* as systems for representing class interests and for waging the class struggle. At that point, the end of ideologies need not be presented as an eschatological concept; it can be presented, instead, in the same terms as the disappearance of the state, that is, as a function of the end of class struggle. We know now, even after the establishment of the dictatorship of the proletariat, that this end is a long way away. The experience of the Cultural Revolution has taught us something on that point. It showed us that ideology's supposed forms of existence in a classless society are in fact forms through which the class struggle is relentlessly waged within a socialist society. The rejection of the 'ideological' theme of the end of ideologies forecloses the examination of the essential problem of the forms assumed by the class struggle in socialist societies. The Chinese experience has shown us the critical importance of the ideological forms of this struggle: the socialist revolution engages the struggle against various forms of bourgeois ideology – be they traditional ideologies of individualism or obedience, or 'modern' ideologies of skills and technicities – which continue to sprout even after the takeover of political power. All these problems ultimately concern the ideological effects of the class division. They have nothing to do with the disappearance of illusion or of subjectivity. That is not to say that the question should not be raised. But it forms no part of the problematic of the Marxist theory of ideologies. The latter is no more a theory of the subject than it is a theory of science, or of 'society'. Althusser wants to fight against the anthropological ideologies that make a theory of the subject out of the theory of society. But the only subversive effect of his discourse is that it re-establishes the theory of science as the mediator that regulates the relationship between the two terms.

This theory of science stands on the same ground as the ideologies it pretends to combat. In its own way, then, it reflects the class position of the petit-bourgeois intellectual, a position that oscillates between two camps. The camp of the bourgeoisie, to which the petit-bourgeois intellectual is tied by his class situation, by the area he works in and by his theoretical problematic – which itself reflects his function within the ideological bourgeois apparatus. And the camp of the proletariat, which the petit-bourgeois intellectual would like to join, but whose interests he can only adopt by assimilating them to the objectivity and universality of 'science'. This means that, so long as he remains a petit-bourgeois intellectual – so long as he does not participate *materially* in the class struggle – he can only join the proletariat mythically, by orchestrating the coincidence of the revolutionary goal with this ideal point whose search justifies his own practice as a petit-bourgeois intellectual: the Ideal of Science. In other words, he adopts the 'positions of the proletariat' only at the level of the denegation of his own class practice. But to join the proletarian struggle at the level of this denegation means joining the camp of bourgeois politics disguised as proletarian politics. In other words, the camp of revisionism. An ideal convergence that corresponds to a very specific reality in a country like France, where the petit-bourgeois intellectual finds access to the working class to be doubly guarded: by his own integration in the system of bourgeois ideological domination, and also by the fact that the revisionist apparatus – as the 'representative' of the working class – intervenes between him and the proletariat. At both ends, the 'Marxist' petit-bourgeois intellectual is excluded from participation in the proletarian struggle, excluded, that is, from the only thing that in the end can guarantee the Marxist rigour of his discourse. The operation that transforms Marxist theory into a discourse on science reflects this double limitation: a general limitation related to the position of the intellectual cut off from the masses and integrated into the system of bourgeois ideology, and a particular limitation related to the way revisionism has surrounded the proletarian struggle. The 'scientific' rigour of this discourse is thus nothing more than the flip side of its inability to function as a rigorous Marxist theory – in other words, as revolutionary. It does not give the discourse the power to transgress the double limitation that binds it. Quite the contrary, in fact: it is only in light of its incoherence that a petit-bourgeois ideology can acquire, under particular circumstances, a progressive function. But when it attains its basic rigour, it is revealed for what it really is: a bourgeois rigour. In the end, Marxist discourse resolves to be the justification of academic knowledge and of the authority of the Central Committee. 'Science' becomes the slogan of the ideological counter-revolution.[39]

Without revolutionary theory there can be no revolutionary practice.[40] We have repeated this sentence over and over again, thinking it might set our minds at ease. But now we must heed the lesson taught by the Cultural Revolution and the ideological revolt of the students: cut off from revolutionary practice, there is no revolutionary theory that is not transformed into its opposite.

# Notes

FOREWORD

[1] Rancière is alluding to André Glucksmann's *The Master Thinkers*, first published in France in 1977. – Trans.

[2] I try to give a systematic account of this second aspect in *The Emancipated Spectator*, trans. Gregory Elliott (London: Verso, 2009). See, in particular, the chapter entitled 'The Misadventures of Critical Thinking' (25–49).

[3] See page 123 of this volume.

[4] 'On the Theory of Ideology: Althusser's Politics first appeared in a collection of essays on Althusser published in Argentina entitled *Lectura de Althusser* (Buenos Aires: Editorial Galerna, 1970). For more about this text, please see the conclusion to the original Preface (p. XXII) and the brief introduction written especially for this edition (p. 127–8). – Trans.


PREFACE

[1] Louis Althusser, *Reply to John Lewis*. (The *Reply to John Lewis*, which appeared as a book in France in the summer of 1973, is a reworked and expanded version of two articles Althusser first published in 1972, in the October and November issues of *Marxism Today*, the theoretical journal of the British Communist Party. Althusser's articles (they bore the same title as the book) were replies to two articles John Lewis

had published in the same journal earlier that year: 'The Althusser Case Part I, Marxist Humanism', *Marxism Today* 16:1 (1972): 23–8, and 'The Althusser Case [Part II]', *Marxism Today* 16:2 (1972): 43–8. The translation of the *Reply* in *Essays in Self-Criticism* follows the revised and expanded version. – Trans.)

2  The terms 'leftist/leftism' (*gauchiste/gauchisme*), 'communists' and 'the left' or 'left-wing(ers)' (*la gauche* and *de gauche*) are not interchangeable; each designates a different tendency or faction within Marxism, and these, in turn, allow for still further subdivisions. The distinctions, by no means original to Rancière, were commonplace markers that reflected the reality of Marxism as a system of thought and a political practice at the time the book was written. 'The left' and 'left-wing(er)' are the most general terms: they cover the entire spectrum of the left, from its radical or revolutionary to its more conventional elements. Members of the socialist party with no interest in revolution see themselves as being on 'the left' and describe themselves as 'left-wingers' (*de gauche*). 'Communist' refers to members of Communist Party or to political and theoretical positions aligned with the Party and its 'orthodoxy' (what communist 'orthodoxy' might be is the topic of the first chapter). Lastly, 'leftist' and 'leftism' (*gauchiste/gauchisme*) refer to political factions and theoretical positions that are, as it were, to the left of the Party. The PCF revived the terms 'leftist' and 'leftism' – which Lenin uses pejoratively in *'Left-Wing'* [i.e. *Leftist*] *Communism: An Infant Malady* (in French: *La Maladie infantile du communisme: le gauchisme*) – to designate the actors of May 68 and their followers and supporters. It would be correct to render these terms with such expressions as the 'radical' or 'ultra' left; this is often done, in fact, and I do use these expressions on occasion. But if this is the meaning, making the expressions work for every case ultimately demanded too many awkward acrobatics, and I have consequently decided for the most part to use the straightforward translation, 'leftist' and 'leftism'. The political and theoretical problems raised by the positive appropriation of these terms in France in the 1960s, when leftists of various stripes pit a radical form of communism against the (revisionist) politics of the PCF, is a crucial element in the argumentation of the book, particularly of Chapter Two, where Rancière explores Althusser's strategies to debunk that 'perversion of Marxism' known as *leftism* (p. 26 of this book). – Trans.

[3] Lip is a French watch and clock company based in Besançon. The strikes led by Lip workers, their occupation of the factory and their eventual takeover of all operations making Lip a worker-managed company, are events Rancière returns to several times in the book. He is referring to events at the Lip factory when he mentions Besançon in the next paragraph. – Trans.

[4] The Union de la Gauche (1972–1977) was a political alliance between the Parti socialiste (PS), the Mouvement des radicaux de gauche (MRG) and the PCF. For more about its core principle, the 'common programme of government', see *Programme commun de gouvernement* (Paris: Flammarion, 1973). – Trans.

[5] The Larzac gathering – the *rassemblement du Larzac* – refers to the gathering of militants from all over France on the plateau of Larzac in the summer of 1973; they gathered there to protest, alongside farmers from the area, the government's plan to extend a military camp onto local farmland. – Trans.

[6] See, especially, François Fourquet, 'Généalogie du *Capital*. 2: L'idéal historique' in *Recherches* 14 (January) 1974. (The first instalment of this 'genealogy' appeared in *Recherches* 13 and bore the title: 'Génealogy du *Capital*. Les équipements du pouvoir'. *Recherches* (1966–1981) was the journal of the Centre d'Études, de Recherche et de Formation Institutionelles (CERFI) – Rancière mentions it just below. Félix Guattari was one of founders of the Centre and the journal. – Trans.)

[7] The transformation of consciousness through practice is a general topos of Marxism – present in the 'Theses on Feuerbach', for example – which had been rejuvenated by Maoist discourse, notably by Mao Tse-tung's *Where do Correct Ideas Comes From?* – Note supplied by the author.

[8] Throughout this book, I use the concept of *revisionism* to designate the ideology and practice of the PCF. I am well aware of the inconveniences attached to this term, which does not offer a positive definition of the functioning of a political apparatus, but instead characterizes it through the ambiguous criteria of faithfulness to texts. That said, it seemed to me that it would be clearer, politically speaking, to retain the concept – at least until revolutionary practice invents another – through which the revolutionary left, in China and the rest of the world, became aware of the practice common to the Soviet state apparatus and to the parties

that supported it. The term, meanwhile, remains the most suitable we have for revealing an element that is central to this ideology: the use of a revolutionary discourse to justify a politics of power sharing within the capitalist system.

[9] For more on Rancière's decision to print 'On the Theory of Ideology' as an appendix in this edition, please see pp. XVII–XVIII and 127–8. – Trans.

CHAPTER ONE

[1] From 1962 to 1982, Georges Séguy was Secretary General of the CGT, a trade union entirely subservient to the PCF. – Note supplied by the author.

[2] Althusser, RJL, 46, n9.

[3] The passage is taken from a summary of the original English work produced at the request of the Constituent Assembly, and printed in 1791 under the title *Panoptique. Sur un nouveau principe pour construire des maisons d'inspection et notamment des maisons de force*. The panopticon, the reader will recall, is a circular structure that allows an inspector situated in the central tower to hold everyone under surveillance simultaneously and at all times. Its basic principle is applicable 'without exception, to all establishments whatsoever, in which, within a space not too large to be covered or commanded by buildings, a number of persons are meant to be kept under inspection': prisons, workhouses, manufactories, schools, madhouses, houses of correction and so on. (The summary Rancière is citing from exists in English, and can be found in Basil Montagu (ed.), *The Opinions of Different Authors upon the Punishment of Death* (London: Longman, Hurst, Rees, Orme and Brown, 1813), 321–73. The passage cited occurs on page 324. – Trans.)

[4] The reader will easily recognize in these remarks the teachings of Michel Foucault at the Collège de France. Any misuse of these teachings is entirely my responsibility.

[5] *Panoptique*, 14; for English, see Montagu (ed.), *The Opinions of Different Authors upon the Punishment of Death*, 333.

[6] The reference is to Marx, C1, 280. – Trans.

7  Karl Marx, 'Theses on Feuerbach', in MECW 5, thesis III. (The reference to Robert Owen was added later by Engels, and is not to be found in most English translations. – Trans.)

8  The line that runs from Helvétius to Owen, passing through Bentham, is clear and well known. The question raised here, though, affects each and every 'utopian socialism', as these are all grounded in the same source: philanthropic bourgeois thought. Some people today try to find in the 'Fourierist subversion' the answer to certain of Marxism's adventures, but Charles Noiret, in 1841, gave powerful expression to what the phalanstery represents to the thoroughly coherent proletarian revolutionary: an extreme form of the link between capital and labour which is, ultimately, a most refined form of slavery. 'Each phalanstery would become a Russian fiefdom or an American plantation', Noiret writes. See Charles Noiret, 'Deuxième lettre aux travailleurs' [1841], in Faure and Rancière, PO, 95.

9  Karl Marx and Friedrich Engels, *The Holy Family*, in MECW 4, 131.

10  Althusser, RJL, 97.

11  Karl Marx, *Economic and Philosophic Manuscripts of 1844*, in MECW 3, 105.

12  Cf. Antonio Gramsci, *Prison Notebooks* 3, ed. and trans. Joseph A. Buttigieg (New York: Columbia University Press, 2007), 177. 'Reading the *Popular Manual*, one has the impression of someone who is bored, who is kept from sleeping by the moonlight, and who busies himself slaying fireflies in the belief that the brightness will dim or go away.' – Trans.

13  See Althusser, RJL, 54. ' ... *Marxism-Leninism has always subordinated the dialectical Theses to the materialist Theses.'* – Trans.

14  Althusser, RJL, 55.

15  Althusser, RJL, 55.

16  Marx, C1, 493 n4 (italics added). Towards the end of this chapter, we shall look at how Marx contrasts the materialism he founds on these premises with the 'abstract materialism of natural science'.

17  It used to be the case that, when Marx's texts said the very opposite of what they should say, we would spare no efforts to explain away the discrepancy. Later on, we learned that we should not mistake *words* for *concepts*. As the concepts themselves came under fire, we introduced the notion of 'index-concepts'. And, when all else failed, we appealed to the claim of last resort: Marx did not understand the

concepts he 'produced', and this spoiled the product. Now that 'theoreticism' has been rejected, there is a still more expedient method: leave Marx alone and give the floor to M-L.

18  Karl Marx, 'Letter to Annenkov, 28 December 1846', in MECW 38, 95.

19  The song is sugar-sweet in the very paternal Montfalcon: 'The science of things and of men is, of all other sciences, the most difficult and serious ... How could workers have an opinion about the principles of government or about what system to follow, when these problems remain unresolved even though history's most intelligent men have long debated them?' Jean-Baptiste Montfalcon, *Code moral des ateliers, ou, Traité des devoirs et droits des classes labourieuses* (Lyon: G. Rossary, 1835), 83. In Michel Goudchaux – a 'democratic' banker who would become Finance Minister and firing-squad member in 1848 – the song is cynical: 'When it comes to industry and labour, you are everything, on account of your intelligence and strength. You take a piece of mineral, and in your able hands it comes to be worth a hundred crowns. But we think you are incapable of self-governance. Indeed, we do not want workers to govern themselves.' Cited by Auguste Desmoulins, 'Le Capital et les Associations partielles', *Almanach des Corporations nouvelles* (Paris: Bureau de la Société de la Presse du travail, 1851).

20  The Fleurvilles and the Rosbourgs are fictional characters created by the Comtesse de Ségur. They figure in *Les Petites filles modèles* and *Les Vacances*, classics of edifying children's literature in France. – Note supplied by the author.

21  Althusser, IT, 23.

22  The reference is to Martial Guéroult's book, *Descartes selon l'ordre des raisons*, translated into English as: *Descartes' Philosophy Interpreted according to the Order of Reasons*. Althusser alludes to Guéroult's book in the lecture entitled: 'The Philosophical Conjuncture and Marxist Theoretical Research', printed in *The Humanist Controversy and other Writings (1966–1967)*. – Trans.

23  We can hear echoes of this position in the declarations of two of Althusser's 'comrades': in Professor André Gisselbrecht, who was summoned to the university at Vincennes in 1969 to explain himself before the masses about a particularly damning anti-leftist article, 'Les masses, qu-est que c'est?' ('The Masses: What Are

They?'), and in the words of a student at Vincennes and a member of the UEC. Following the rejection by the mass of students of a movement by a 'communist' organization to impose university elections, this student had said, 'There are no masses at Vincennes.' He meant that only a handful of students were members of the UEC.

24  For this concept, see *Lenin and Philosophy*, 183 (and pp. 132, 182, for the 'socio-technical' division of labour; Rancière discusses this division at length in 'On the Theory of Ideology: Althusser's Politics'). – Trans.

25  See Althusser, SP, 14, and the appendix to this book: 'On the Theory of Ideology: Althusser's Politics'.

26  Cf. Althusser, RJL, 61. 'These Theses do not paralyse research: they are *on the side of* a scientific understanding of history.' – Trans.

27  Marx, C1, 493 n4.

28  Marx, C1, 494 n4.

29  Cf. Marx, 'Preface' to *A Contribution to the Critique of Political Economy*, in MECW 29, 263. 'It is not the consciousness of men that determines their existence, but their social existence that determines their consciousness.' – Trans.

30  Althusser, RJL, 62.

31  It may bear stressing, once again, that I am not interested in defending some sort of 'paleo-Marxism'. It may very well be that Marx is wrong and that Althusser is perfectly right to correct him. But to do that, he must actually confront Marx. History, however, had taught Althusser that it was best to leave Marx alone – it's impossible to tell what will come up when one starts stirring things up there. Hence his forward flight: better talk about Gramsci than about Marx, about Lukács than about Gramsci, about Garaudy than about Lukács, about John Lewis than about Garaudy. This forward flight takes him further and further away from the question: where are we with Marx? Ultimately, this question can be rephrased as follows: where are we with the revolution?

32  Mao Tse-tung, *On Coalition Government*, in SWM 3, 207.

33  It may help the reader to know that the French translation of Mao's text reads as follows: 'Le peuple, le peuple seul est la force motrice, le *créateur* de l'histoire *universelle*' (italics added). When Rancière mentions 'creativity', he is of course referring back to the word in the translation of Mao's

text. Similarly, *universal* history has a much stronger 'Hegelian' ring to it than the English 'global history'. – Trans.

34  Lin Piao, *Selected Works of Lin Piao*, ed. China Problems Research Center (Hong Kong: Chi Luen Press, 1970), 130.

35  Cf. Edgar Snow, *Red Star over China* (1938) and *The Long Revolution* (1972), and Jan Myrdal, *Report from a Chinese Village* (1963; English translation, 1965). – Note supplied by the author.

36  If this thesis, which states that victory is necessary, does not figure in Marx, it is because its place in Marx is occupied by another thesis: the development of productive forces, coupled to the contradictions that stem from this development, necessarily lead to the dictatorship of the proletariat. Marx grounds the inevitability of victory on a 'science' of the natural history of humanity, one which demonstrates that superior forms cannot but be born from the development of inferior forms. We know the fate that awaited this thesis at the hands of Marx's descendants. 'It is the masses which create history': this, too, invites, and bears out, a thorough reassessment of all the theories and practices founded on a mechanistic understanding of the development of productive forces.

37  The *capitalist* relation of science to labour cannot be reduced to the use of science to oppress the worker, or to the idea that the privilege of science goes to those who live from the redistribution of surplus value. The appropriation of the knowledge and inventions of the worker is also an important aspect of this relation. Capitalism does not impose from above a scientific work method that replaces the 'artisanal' methods of workers: it forms this scientific work method by constantly appropriating the inventions born from workers' practices. To gain a sense of how Chinese texts celebrate the inventions of workers, one could do worse than to reread Sophie Ségur's *La Fortune de Gaspard* [*Gaspard's Fortune*].

38  Cf. Marx, 'Marx to Ludwig Kugelman in Hanover, 12 April 1871', in MECW 44, 132. Discussing the Paris Commune, Marx writes: 'Compare these Parisians, storming the heavens, with the slaves to heaven of the German-Prussian Holy Roman Empire.' The passage about John Lewis's 'little human god' is in Althusser, RJL, 43–4. – Trans.

39  Althusser, RJL, 63–4. (I have reworked the translation in order to bring out the insistent use of *on*, 'one', Rancière wants to draw attention to. – Trans.)

[40] I refer the reader to what Marx in *The German Ideology* has to say about the uses that speculative philosophy can make of pronouns like 'one': '"One!" We have here the second impersonal person which, together with the "It", is in Stirner's service and must perform the heaviest menial work for him. How these two are accustomed to support each other is clearly seen here. ... "It" gives the signal and immediately "one" joins in at the top of its voice. The division of labour is classically carried out' (MECW 5, 123).

[41] See Althusser, RJL, 36. 'When he [John Lewis] talks about philosophy, he talks about philosophy. Just that. Full stop. It has to be said that this is precisely what the majority of so-called philosophy teachers do in our bourgeois society. The last thing they want to talk about is politics! They would rather talk about philosophy. Full stop.' – Trans.

[42] Rancière is referring to a discussion in *Reading Capital* vol. 2, 120–9. – Trans.

[43] For the passages Rancière is alluding to, see Althusser, RJL, 59 and 98, respectively. – Trans.

[44] At that time, the 'orthodoxy' zeroed in on Sartre's 'opaque' conscience to accuse him of anti-humanism; today, conversely, it seizes upon his 'transparent' praxis to accuse him of being a humanist. This gives us a sense of how easy it is to say anything at all when one forsakes historical-material analysis in favour of the tribunal of rhetorical verisimilitude.

[45] Here, for example, is an interesting fact. In the debates of 1961, *Vigier* and *Garaudy*, two future 'renegades', defended the 'orthodox' position on the dialectic of nature.

[46] Algeria's Front de Libération Nationale or National Liberation Front. The FLN has ruled Algeria from before the battles for independence through today. The 'Declaration of the Right of Insubordination in the Algerian War' dates from 1960. – Trans.

[47] Sartre became editor-in-chief of *La Cause du peuple* in 1970, after Jean Pierre Le Dantec and Michel le Bris, its first two editors, had been arrested. – Trans.

[48] Sixteen miners were killed as a result of an explosion at Fouquières-les-Lens, on 4 February 1970. Two weeks later, on 17 February, members of the Nouvelle résistance populaire (NRP) burned the offices of the (state) company in charge of the mine. Six people were

arrested and charged and their trial date set for 14 December. At a 'Popular Tribunal' staged at Lens on the same day as the state trial, Sartre played the prosecutor arguing the case against the mining company. My source for this information is Julian Bourg, *From Revolution to Ethics: May 1968 and Contemporary French Thought* (Montreal: McGill-Queen's University Press, 2007), 72ff. *Libération* was founded in 1973. – Trans.

49 PCF leaders voted on 12 March 1956 to give Guy Mollet 'full powers' to carry on the war against the Algerian people. – Trans.

50 Whether Althusser wants it or not, he occupies a clearly determined place in the distribution of tasks entrusted to 'communist' intellectuals: he writes for those whom his colleagues fail to convince. When he writes for the paper of the Communist Party, he needs to give his position a leftist hue and come across as anti-establishment. We have, for example, two texts Althusser wrote about May 68, both dated the same day (15 March 1969). One, written for an Italian publication, shamelessly rehashes Marchais's ideas and style: the working class can take care of itself; it is high time 'students understood this and minded their own business'; students – all petit bourgeois – can be cured by being treated with a dose of the right medicine. By the end of the letter, however, a small problem appears: the Party has lost touch with young people (see Althusser, DMAb, 301–20). The tone changes in the text published in *La Pensée* ('A propos de l'article de Michel Verret sur "Mai étudiant"', June 1969). No need there to impress upon students that they should mind their own business; Pierre Juquin (PCF deputy and spokesperson in matters pertaining to intellectuals and to higher education) and his troops did that well enough on their own. Althusser's piece concentrates on the widening gap between students and the Party: he critiques Verret's attacks and underscores the progressive character of the student movement. Thus, Althusser manages to kill two birds with one stone: in the text published abroad, he puts his stamp on Marchais's theses, which would not be easily exported without it; in the text published in France, his goal is to say something else: we've recruited as much from the right as we can, so let's start canvassing on the left.

51 Althusser, RJL, 63–4.

52 Mao first described 'imperialism and all reactionaries' as 'paper tigers' in an interview with American journalist Anna Louise

Strong. He says there, 'All reactionaries are paper tigers. In appearance, the reactionaries are terrifying, but in reality they are not so powerful. From a long-term point of view, it is not the reactionaries but the people who are really powerful.' See 'Talk with the American Correspondent Anna Louise Strong', in SWM 4, 100. – Trans.

53  Althusser, RJL, 64.

54  Althusser's thesis also has its credentials, of course. It is a 'Leninist' thesis and, like with many another Leninist thesis, its source is clearly indicated in Lenin: Karl Kautsky. See Lenin, *One Step Forward, Two Steps Backwards*, in LCW 7, 397–9.

55  How does Althusser define May 68? As the largest strike in world history. But why the largest? Because there were nine million strikers. It is of no concern to Althusser that a good many of these nine million were reluctant strikers, or that a good many others had no initiative at all. What matters is the number of people who did not go to work. This collection is 'the working class' for Althusser (it is not surprising that he thinks Sartre is making a mountain out of a molehill with his groups and series). What *novelty* was there in the May strikes? What specific contradictions influenced its unfolding? It does not matter; what matters is the number.

56  'But you can't read,' left-wing Althusserians will cry out, 'Althusser writes "the Party", yes, but he does not say which party. He seems to be talking about the PCF, when, in fact, he is speaking about the *real* Communist Party, which is not to be confused with the PCF.' It's all a smokescreen, then, and not a new one either. After all, had not Eric Weil explained to us that the state Hegel talks about is not the Prussian State that was all around him, and that the *Philosophy of Right* is in fact a critique dressed up as an apology? For the final word on the ruses philosophers play with politics, the reader should consult the magisterial analysis – in the *Critique of Hegel's* 'Philosophy of Right', – in which the young Marx lays bare the philosophical game of empiricism and speculation. Philosophy duplicates the reality of sovereignty in its *idea*, so as to be able to incarnate it again in an empirical existence (the monarch). As a result of this game, philosophy is always in a position to doubt this incarnation, to think the ideality only there where it seems to praise reality – the very possibility of such scepticism rests in the 'positivism' that defines philosophy's relationship to power. The heart of specula-

tion is the existence of a point of reality that is posited as the immediate existence of a concept.

Such is, indeed, the secret to the dialectic of armchair Marxists. Once they have stipulated, from their chairs, the need for the working class to organize and for the working class, its Party, proletarian ideology, and so forth, to play a 'leadership role', they are perfectly free to see the instantiation – or not – of these abstractions in this or that empirical reality. That is why 'communist' theorists and their 'Marxist-Leninist' colleagues can use the same discourse to justify – and it can justify just about anything – different political positions.

We see why rejecting the young Marx by associating him with petit-bourgeois ideology is so vital to these theoreticians. Their entire discourse trades on the possibility of oscillating between empiricism and speculation – and such oscillation, according to the young Marx, is what is at the heart of Hegelian mystification. For an illustration of it, see *Class Struggle in the USSR*, where Charles Bettelheim explains the Bolshevik Party's confiscation of the power of the Soviet Central Executive Committee in the same way Hegel deduces the necessity of hereditary monarchy from the abstract idea of government (see *Hegel's Philosophy of Right*, trans. and ed. T. M. Knox (Oxford: Oxford University Press, 1973), pp. 185–8, 196 [§280–6; §301]). (For Marx's laying bare of the 'philosophical game of empiricism and speculation', see his comments on §279, in the *Critique of Hegel's* 'Philosophy of Right'. – Trans.)

[57] Althusser, RJL, 46.
[58] A programme adopted by the PCF during a session held at Champigny in December 1968. The programme aimed to replace the bourgeois/ proletariat opposition with the idea of a vast conglomeration from every social stratum against the monopolizing capitalist majority. This conglomeration was supposed to include medium- and low-level managers, cadres and a whole series of intermediaries in charge of subjecting the masses to the capitalist order. The *Champigny Manifesto*, which circulated widely in 1969, became the basis for the common programme of the Union de la Gauche (see Preface, note 4). – Note supplied by the author.
[59] A political alliance operative from 1972–1977 (see Preface, note 4). – Trans.

## CHAPTER TWO

1. From Jacques Rancière: 'My "citation" is in fact a summary; as often happens with very famous passages, that is how they circulate, and how we hear and remember them.' Readers can find the full passage in the *Republic* (499ab). – Trans.

2. Roland Leroy was an important figure within the PCF. He was a member of the Central Committee, the Political Bureau and the Secretariat; he was also editor-in-chief of *L'Humanité* (a 'central organ of the PCF' was its running epigraph) from 1974–2004. – Trans.

3. See Althusser, LP.

4. See Althusser, LP, 64ff. – Trans.

5. The 'theoreticist deviation' (which Althusser also calls *error* and *tendency*) figure prominently in the *Essays in Self-Criticism*; the reader should not confuse the 'theoreticist' deviation (a key element in Althusser's self-criticism) with Althusser's discussion, in 'Lenin and Philosophy' for example, of such 'theoretical' deviations as economism and humanism. – Trans.

6. Althusser develops the notion that Marxism is a theory of the production of knowledges in, among others, *Reading Capital* vol. 1 (pp. 41ff), and in 'Theory, Theoretical Practice, and Theoretical Formation: Ideology and Ideological Struggle', in PSPS. – Trans.

7. The Union des Jeunesses Communistes (Marxiste-Leniniste), or UJ, was not the first Maoist organization in France. In 1966, when the UJ was formed, two organizations inspired by Chinese communism had already been established: the MCF (Mouvement Communiste Français, which issued from the Féderation des cercles marxistes-leninistes) and the CMLF (Centre marxiste-léniniste de France). The UJ, however, was France's first Maoist *student* organization.

8. In Italian in the original; *aggiornamento* means to 'bring up to date', 'modernize', 'update'. The word is commonly used in connection with the Second Vatican Council of the Catholic Church. The PCI is the Partito communista italiano or Italian Communist Party. – Trans.

9. Althusser, IT, 21.

10. Cf. 'On the Materialist Dialectic', in FM, 161–218. (The 'polemic with Mury' is in the first twenty or so pages of the essay. – Trans.)

11  The expression occurs several times in *For Marx*, as well as in other texts by Althusser, always in dialogue with Lenin and Lenin's brief text 'On the Current Moment', that is, on the 'current situation'. For Lenin's text, see LCW 9, 286–7. – Trans.

12  For Althusser on French 'misery' and 'provincialism', see IT, 23 and 27–8, respectively. – Trans.

13  Althusser, IT, 22, 27, 23, respectively.

14  Althusser, IT, 22 (translation slightly modified).

15  Althusser, IT, 22. The 'old Left-wing [Leftist] formula' is: 'Bourgeois science, proletarian science.'

16  Althusser, IT, 22.

17  Althusser, 'Lettre à Bruno Queysanne' ['Letter to Bruno Queysanne'], unpublished mimeographed text. (This unpublished letter offers a first formulation of the arguments Althusser develops in the essay 'Student Problems', discussed at various points in this book. – Trans.)

18  In 1948, Jules Moch was France's Interior Minister. In the event Rancière is referring to, Moch used overwhelming force against coal miners on strike, especially in the north of the France; Moch mobilized over 60 thousand guards and soldiers to crush a strike 15 thousand strong. – Trans.

19  The first issue of *La Nouvelle Critique*, from 1948, develops the opposition between bourgeois science and proletarian science. – Note supplied by the author.

20  There was nothing spontaneous about this acceptance. For more on the efforts undertaken by the leaders of the PCF and the CGT to convince the miners to forego their demands (particularly the demand to be purged of collaborators), see Anonymous, *Mineurs en lutte* (Paris: Éd. Gilles Tautin, 1972).

21  See Althusser, 'PRW, in LPOE, 13. – Trans.

22  See Althusser, IT, 23. – Trans.

23  Michurian biology (named after Ivan Vladimirovich Michurin), particularly its theory of hybridization, was the 'official' biology of the Soviet regime, even though its principles had been universally rejected. – Trans.

24  Rancière is alluding to Section III, Part 3 of the *Manifesto of the Communist Party*: 'The Socialist and Communist systems, properly so called, those of Saint-Simon, Fourier, Owen, and others, spring into existence in the early undeveloped period, described above, of the

struggle between proletariat and bourgeoisie. The founders of these systems see, indeed, the class antagonisms, as well as the action of the decomposing elements in the prevailing form of society. But the proletariat, as yet in its infancy, offers to them the spectacle of a class without any historical initiative or any independent political movement' (MECW 6, 514–5). As the movement develops, these systems become an 'obstruction'. – Trans.

[25] Cf. Althusser, MD, 180; Althusser, RJL, 74.

[26] See Althusser, OYM, 62–3. Althusser returns to this discussion in a later text, 'Marx in his Limits', in *Philosophy of the Encounter: Later Writings, 1978–1987*, eds François Matheron and Oliver Corpet, trans. M. G. Goshgarian (London and New York: Verso, 2006), 26. – Trans.

[27] 'To organize student groups ... without first asking whether, perhaps, certain forms of collective work are not actually an obstacle to discovery (this is *sometimes* the case, and generally so in the case of new scientific insights powerful enough to bring to light, and critique, the crushing ideological illusions which hold *the entire world prisoner* – it was under these circumstances that Marx was necessarily alone, that Lenin was necessarily alone, for example at the moment of the *April Theses*, that Engels was necessarily alone during the publication of the *Critique of the Gotha Programme*) is to run the risk of a deception that can discourage the most generous efforts' (Althusser, PE, 87). We see quite well here how Althusser goes from an empirical consideration (the difficulty of organizing common research projects in the absence of shared basics) to a philosophical thesis (everybody lives in an illusion; the solution can only come from the heroes of theory).

[28] Rancière is alluding to Descartes' *Discourse on the Method*: 'Likewise, lest I should remain indecisive in my actions while reason obliged me to be so in my judgments ... I formed for myself a provisional moral code.' In *The Philosophical Writings of Descartes* vol. 1, trans. John Cottingham et al. (Cambridge and New York: Cambridge University Press, 1985), 122; AT VI; 22. – Trans.

[29] The Langevin-Wallon Plan is the name for a project first drafted at the end of World War II and aimed at entirely reforming the French educational system. The Plan is named after Paul Langevin and Henri Wallon, both of whom presided, at different times, over the committee drafting the plan, and both of whom had ties to the PCF. – Trans.

## NOTES

[30] We should perhaps correct the ambiguity of the words. The ruse was not a purposeful act of dissimulation carried out by camouflaged opponents, nor was the provisional moral code the result of a carefully calculated waiting game. It was an actual bisection of politics. When the enthusiasm for the struggle lagged, there was the enthusiasm for 'the party of the working class' and for the path traveled to reach it.

[31] The Cold War period, when intellectuals had two choices: play ball or go. – Note supplied by the author.

[32] Alain Forner was elected Secretary General of the UEC in 1962, a position he exercised until he was replaced by Pierre Kahn in 1964; both Kahn and Forner favoured the liberal 'Italian' agenda or *aggiornamento*. – Trans.

[33] This policy will bear fruit. After May, the intellectuals of *La Nouvelle Critique* – the 'Freemen' Gisselbrecht, Prévost and Verret – will turn out to be the most zealous ideological representatives of anti-leftist hysteria and of the call for the restoration of order at the university. They had carved out for themselves a certain political freedom within the Party, and they were not about to yield to the naïve demands of students who were eager to test their theoretical activity against the touchstone of political questions.

[34] The syndicalist left was not a union or organization as such; rather, it was made up of a part of the students in the UNEF. – Note supplied by the author.

[35] Mao called the 'three As' (Africa, Asia and Latin America) the 'zone of revolutionary storms'. – Trans.

[36] Cf. the extracts published by Patrick Kessel in *Le Mouvement Maoïste en France* (Paris: UGE, 1972), 64–6.

[37] Althusser discusses this concept, and what he calls the 'logic of sighting [*vue*] and oversight [*bévue*]', in *Reading Captial* vol. 1. See, especially, pages 12–30. – Trans.

[38] Later on, when the 'autonomy of theory' poked a hole in the authority of revisionism, theory was obliged to thwart its own effects. Althusserianism thus became the cloth Penelope weaves: an undertaking informed by the hope that the hero, and not the masses, will eventually arrive to save the day. What we must not forget, of course, is that, should no hero arrive, the entire undertaking only benefits the suitors.

[39] The Fédération des Groupes d'Études de Lettres de UNEF, headed by the communist students of the syndicalist left. (FGEL represented the Sorbonne, hence the slogan, and also its name: the Letters Faculty was at the Sorbonne. – Trans.)

[40] The seminar Rancière is referring to is the source for Pierre Bourdieu, Jean-Claude Passeron and Monique de Saint Martin, *Academic Discourse: Linguistic Misunderstanding and Professional Power*, trans. Richard Teese (Stanford: Stanford University Press, 1994 [1965]). – Trans.

[41] 'Scientific practice (theory, research), when directed at the following object, the structure of the university (with all its implications), cannot, under any circumstances, be confused with any other practice used to approach an object, for such confusion leads to theoretical mistakes with serious theoretical and political repercussions. In particular, the structure of the university must not be confused with syndicalist, ideological and political practices which aim at the transformation of this concrete object.' Althusser, 'Lettre à Bruno Queysanne' ['Letter to Bruno Queysanne'], unpublished mimeographed text. *Knowledge of an object is independent from its transformation*: this quite '*un*orthodox' thesis was not called into questions as part of the critique of 'theoreticism'.

[42] See the appendix, 'On the Theory of Ideology: Althusser's Politics', pp. 125–54.

[43] The Cercle d'Ulm was the circle of communist students of the École Normale Supérieure on the rue d'Ulm. What interests us here is not to tell the history of this circle or the prehistory of the Maoist student movement, but to describe how certain Althusserian notions were put to work politically.

[44] 'Fellow-travellers' is an expression with a history. There is a passage in Trotsky's *Literature and Revolution* that suggests why Rancière reaches for the expression here: 'They are not the artists of the proletarian revolution, but her artist "fellow-travellers". ... As regards a "fellow-traveller", the question always comes up – how far will he go?' And the answer is: not that far, in most cases. For this passage and for a detailed account of the 'fellow-travellers', see: David Caute, *The Fellow-Travellers: Intellectual Friends of Communism* (New Haven: Yale University Press, 1988). – Trans.

[45] The science in question is not only of the bookish sort. The concrete experience lived through in Algeria by our own Robert Linhart is

what will lead us, later on, to a positive appreciation of the Chinese Revolution. This appreciation would be founded not only on that Revolution's faithfulness to Marxist texts, but also on the original solution it developed to the problems of agrarian collectivization.

46  A resolution drafted by the Cercle d'Ulm and circulated internally. It is not published anywhere. – Note supplied by the author.

47  Guy Hermier was National Secretary of the UEC from 1965 to 1967, and Jean-Michel Cathala was General Secretary during the same period; they unseated the 'Italians'. – Trans.

48  Cf. Marx, *Introduction to a Contribution to a Critique of Hegel's* 'Philosophy of Right', in *Critique of Hegel's* 'Philosophy of Right', ed. Joseph O'Malley, trans. Annette Jolin and Joseph O'Malley (Cambridge: Cambridge University Press, 2009 [original edition 1970]), 138. 'Philosophy cannot be actualized without the abolition [*Aufhebung*] of the proletariat; the proletariat cannot be abolished without the actualization [*Verwirklichung*] of philosophy.' 'Actualization' is sometimes translated as 'realization'. – Trans.

49  The slogan was a running epigraph of the *Cahiers*. Althusser mentions it twice in the *Essays in Self-Criticism* (pp. 138 and 170), attributing it to Lenin. – Trans.

50  Cf. Étienne Balibar, 'The Rectification of the *Communist Manifesto*', in *Partisan* (Manchester) 1975. (Text originally appeared in *La Pensée* 164, August 1972; the English translation, although referenced in a handful of places, has eluded all my efforts to find it. – Trans.)

51  See Althusser, PE, 82.

52  The event Rancière is referring to happened in March 1966, when the Central Committee pronounced its position on the dispute between Althusser and Garaudy over the faults and merits of humanism. The Party sought a conciliatory, and not a 'brutal', resolution, assigning 'high' and 'low' marks (as we see below) to each position: Althusser's theoretical anti-humanism and Garaudy's humanism. One criticism of Garaudy is that he saw too great a confluence between Marxism and Christianity (his 'ecumenical mission'). This entire episode, including Louis Aragon's final declaration, is documented in the May–June issue of *Cahiers du communisme*, which Rancière will cite shortly. – Trans.

53  *Cahiers du communism*, May–June 1966, 122.

54  Ibid.

55  Ibid., 123.

[56] Louis Aragon, a poet and novelist, was elected to the PCF's Central Committee in 1950; his responsibilities within the Party centred on artistic, literary and intellectual matters. – Trans.

[57] The PCF's decision to endorse Mitterrand's presidential bid in December 1965 was the beginning of the breakup of the UEC. The Letters chapter openly opposed this decision, provoking a secession that eventually led to the formation of the JCR. The Cercle d'Ulm, for its part, tried to keep this issue from fissuring the UEC by rehashing the old argument of reserve and circumspection: the UEC is a student organization and should not take a position on issues outside of its domain. Defeated on this front, the Cercle abstained from intervening any further in the conflict.

It may be worth recalling that Mitterrand campaigned on an openly reactionary platform (the defence of Atlanticism). The PCF, for its part, multiplied its concessions to Altanticism: withdrawal from NATO was not a prerequisite for the alliance with socialists, or for the establishment of a 'true democracy'. As we all know, de Gaulle settled the matter.

[58] Although the context makes this clear, it will not hurt to stress that the reader should not confuse *ouvriérisme/ouvriérist* with *operaismo* or 'workerism'. Indeed, French translations of the Italian prefer to render *operaismo* by *operaïsme* precisely to avoid any confusion with *ouvriérisme*, which in French, as we see here, has a pejorative connotation. Specifically, by *ouvriérisme* we are to understand a narrow position characterized by the cult of the worker as the sole political subject and by the conviction that the anti-capitalist struggle is factory-based. The term also carries a strong anti-intellectual bias, as Althusser himself notes in the introduction to *For Marx*: the PCF, he says, had to devote 'a long and courageous struggle to the reduction and destruction of a reflex "*ouvriériste*" distrust of intellectuals' (25). – Trans.

[59] Cf. Althusser, 'On the Cultural Revolution'. (The essay appeared in *Cahiers marxistes-leninistes*, November–December 1966; a translation of it by Jason E. Smith has just appeared in the new journal, *Décalages* 1:1 (2010). – Trans.)

[60] Rancière is referring to the fact that the piece was unsigned, and to the fact that the *Cahiers marxistes-leninistes* was an organ 'outside' the PCF; indeed, by 1966, it had become openly antagonistic to the 'revisionism' of the Party. – Trans.

[61] In the literature of the PCF from 1967, I have only been able to find one very veiled allusion to the relationship between Althusserianism and Maoism, in an article by Claude Prévost, 'Portrait robot du maoïsme en France' in (*La Nouvelle Critique*, June 1967 ['An Identikit of Maoism in France']). 'There was at first a great deal of enthusiasm for a reading of Marx which privileged the moment of rupture with earlier ideologies. But, by giving this reading too leftist an inflection, its authors rendered it absurd: they made Marxism some sort of absolute beginning, even though such wholesale denial of past culture flew in the face of hundreds of texts by Marx and Lenin. They found themselves, as a result, having to establish a new "great bond". It was at that point that "Mao's thought", or at least that part of it which they highlight, was seen to be serviceable to their project, because it could lend to it its linearity and schematism.' Between the lines, we notice a personal absolution of Althusser, and a warning against the leftist risks inherent to his approach. We should note, in passing, that in this same text, Prévost, to show how ridiculous the 'pubescent Doctors' of the UJC (ML) were, chose as his target nothing other than Althusser's unsigned text, 'On the Cultural Revolution'.

CHAPTER THREE

[1] Althusser uses 'denegation' as a technical term in *Lenin and Philosophy*. The process it names, pertinent to the argument of this chapter, leads Althusser to claim that the philosophy that 'interprets' the world might be called 'the philosophy of *denegation*'. See Althusser, LP, 65–7. – Trans.

[2] Cf. Althusser, 'Letter from Louis Althusser [about *Revolution in the Revolution?*]', in Régis Debray, *A Critique of Arms*, trans. Rosemary Sheed (Harmondsworth and New York: Penguin, 1977), 258–67; Althusser, DMAa, 21–3. I cite the English edition because it has become impossible to find the Italian edition, and because the French edition was published without Althusser's letters. (Régis Debray published *Revolution in the Revolution? Armed Struggle and Political Struggle in Latin America* in 1967; it appeared in English that same year. – Trans.)

[3] The passages from the 'Philosophy Course for Scientists' cited in this chapter are from mimeographed texts of the lectures distributed as the course was ongoing in 1967–1968. These notes have recently been published (1974) under the title 'Philosophy and the Spontaneous Philosophy of Scientists', with some of the cited passages omitted, and others reworked. The passages cited on pages 57–8 and 66 did not make into the published text; those on page 65 were substantially revised; lastly, the long passage on page 66 remained identical. (In the original, this note appears at the end of the chapter. I have followed Rancière's citations, but have given in notes the reworked passages as they appear in the English translation of 'Philosophy and the Spontaneous Philosophy of Scientists'. Some of the material that did not make it into the published text has since been published in Althusser, *Écrits philosophiques et politiques*, ed. François Matheron (Paris: Stock; IMEC, 1994); – Trans.)

[4] The themes discussed in this lecture became the basis for Monod's *Chance and Necessity: An Essay on the Natural Philosophy of Modern Biology*, trans. Austryn Wainhouse (London: 1972 [1970]). For Althusser's discussion of Monod, see PSP, 145–165. – Trans.

[5] Cf. Althusser, PSP, 111. 'Like Teilhard de Chardin, palaeontologist and priest, authentic scientist [*savant*] and authentic clergyman, exploiting science for the profit of his faith: directly.' – Trans.

[6] Dominique Lecourt, *Une crise et son enjeu* (Paris: F. Maspéro, 1973). (Althusser discusses this very point in PSP, 132–3. – Trans.)

[7] *Materialism and Empirio-Criticism* is a critique of the 'Machist' Bogdanov. Three sections are specifically devoted to Mach, but his ideas are discussed throughout the book. – Trans.

[8] For Georges Sorel's use of Bergson in the development of his theory of 'myths', of how 'images' or 'pictures' provide an understanding (an intuition) of 'the activity, the sentiments and the ideas of the masses as they prepare themselves to enter on a decisive struggle', see *Reflections on Violence*, ed. Jeremy Jennings (Cambridge: Cambridge University Press, 1999), 28 (for the passage just cited). – Trans.

[9] Georgy Valentinovitch Plekhanov (1856–1918) was a Marxist theoretician and revolutionary. A Menshevik, he opposed the Bolshevik takeover of 1917, and died in exile. Jules Guesde (1845–1922) was an organizer and early leader of the Marxist wing of the French workers' movement. – Trans.

## NOTES

10  In the section 'Ernst Haeckel and Ernst Mach' of *Materialism and Empirio-Criticism*, Lenin stages the comparison between the materialist 'scientist' Haeckel and the idealist 'philosopher' Mach; Haeckel's *The Riddle of the Universe*, Lenin says, brought out the *'partisan character* of philosophy in modern society'. – Trans.

11  Cf. Althusser, PSP, 135. The 'spontaneous philosophy of scientists' contains 'both an "intra-scientific" element and an "extra-scientific" element – the one originating in their practice, the other imported from the outside'. – Trans.

12  See Althusser, PSP, 134ff. – Trans.

13  Vasil Bilak (1917–) leader of the 'hardliners' inside the Czech Communist Party (KSC), was among the politicians who called for the Russian invasion that put an end to the Prague Spring in August 1968. – Trans.

14  Althusser, 'Cours de philosophie pour les scientifiques' (mimeograph), 37. The reworked passage in 'Philosophy and the Spontaneous Philosophy of Scientists' reads: ' … has as its kernel the unity of three terms – an external object with a material existence/objective scientific knowledges or theories/scientific method, or, more schematically, object/theory/method – they have the impression of hearing not a scandalous language but a language that sounds foreign to them, that has nothing to do with the content of their own "experience"' (PSP, 135).

15  Althusser, 'Cours de philosophie pour les scientifiques' (mimeograph), 37. Reworked passage reads: 'A hundred years ago, physicists and chemists employed a very different language' (PSP, 136).

16  It may be worth reminding the reader here that, at the beginning of PSP, Althusser argues that philosophical theses (as opposed to scientific theses) 'cannot be said to be "true" (demonstrated or proved as in mathematics or in physics). They can only be said to be "correct" [*justes*]'. Hence thesis number 2 reads: 'Every philosophical thesis may be said to be correct or not' (PSP, 74). – Trans.

17  Cf. Jean-Toussaint Desanti, 'Qu'est-ce qu'un problème épistémologique?' Originally published in *Porisme*, the text is reprinted in *La Philosophie silencieuse: ou, Critique des philosophies de la science* (Paris: Le Seuil, 1975), 110–32. (Althusser's discussion of Desanti did not make it into the published version of the course; indeed, Desanti is not mentioned at all in PSP. – Trans.)

[18] This expression enters Althusser's vocabulary with the joint project of rectification, partisanship in philosophy, and self-criticism. See, for example, LP, 68. 'What is new in Marxism's contribution to philosophy is a new *practice of philosophy. Marxism is not a (new) philosophy of praxis, but a (new) practice of philosophy.*' – Trans.

[19] Althusser, PSP, 156.

[20] Nikolay Ivanovich Yezhov (1895–1939) was Chief of the NKVD (or People's Commissariat for Internal Affairs) during the worst moments of the great purges. – Trans.

[21] Althusser mentions Husserl's image of the philosopher as a 'civil servant of humanity' in LP, 64. For the passage in Husserl, see *Crisis of European Sciences and Transcendental Phenomenology*, trans. David Carr (Evanston, IL: Northwestern University Press, 1970 [1935]), §7, p. 17. 'In *our philosophizing,* then – how can we avoid it? – we are *functionaries of mankind.*' – Trans.

[22] Cf. Althusser, PRW, 22. – Trans.

[23] Althusser, DMAb, 309. (The 'first' problem Althusser mentions is that of the demands for better wages. – Trans.)

[24] Althusser, DMAb, 302.

[25] Alain Geismar and Daniel Cohn-Bendit. For Althusser's explanation of why the May occupation of the Sorbonne depended on the workers, see DMAb, 304–5. – Trans.

[26] Althusser, DMAb, 304.

[27] Althusser, 'A propos de l'article de Michel Verret sur "Mai étudiante"', *La Pensée* 145 (June 1969): 10. (Althusser is replying to Michel Verret, 'Mai étudiant ou les substitutions', *La Pensée* 143 (February 1969): 3–36. – Trans.)

[28] Ibid., 12.

[29] Faure Law, named for Edgar Faure, who had been appointed Minister of Education after the events of May 68, was adopted in November of that year, and remained in vigour until it was replaced by Savary Law in 1984. The experimental Vincennes University (or Paris VIII) was a direct result of Faure Law, which, among many other things, stated that the university system should be run on the model of a democratic society, and that voting rights should be extended to all its 'citizens', students included. This is the 'participation' that had to be 'imposed' mentioned in the next sentence. – Trans.

[30] Prevost's book appeared in 1969. – Trans.

31 There was talk at this time of creating an SNE (sup) [the Syndicat national de l'enseignement (supérieure), a leftist union for university lecturers and professors] local among the students of the École Normale Supérieure. This local would have supported the flagging leftist majority of the SNE (sup). Althusser campaigned against this project, thus helping the PCF to gain a majority at the SNE (sup).

32 Needless to say, this game redoubles on itself: if the point is to bring back certain leftists, it must be in order to change the Party. In this redoubling to infinity, worthy of 'The Purloined Letter', one thing appears, unfortunately, to be quite clear: Althusser has as many chances of catching up to the revolution as Achilles has of catching up to the turtle.

33 This choice, of course, incurred other problems and contradictions. We cannot treat them here, but the history of the last few years has sufficiently brought them to light. (The Gauche prolétarienne (Proletarian Left) was founded by former members of the UJC (ML) in 1969; it dissolved four years later. The Secours rouge (Red Aid or Assistance) was an organization created by the Gauche prolétarienne in 1970 (Sartre was one of its founders); it should not be confused with the Marxist-Leninist organization of the same name founded in 1922 by the PCF and eventually renamed Secours populaire, or with the Secours rouge operative today, which has no relation to either of the organizations mentioned. – Trans.)

34 See the appendix to this book, 'On the Theory of Ideology: Althusser's Politics', 125–54.

35 Cf. Althusser, ISA, 142; see note 7 on the same page for the discussion of Gramsci. – Trans.

36 Cf. Althusser, ISA, 153 for cited passages. – Trans.

37 Ibid., 155.

38 An example of this solidarity between a theory and a practice: the solidarity between Althusser's views of Edgar Faure's politics, and the support this politics received from the PCF. Commenting on the 'disintegration' of the student movement in the letter about May 68 to Maria Antonietta Macciocchi, Althusser says: 'We can count, moreover, on the (bourgeois) intelligence of E. Faure to contribute to it with all his [sic] might, at least in the universities' (DMAb, 310). We recognize the old thesis: the students involved in the revolts are sure

to be trapped by the intelligence of bourgeois reformists. But we also know that Edgar Faure's 'bourgeois intelligence' was only able to make Vincennes the practical confirmation of Althusser's 'theoretical' predictions by becoming a 'material might': the shock troops of Mr Pierre Juquin.

39  Althusser, ISA, 158.

40  Ibid., 181.

41  Rancière is referring to the concluding section, in the English translation, of RJL, the 'Remark on the Category: "Process without a Subject or Goal(s)"', which Althusser added in May 1973. See RJL, 94–9. The French text, conversely, ends, not with the 'Remark', but with the 'Note on the "Critique of the Personality Cult"'. The concluding paragraph of Althusser's 'Remark' reads, in part: 'History really is a "process without a Subject or Goal(s)", where the given *circumstances* in which "men" act as subjects under the determination of social *relations* are the product of the *class struggle*. History therefore does not have a Subject, in the philosophical sense of the term, but a *motor*: that very class struggle.' – Trans.

42  'If Marx did not deem it necessary to establish terminological differences it is because he never rigorously thought the difference between his discourse and the anthropological discourse of the young Marx.' Jacques Rancière, 'The Concept of Critique and the "Critique of Political Economy" (From the *Manuscripts* of 1844 to *Capital*)', trans. Ben Brewster, in *Ideology, Method and Marx: Essays from Economy and Society*, ed. Ali Rattansi (London and New York: Routledge, 1989), 167.

43  Cf. Althusser, RJL, 70–1. – Trans.

44  Ibid., 69.

45  Ibid., 66.

46  The reference is to the letter from 5 May 1846 (MECW 38, 38). – Trans.

47  Althusser, RJL, 72.

48  Rancière is alluding to Jacobus de Voragine's *The Golden Legend*, a thirteenth-century collection of hagiographies. Althusser, in other words, is claiming a noble lineage for his concept. – Trans.

49  Althusser, RJL, 71.

50  Ibid., 73.

51  Cf. Althusser, RJL, 65. – Trans.

52 Cf. Marx, *The Civil War in France* (first draft), in *Selected Writings*, ed. David McLellan (Oxford and New York: Oxford University Press, 2000), 553. 'This was, therefore, a revolution not against this or that, legitimate, constitutional, republican or imperialist form of State power. It was a revolution against the State itself, of this supernatural-ist abortion of society, a resumption by the people for the people of its own social life.' The indubitable 'origins' for the ideas Marx turns to in this text from 1871 are to be found in Feuerbach's critique of Hegel, a critique that, according to Althusser, should have lost its grip on Marx following the break of 1845. – Trans.

53 For a more detailed analysis, I refer the reader to my essay, 'How to Use *Lire le Capital*', trans. Tanya Assad, in *Ideology, Method and Marx*, 181–9. (This piece was originally published in *Les Temps modernes*, November 1973. – Trans.)

54 Joseph Barberet, *Le travail en France. Monographies professionelles* (Paris: Berger-Levrault et Cie., 1886), vol. 2, 134. (The bronze workers' strike began in February 1867, the same year that saw the publication of *Capital* 1. – Trans.)

## CHAPTER FOUR

1 Althusser, RJL, 88.

2 Cf. Althusser, SC, 130, 143. – Trans.

3 A line from 'The Internationale', by Eugène Pottier. – Trans.

4 Althusser, RJL, 51.

5 See, for example, how Jean-François Lyotard praises Deleuze and Guattari for having rid Marxism of surplus value: 'Its [*Anti-Oedipus*'] muteness on surplus value springs from the same source: looking for the creditor is wasted effort, the *subject* of the credit would always have to be *made to exist*, the proletariat to be incarnated on the sur-face of the *socius*, that is, represented in the representative box on the political stage.' Jean-François Lyotard, 'Energumen Capitalism' (1972), trans. James Leigh, in *Deleuze and Guattari: Critical Assessments of Leading Philosophers*, ed. Gary Genosko (London: Routledge, 2001), 590–1.

[6] *Hypokhâgneux* are first-year students in the *khâgne*, a two-year prepara-tory course for entry into the humanities section of the École Normale Supérieure, whose admission examinations are notoriously difficult. These are elite students, in other words. – Trans.

[7] Althusser, PRW, 21 (translation slightly modified).

[8] Cf. Althusser, RJL, 69, 71. More examples can be found in the *Reply*, as well as in the essays in *Lenin and Philosophy*. – Trans.

[9] Althusser, RJL, 83.

[10] Saül Karsz, *Théorie et politique: Louis Althusser* (Paris: Fayard, 1974), 267.

[11] Ibid., 214.

[12] The Le Chapelier Law (named after Jean Le Chapelier) prohibited the formation of workingmen's associations and abolished craft guilds. – Trans.

[13] A famous speech to the Convention by representative Thibaut: 'There is a major vice in the papermaking industry that you must eliminate so as to leave no vestige of despotism on the face of the Republic. I am referring to the workers' guilds, whose practices, regulations, preju-dices, and laws are a menace to the tranquility and stability of the workshops. ... When there is disagreement between the entrepreneur or manufacturer and the workers, the shop is 'banned': the workers abandon it, and anyone bold enough to continue working in a banned shop is exiling himself, and will only be able to find work by paying a very high tax.' Cited by Daniel Guérin, *La lutte de classes sous la Première République*, vol. 2 (Paris: Gallimard, 1946), 158.

[14] Bourgeois law not only distinguishes between 'people' based on whether they are employers or workers, it also distinguishes between the actions exercised on 'things' by different categories of people. During the Lip affair, jurists noted that the law of 28 April 1832, which qualified theft by a worker in the workplace as a crime pun-ishable with five to ten years' imprisonment, had not been repealed (being robbed by a burglar is different than being robbed by one of *your* employees). As the law had not been repealed, it could be applied to the theft of watches that, coming from the employers, was given the more noble name, embezzlement of assets. (Lip, the reader will recall, made, and continues to make, watches and clocks. – Trans.)

15 *Le Journal des Débats*, 8 December 1831. (Almost the entire archive of *Le Journal des Débats*, including the issue just cited, is freely available on Gallica. – Trans.)

16 Cited by Grignon, *Réflexions d'un ouvrier tailleur sur la misèr des ouvriers en général* ... (Paris: 1833), 1 (italics are Grignon's). Reprinted in Faure and Rancière, PO, 343 n11. (Grignon cites the passage from Persil in a footnote keyed to the passage Rancière will cite shortly, note 19. – Trans.)

17 J-F. Barraud, 'Étrennes d'un prolétaire à M. Bertin aîné' (Paris: 1832), 4. Reprinted in Faure and Rancière, PO, 48–9.

18 Also a line from 'The Internationale', by Eugène Pottier. – Trans.

19 Grignon, *Réflexions d'un ouvrier tailleur*, 1. Reprinted in Faure and Rancière, PO, 55–6.

20 Grignon, 'Réponse au manifeste des maitres-tailleurs', *La Tribune politique et littéraire*, 7 November 1833. Reprinted in Faure and Rancière, PO, 61 and 63, respectively.

21 Ibid., 61.

22 The strike Rancière is referring to happened in the fall of 1833; Rancière discusses it in *The Nights of Labour*. – Trans.

23 From the argument of Mr Claveau, lawyer for the masters in the trial of the striking tailor-workers. Cited in Jean-Pierre Aguet, *Les Grèves sous la Monarchie de Juillet* (Geneva: E. Droz, 1954), 84.

24 A CET, short for Collège d'enseignement technique, is a technical school. – Trans.

25 Jean-Baptiste Montfalcon, *Code moral des ouvriers, ou, Traité des devoirs et des droits des classes labourieuses* (Lyon: G. Rossary, 1835), 37–8.

26 Charles Noiret, *Aux travailleurs* (Rouen: Bloquel, 1840), 4.

27 Generally speaking, the processes through which the dominant ideology 'interpellates' individuals do not have for their primary function to exalt the omnipotence of 'men', but to establish what is worthy and unworthy. Traditional testing systems, for example, are much less concerned with validating the knowledge of the students than with making them aware of their ignorance and of the indulgence of their instructors. Bourgeois law, for its part, interpellates the mass of individuals, not as 'free', but as guilty, subjects. In police courts, when the magistrate explains to immigrants whose names he pretends to be unable to pronounce that 'France must not become the dump-

ing ground for all these drunkards', and when the deputy public prosecutor barely rises from his chair to mumble out 'in compliance to the law', it is not the ideology of the free subject and of equality that reigns over the whole, but the ideology of a difference – suggested almost as a difference in kind – between the guardians of the law and its subjects. (This explains why there is always a certain storm when an officer of the law finds him/herself behind bars.)

Bernard Edelman has tried to show that legal practice bears out Althusser's theses. But, to do so, he was obliged not only to concentrate on civil law, that is to say, on the sphere of law that applies essentially to relations among the bourgeoisie, but also to focus on a privileged object: the reduplication of property in the image. See his *Ownership of the Image: Elements for a Marxist Theory of Law*, trans. Elisabeth Kingdom (London: Routledge, 1979).

[28] Charles Piaget, in an interview given to *Le Monde*, 18 September 1973.

[29] Palente is the neighbourhood of Besançon where the Lip factory is located. – Trans.

[30] Henri Tolain was one of the signers of the 'Manifesto of the Sixty', a manifesto signed by 60 workers in 1864 (among other things, it called for the repeal of the articles in the penal and civil code Rancière mentioned earlier); Eugène Varlin was a member of the Paris Commune and of the First International. – Trans.

[31] See Chapter 1, note 38. – Trans.

[32] Cf. Jacques Rancière, 'How to Use *Lire le Capital*', trans. Tanya Assad, in *Ideology, Method and Marx*, 181–9. (*Capital* 1 was published in London just as the bronze workers were striking in Paris in 1867. – Trans.)

[33] The Freemen (*Die Freien*) is the name given to the group of young Hegelians gathered around the Bauer brothers, Bruno and Edgar; Marx had no sympathy for them. – Trans.

[34] Althusser, RJL, 85. (Althusser claims to be citing Marx, but I could not find the reference. – Trans.)

[35] Althusser, RJL, 77. Taken literally, Althusser's sentence can only mean two things: either that the Czech people only wanted to give their society a nice face, and could live with the disfigured body, or that the body was unharmed and only the face was vulnerable to the 'unworthy' practices, a suggestion that would run entirely counter to Althusser's views concerning the roots of the 'Stalinist deviation'.

[36] For 'integral humanism', see Althusser, RJL, 83. – Trans.

[37] The common programme is the programme adopted by the Union de la Gauche; see Preface, note 4. – Trans.

[38] The Fête de l'Humanité is an annual fundraiser for the PCF. It takes its name from the daily newspaper *L'Humanité*, which retains strong ties to the PCF even though it is has not been directly run by the Party since 2004. – Trans.

[39] Grahame Lock prefers 'Stalinian deviation' in his translation of the *Reply to John Lewis*, but, for the sake of consistency with the rest of this translation, I will use 'Stalinist' instead of 'Stalinian'. – Trans.

[40] Cornelius Castoriadis, 'The Relations of Production in Russia', in *Political and Social Writings*, vol. 1, *From the Critique of Bureaucracy to the Positive Content of Socialism*, trans. David Ames Curtis (Minneapolis: University of Minnesota Press, 1988).

[41] Stakhanovism was a measure established in 1935 and aimed at significantly increasing industrial production; it is often compared to Taylorism. – Trans.

[42] Naturally, many of these works owed their problematic to Althusserianism. What interests us here, though, is not to settle questions of theoretical paternity, but to capture the specific contribution of the *Reply to John Lewis*. (Rancière is referring to Maria Antonietta Macciochi, *Dalla Cina (Dopo la rivoluzione culturale)* [*From China (After the Cultural Revolution)*] (1971); Alberto Jacoviello, *Capire la Cina* [*Understanding China*] (1972); K. S. Karol, *China: The Other Communism* (1966) and *The Second Chinese Revolution* (1973). – Trans.)

[43] For more on this subject, see *Reading Capital* and 'Philosophy as a Revolutionary Weapon'.

[44] An organization of socialist labour parties in Paris formed in the wake of the dissolution of the First International; it was operative until 1916. – Trans.

[45] Althusser, RJL, 89.

[46] Ibid., 90.

[47] Cf. Althusser, RJL, 90. – Trans.

[48] Émile Pouget was a French communist. He was the vice-secretary of the CGT from 1901 to 1908. – Trans.

[49] See Lenin, 'How to Organize Competition', in LCW 26, 404–15, and 'The Immediate Tasks of the Soviet Government', in LCW 27, 235–77.

50 See Lenin, '"Left-Wing" Childishness and Petty-Bourgeois Mentality', in LCW 27, 323–34.

51 See Marx, *Capital* 2.

52 Cf. Lenin, *One Step Forward, Two Step Back*, in LCW 7, 391–2. ('For the factory, which seems only a bogey to some, represents that highest form of capitalist co-operation which has united and disciplined the proletariat, taught it to organize, and placed it at the head of all the other sections of the toiling and exploited population. ... The discipline and organization which come so hard to the bourgeois intellectual are very easily acquired by the proletariat just because of this factory "schooling".' – Trans.)

53 We had expected Bettelheim's book (*Class Struggles in the USSR*) to offer precisely this materialist analysis of class relations and thus free us from the abstractions that histories of Leninism trade on. Unfortunately, though, it does not help us get any further with the Althusserian problematic: first, because the book introduces no new documentary evidence, but instead proceeds by and large by summarizing already existing syntheses like Carr's; secondly, because the book is dominated by the *a priori* conviction that Lenin always embodied the right line in the face of the 'economism' of his opponents; and, finally, because Bettelheim's method consists of filling the gaps left open in the documentation with purely abstract deductions about Bolshevik leaders, about the soundness of the decisions they took in such or such circumstances, about their ties to the masses – in sum, about the being in-and-for-itself of a proletarian party.

54 Althusser, RJL, 73.

55 Ibid., 90.

56 Rancière is alluding to the section entitled 'Remark on the Category: "Process without a Subject or Goal(s)"' of RJL (94–9). – Trans.

57 See Althusser, RJL, 58 n18. 'Philosophy works in quite a different way: by modifying the *position* of the problems ... ' – Trans.

58 Leonid Illich Brezhnev (1906–1982) was a Soviet statesman and official of the Communist Party; Philipp Scheidemann (1865–1939) was a German social democrat politician; Rosa Luxemburg (1871–1919) was a Polish-born German revolutionary and agitator who played an important role in founding the Polish Social Democratic Party and the Spartacus League, which became Germany's Communist Party; Pierre Overney (1948–1972) was a militant Mao-

ist and member of the Gauche próletarienne who was shot dead on 25 February 1972 by a security guard of the Renault plant in Billancourt (Rancière mentions Overney several times in the next chapter). – Trans.

59 Rancière is referring to the fact that Daix's trajectory exemplifies the point about the spokespersons in the sentence before: Daix goes from denying Soviet labour camps to breaking with the PCF in 1974 over the publication of his book *Ce que je sais de Soljenitsyne* (*What I Know from Solzhenitsyn*), which he published the same year Solzhenitsyn's *The Gulag Archipelago* appeared in France (1974), and the same year Solzhenitsyn was exiled from Soviet Union. – Trans.

60 Althusser, RJL, 92.

61 Ibid.

62 Nothing shows the philistinism of a good many of our Marxists better than the 'leftist' critiques they level at Soviet dissidents. The problem, they explain, is that their dissent is right-wing. They demand freedom and human rights; they fill their heads with illusions about Western democracies; and they don't rely on the masses. What are they asking for, anyway? They want to have the privileged status of Western intellectuals (that is indeed the height of insolence: they want to be intellectuals like us, they dare imagine that the condition of the Marxist intellectual in the West is not just awful).

Our 'Marxists' don't trouble themselves for an instant to find out what sorts of relationships Soviet intellectuals are allowed to have with the masses, what knowledge they command, what theoretical weapons they can use in their critique of the Soviet regime. To ask them to articulate a 'Marxist' critique when Marxism is for them *raison d'état* is simply ridiculous. Soviet dissident intellectuals attest, in their way, to the oppression that weighs on the Russian people. In our ignorance of the real conflicting ideologies at work and of their precise social roots, we should in any case forgo exacerbating the 'Marxist' censure of whatever acts of repression are carried out by Brezhnev's state apparatus.

63 This is not to say that such a place exists elsewhere. But a 'communist' philosopher is susceptible to illusions about his discourse's capacity to change the world that his colleagues may be less prone to.

64 Althusser, RJL, 92.

## CHAPTER FIVE

[1] For Pierre Overney, see Chapter 4, note 58. – Trans.

[2] Althusser, IT, 27.

[3] Rancière is referring to a review of Althusser's *Reply to John Lewis* that appeared in *France Nouvelle*, the Party weekly, on 9 October 1973. – Trans.

[4] Rancière discusses Althusser's speech and his chiding of Pierre Daix over the Solzhenitsyn affair in Chapter 4 (p. 97); for the Fête de l'Humanité, see Chapter 4, note 38. – Trans.

[5] Cf. Michèle Manceaux and Jacques Donzelot, *Cours camarade, le P.C.F est derrière toi* [*Run, Comrade, the PCF Is after You*] (Paris: Gallimard, 1974). The book cites an exemplary speech by a CGT delegate, who evidently attended the best schools, about the strike sparked when a leftist worker was laid off: 'They went on strike of their own initiative, but they were striking for the wrong cause, for a cause that would take them nowhere and that, at the end of the day, was not even the real cause of their frustration. What they were really frustrated about was their salaries' (20). Or, 'We asked the workers who had joined the strike: "Is this really what is troubling you?" And they had to say no. That was a part of it, yes, but the real problem is that they wanted better wages than what they were getting' (19). What we see, *in nuce*, in this displacement of targets is the very same mechanism that governs Althusserian idealism.

[6] It is well known that the reference to the abolition of wage labour has recently disappeared from the statutes of the CGT. But the event was too minor for the doctors of Marxism-Leninism, ever so busy with their critiques of the 'economism of the Communist Party' and their punctilious defense of 'Leninism', to pay any attention to it.

[7] Rancière means the votes of the communist left; the PCF also wants to win the votes of those whose positions are to the left of the Party line: leftists, Maoists and so on. See Chapter 1, pages 19–20 and note 50, for a longer discussion. – Trans.

[8] There is good news on this front, incidentally, for revisionist thinkers, as the official theoreticians of the PS and of the CFDT have relieved them of this task. Now it is the self-managing unionist Edmond Maire (he was Secretary General of the CFDT from 1971–1988) who believes

that a worker does not necessarily have the qualities to become president of the Republic. And Régis Debray, the in-demand socialist of the moment, can be found rehashing in the pages of *Le Nouvel Observateur* Prévost's and Gisselbrecht's arguments against the 'Messianism' of petit-bourgeois leftists who play at revolution (you have to make do with what you have).

9  The hour-long occupation of the Chilean Embassy in Paris took place on 8 December 1973. – Trans.

10  I stress *alongside*. There is no need, in fact, for anti-economist philosophy to bother itself with the economic theses of the Party. An overly enthusiastic reader of the *Reply to John Lewis*, Nicole-Édith Thévenin, had the strange idea that it was possible to extract from the anti-economist theses of the *Reply* a critique of the official theoreticians of state monopoly capitalism (Boccara and Herzog). The April 1974 issue of *La Nouvelle Critique* set the record straight. Without uttering a word about the theses of the master, it reprimanded the student for completely misunderstanding 'the current realities of state monopoly capitalism'. (For Boccara and Herzog on state monopoly capitalism, see Paul Boccara, *Études sur le capitalisme monopoliste d'État, sa crise et son issue* (Paris: Éditions Sociales, 1973), and Philippe Herzog, *Politique économique et planification en régime capitaliste* (Paris: Éditions Sociales, 1972). – Trans.)

11  See, for example, Emmanuel Terray, *Marxism and 'Primitive' Societies: Two Studies*, trans. Mary Klopper (New York: Monthly Review Press, 1972). – Trans.

12  Michel Foucault, 'Intellectuals and Power: A Conversation between Michel Foucault and Gilles Deleuze', in *Language, Counter-Memory, Practice: Selected Essays and Interviews*, ed. Donald F. Bouchard (Ithaca, NY: Cornell University Press, 1992), 209.

13  The expression is Marx's. See *Introduction to a Contribution to a Critique of Hegel's* 'Philosophy of Right', 131. – Trans.

14  We see this play at work in 'Philosophy as a Revolutionary Weapon', where the dogmatic discourse of proletarian philosophy grounds itself on the humiliation of the petit-bourgeois conscience of the philosophy professor.

## APPENDIX

1. Martin Jordin translated this essay in 1974, and it was published, under the title 'On the Theory of Ideology: The Politics of Althusser', in *Radical Philosophy* 7 (1974). Jordin's translation has since been reprinted in Roy Eldridge and Peter Osborne (eds), *Radical Philosophy Reader* (London: Verso, 1985), 101–36; and in Terry Eagleton (ed.), *Ideology* (London: Longman Group, 1994), 141–61 (Eagleton omits the last third of the essay). I would like to acknowledge my debt to Jordin's translation, whose elegant and clear solutions I have on occasion adopted, unable to improve on them. – Trans.

2. Marx, Theses on Feuerbach, in MECW 5, thesis VIII. Althusser uses this very same passage as an epigram to 'On the Materialist Dialectic'. – Trans.

3. Cf. Chapter 3, p. 81. – Trans.

4. 'For now we see only a reflection as in a mirror; then we shall see face to face' (1 Cor. 13.12, New International Version). – Trans.

5. Althusser, TPF, 28.

6. Cf. Nicos Poulantzas, *Political Power and Social Classes*, trans. Timothy O'Hagan (London: Verso, 1978).

7. Althusser, TPF, 28–9.

8. Ibid., 25.

9. Ibid., 29.

10. Naturally, this class relationship must be carefully distinguished from the forms (political, economic, ideological) through which the class struggle is fought, and which are its effects. The fact remains, though, that relations of production can only be understood as class relations, lest they are transformed into a new netherworld (*arrière-monde*). Such a transformation is precisely what results from Poulantzas's distinction, in *Political Power and Social Classes*, between relations of production and 'social relations'. Poulantzas begins from the quite correct premise that relations of production are not 'human relations', only to fall into the dilemma mentioned earlier: transparency or opacity? The relations of production, consequently, appear as withdrawn into that netherworld represented by the 'structure'. At their limits, Althusser's or Poulantzas's analyses confront us with a truism: the structure is defined by nothing more than the opacity manifested in its effects. In other words, the structure's opacity is what renders it opaque.

This quasi-Heideggerian retreat of the structure might very well not be politically innocent. The PCF is happy to argue the following: the student struggle aims only at the effects of capitalist exploitation; similarly, grass-roots struggles in factories against hierarchy, automation and harassment aim only at effects. The real target, however, is the cause of exploitation itself: capitalist relations of production. But only science – meaning the wisdom of the Central Committee – can pierce through to this dimension of the problem. The retreat of the structure thus becomes Kant's *focus imaginarius*, the inverted image, condensed to a point, of an endless future: France's peaceful march towards socialism.

11 Cf. Rancière, 'How to Use *Lire le Capital*', in *Ideology, Method and Marx*, 183. – Trans.

12 The evil genius is that of the first of Descartes' *Meditations*; the cunning of reason is a concept in Hegel. – Trans.

13 The 'law' or notion of determination 'in the last instance' occurs in different texts by Althusser. The most pertinent in light of the discussion here is 'Contradiction and Overdetermination', in *For Marx*. – Trans.

14 Althusser, MH, 232.

15 ' ... ideology is not only divided into regions, but also divided into *tendencies* within its own social existence' (TPF, 30).

16 Althusser, TPF, 28–9.

17 A substitutive understanding of contradiction founded, of course, on a misunderstanding of the real contradiction.

18 Althusser, SP, 14; PE, 83.

19 Althusser, SP, 14–5 (translation modified); PE, 84.

20 Similarly, Althusser deduces in the same article the 'technical' necessity of every industrial hierarchy. Further on, we shall have to examine the essential reasons that make the existence of the university in a socialist society a necessity.

21 Althusser, SP, 18; PE, 89.

22 Althusser, SP, 22 (translation modified); PE, 94. It is interesting to note the complicity, even at the rhetorical level, between the metaphysical 'as if' structure and the classical rhetorical trope the PCF loves to use: 'It is not by chance that ... ' Popular wisdom is not mistaken when it says that chance knows what it is doing.

23 It is typical of metaphysical thinking to want to trace a dividing class line across realities (institutions, social groups) that it treats as static.

Revisionists, for example, list social groups according to whether they are revolutionary or not. Dialectics, however, teaches the contrary: unity and division can only be known in the struggle. We can't trace a line of class division in the university, but only in the struggle that puts it at stake.

[24] Althusser, SP, 19 (translation slightly modified); PE, 90.

[25] Althusser, PE, 94 (this passage is not in the translation in *Sublation*).

[26] Althusser, LP, 65.

[27] More precisely: as a critique of the articulation of a certain type of discourse to a practice of power.

[28] In the 'Philosophy Course for Scientists' (held at the ENS in 1967–1968), Althusser develops the idea that philosophy is not concerned with science – an ideological concept – but with *the sciences*. Balibar, in an article published in *L'Humanité* (14 February 1969), rails against those who speak of science as if it were a 'speculative Holy Ghost' incarnated in the various sciences. We might, however, ask ourselves what this strange concept, 'the sciences', really is. Is it possible to say anything about it without passing through the mediation of the concept of 'science'? Putting a concept in the plural does not change its nature – indeed, it only conceals it further. That is the issue here: to replace 'science' with 'the sciences' is to mask philosophy's proper object (science) insofar as it is produced by the denegation of knowledge. The supposedly anti-speculative operation undertaken by Althusser and Balibar has no other effect than to strengthen the philosophical denegation of knowledge. (For the notion of 'denegation', see Chapter 3, note 1. – Trans.)

[29] Ludwig Feuerbach, 'Towards a Critique of Hegel's Philosophy', in *The Fiery Brook*, trans. Zawar Hanfi (New York: Anchor Books, 1972), 75.

[30] See Althusser, MH, 219–41.

[31] Ibid., 238–9.

[32] Ibid., 238.

[33] The expression occurs once in Althusser's 'Marxism and Humanism' (222), where he contrasts 'class humanism' to the 'humanism of the person'. – Trans.

[34] 'The state of all the people' is the slogan introduced in 1961, under Khrushchev, to replace what was then the slogan of the Soviet Revolution, 'the dictatorship of the proletariat'. – Trans.

35 Althusser, MH, 238.

36 Ibid.

37 Cf. Marx, 'Preface' to *A Contribution*, in MECW 29, 263. 'At a certain stage of development, the material productive forces of society come into conflict with the existing relations of production or – this merely expresses the same thing in legal terms – with the property relations within the framework of which they have operated hitherto. From forms of development of the productive forces these relations turn into their fetters. Then begins an era of social revolution. The changes in the economic foundation lead sooner or later to the transformation of the whole immense superstructure. In studying such transformations it is always necessary to distinguish between the material transformation of the economic conditions of production, which can be determined with the precision of natural science, and the legal, political, religious, artistic or philosophic – in short, *ideological forms in which men become conscious of this conflict and fight it out*' (italics added.)

38 Althusser, MH, 232.

39 Just to be clear, assuming it is still necessary: this has nothing to do with Althusser's personal position in a particular set of circumstances, but only with the political line implied by his theory of ideology. It would be hard to find another theory so quickly appropriated by those whose interest could benefit from it. In the name of science, its appropriators opposed the workers' struggle against salary hierarchy: don't they know the scientific law that says that each person should be paid in accordance with the value of his labour power? Similarly, those fighting against hierarchy at the university misunderstand that 'the goal of the professor-student relation corresponds to the advancement of human knowledge, and is indeed its very foundation' (J. Pesanti, 'Problèmes de méthode et questions théoriques liées à la refonte des carrières', in *Bulletin du SNE (sup)*, July 1969). It would be impossible for an admission of what constitutes the 'foundation' of the theory of science one is laying claim to be more naïve than this.

The impasse Althusser finds himself in can be seen in an article he published recently in *La Pensée*, 'A propos de l'article de Michel Verret sur "Mai étudiant"' (June 1969). In it, Althusser defends the progressive character of the May student movement and denounces the reactionary interpretation of this movement by an overly zealous defender of 'science'. But he cannot, or will not, see in Verret's article the simple justification of a reactionary politics. What he sees, instead, is a *shortcoming*: the Party 'wasn't able' to analyse the student movement, or stay in contact with the students, or explain to them the forms of working class struggle, or .... The conclusion of the article shows that he remains bound to the double recourse – to science and to the Party apparatus. It is on the latter that he relies to 'provide the *scientific* explanations that will allow *everyone*, the young included, to understand the events they have experienced, and, if they really want, to find their place, on a correct basis, in the class struggle, by opening up to them correct perspectives, and by giving them the political and ideological means for correct action'.

[40] This sentence from Lenin is sometimes translated: 'Without revolutionary theory, there can be no revolutionary movement.' Althusser cites it often. See, for example: LP, 52; EYM, 161 – Trans.

# Index